PRENTICE-HALL

FOUNDATIONS OF DEVELOPMENTAL BIOLOGY SERIES

Clement L. Markert, Editor

PRINCIPLES
OF
MAMMALIAN
AGING

Second Edition

Robert R. Kohn

School of Medicine
Case Western Reserve University

PRENTICE-HALL, INC., Englewood Cliffs, New Jersey 07632

Library of Congress Cataloging in Publication Data

Kohn, Robert Rothenberg, (date)
   Principles of mammalian aging.

   Includes bibliographies and index.
   1. Aging. 2. Mammals—Physiology. I. Title.
[DNLM: 1. Aging. WT104 K79p]
QP86.K58 1978   599'.03'72   77-20289
ISBN 0-13-709352-7

PRENTICE-HALL
FOUNDATIONS OF DEVELOPMENTAL BIOLOGY SERIES

Printed in the United States of America

10 9 8 7 6 5 4 3 2 1

PRENTICE-HALL INTERNATIONAL, INC., *London*
PRENTICE-HALL OF AUSTRALIA PTY. LIMITED, *Sydney*
PRENTICE-HALL OF CANADA, LTD., *Toronto*
PRENTICE-HALL OF INDIA PRIVATE LIMITED, *New Delhi*
PRENTICE-HALL OF JAPAN, INC., *Tokyo*
PRENTICE-HALL OF SOUTHEAST ASIA PTE. LTD., *Singapore*
WHITEHALL BOOKS LIMITED, *Wellington, New Zealand*

To Willy, Carrie, and the memory of J. B. Kohn

Foundations of Developmental Biology

The first edition of *Principles of Mammalian Aging* appeared in 1971. Since then, a substantial amount of new research has been completed, and many theories and concepts of aging have been refined or rejected. The second edition not only brings us up to date, but also develops a useful and stimulating conceptual appreciation of aging that will surely enlighten our future progress in this area. Moreover, recent advances in related areas of developmental biology have been so rapid and extensive that the phenomenon of aging can now be examined against a new and richer understanding of the molecular, genetic, cellular, and intercellular events that comprise the phenomena of development, including the inevitable last state—senescence.

Research in developmental biology has been characterized in recent years by both unexpected insights and discouraging disappointments. But with all the varied and uneven advances in the field of developmental biology, research on aging has steadily increased in importance. Even so, we are only at the beginning of understanding this phenomenon. All organisms develop, mature, and senesce. Although aging is receiving increasing attention, we still do not know whether the causes are cellular or extracellular, genetic or epigenetic. Whether aging proves to be reparable, preventable, or hopeless, it is in any event a universal characteristic of organisms, particularly mammals and ourselves.

This authoritative second edition of *Principles of Mammalian Aging* by Dr. Robert R. Kohn makes a major and welcome contribution by presenting cogently a large amount of information from diverse sources and by developing significant concepts of aging in a critical and stimulating fashion.

CLEMENT L. MARKERT

Contents

Preface

to the Second Edition

It was apparent shortly after the appearance of the first edition of this text that a number of additional subjects, such as time, amyloid, temporary organs, and non-fatal, age-dependent diseases, should have been included. These are discussed in this revision. It was also clear that more material concerning genetics and evolution should have been presented.

The amount of data acquired since the first edition in many areas of biology such as immunology and molecular biology, as well as in aging itself, has necessitated extensive updating and rewriting.

The second edition is a bigger book than the first, and will be of use as a reference source. But the principles argued in the first edition seem to be holding up pretty well, and it is hoped that the reader will find it useful and enjoyable to read the second edition through and look for these principles, rather than put the book on a shelf only to be consulted as a reference.

Cleveland, Ohio   Robert R. Kohn
June, 1977

Preface
to the First Edition

The writing of this book grew out of lectures given to medical students and the preparation of several articles. These activities and research in the field for around 15 years have compelled me to organize my thinking about aging, particularly about interrelationships of processes at different levels of organization, and cause-and-effect sequences. The big problem has often been in deciding on the most significant questions, and in trying to pose them in specific enough terms for one to know where to look for answers.

It can be quite unsettling to have finished a book on a large, complex, and controversial subject. The anxiety is heightened if the subject is an important one, and it makes a difference if what has been said is true or not. One wonders if there is not, lurking somewhere in the literature, a report that renders untenable some major point in the book. It can be assumed that certain recent papers will make various phenomena and interpretations in the book not exactly as described, and indicate a number of omissions.

If one is presumptuous enough to think he has something to teach, and desires to put it in black-and-white, then perhaps he should be prepared to be wrong and be judged for it. I can take some refuge in the knowledge that scientific conclusions are always tentative and that aging is an important and timely subject, badly in need of a conceptual framework within which theories can be argued and tested. I would be satisfied with a passing grade for effort and intention.

Cleveland, Ohio　　　　　　　　　　　　　　ROBERT R. KOHN
April, 1969

Introduction

The deterioration of objects, animals, and people with the passage of time is a conspicious feature of the world around us. It seems so natural and commonplace that man, as curious as he is, has until quite recently seldom asked why this should be. As more has been learned about the not-so-visible world of molecules, cells, and tissues, we have found that some type of deterioration also occurs with the passage of time in these systems. Again, these changes have appeared to many as not only commonplace and uninteresting but also somewhat depressing. More enthusiasm can be generated for finding out how systems become better, or how some whimsical phenomenon might be explained, than for trying to understand why something goes to pieces, as it were. In biology, in particular, a hidden idealism stimulates our interest in programming and control mechanisms that make systems more highly developed, more efficient, and capable of maintaining steady states or equilibria.

Scientists appear to possess a collective consciousness or awareness that causes large numbers of them to ask the same type of questions and to work toward the same goals during a given period. They also possess collective blind spots that cause them passively to observe phenomena without realizing that some important and challenging questions might be in order. We can imagine the early biologist who reflects momentarily on heredity. He might not consider it exciting that dogs invariably give birth to puppies, and cats have kittens. In order for this observation to be exciting, and to cause one to ask questions, enough basic information and techniques must be available to enable the scientist to advance hypotheses and to perform experiments.

The enormous amount of information that has been accumulated on the basic chemistry and structure of living systems has made the era of modern molecular biology possible. This basic information has also enabled us to formulate hypotheses and to carry out experiments aimed toward understanding aging processes at a variety of levels.

In addition to our acquisition of information and techniques necessary for the study of aging processes, we have become aware of the facts that these processes are widespread in nature and constitute exceedingly important theoretical and practical problems. It is difficult to conceive of any population that does not age. Progressive alteration occurs in the nonliving world in populations of molecules, substances, and objects of all kinds. In living systems we can observe progressive changes in populations of molecules, in cells and tissues, and, at higher levels of complexity, in organelles and in the cells themselves. Many of these processes appear essential for normal development and function. Finally, we can recognize aging processes at the level of the intact organism, where they frequently result in debility and the end point of death. The notion that all human beings die when they get very old is scarcely new. However, during the eras of famines and epidemics, the main concern was to get through youth and middle age. In modern societies where this is assured for most of the people, the population faces death due to the complications of aging—the 100 percent fatal disease that everyone has. The increased awareness of the role of age in disease, debility, and death has, very appropriately, stimulated interest in the mechanisms of the aging processes.

Although questions about aging have only recently begun to interest large numbers of scientists, there is a rich literature on aging that goes back to antiquity. Concepts of aging through history reflect the development of biology and scientific medicine. The earliest concerns were with social and psychological aspects of growing old. Aristotle (quoted in Griffin, 1950), in observing the aged, noted, "They lack confidence in the future; partly through experience—for most things go wrong, or anyhow turn out worse than one expects." He also observed and commented on the definite life spans of various organisms. We are indebted to Aristotle for an important hypothesis of aging, perhaps representing the point of view that makes science possible: "The incapacity of old age is due to an affection not of the soul but of its vehicle, as occurs in drunkenness or disease."

Careful observation was characteristic of the Renaissance. Leonardo da Vinci dissected 30 bodies, and was particularly interested in anatomic changes with age, instructing his students on how various parts of the body should be drawn in the progression of subjects from infancy into old age (Belt, 1952). He paid special attention to connective tissues and blood vessels, and concluded that the cause of aging was "veins which by thickening of their tunics in the old restrict the passage of the blood, and by this lack of nourishment destroy the life of the aged without any fever, the old coming to fail little by little in slow death."

Sir Francis Bacon was also a student of aging, and compiled differences between youth and old age (Strong, 1952). His was more the physiological approach, and he observed, "The diseases of young men are more acute and curable, of old men longer and hard to cure: a young man's wounds soon close, an old man's later; . . . because old men's bodies do neither perspire well, nor assimilate well."

We can follow concepts of aging through the emergence and development of modern experimental biology. Aging has never been the major interest of the community of biologists, but those most interested in this field have frequently attempted to describe or explain aging processes in terms of the general biological phenomena that were under intensive study or that seemed most important at a given time. Thus, when development and growth began to receive a great amount of attention, Weismann (1882) and others distinguished between the germ plasm, which is immortal, and the soma, which ages. Minot (1908) perceived a relationship between growth and aging in that senescence appeared to be related to the slowing or cessation of growth. Similarly, Child (1915) observed that senescence in metazoans was not inevitable—it could apparently be inhibited by growth and regeneration.

When the importance of microorganisms in disease was appreciated, the notion that aging was caused by toxic products from intestinal bacteria was taken seriously by Metchnikoff (1907) and others of his day. The discovery of hormones promoted the "monkey gland" era, during which it was believed that aging was due to endocrine failure, and that transplanted glands or hormone injections would have rejuvenating effects. When biologists were learning chemistry, particularly protein structure and the behavior of colloids, it was argued by Heilbrun (1943) and many others that aging was caused by dehydration or syneresis of body colloids. In the present era of molecular biology and immunology, aging processes are frequently discussed in terms of altered gene transcription or translation, somatic mutation, and autoimmunity or immunologic failure.

The accumulation of empirical data has been enormous. Nathan Shock (1957) compiled a bibliography on aging for the years 1949–1955 that contained 15,983 references. A number of books have been written that have attempted to bring much of this material together and to organize it in some meaningful way. An impressive list of review articles and symposium volumes has also been produced in recent years.

The writing of this book at this time is based on the conviction that we now know enough about aging to argue mechanisms and to present some probable cause and effect sequences. We have acquired so much information about some types of aging that it is no longer sufficient merely to catalogue the various findings and to list the possible mechanisms, any more than it was correct in the last century to argue mechanisms in the absence of knowledge. Although there are some aging systems we know almost nothing about, and there are large gaps of knowledge concerning the systems we know the most about, we do know what kinds of questions to ask. In most cases, in addition, we can advance reasonable hypotheses and utilize conceptual frameworks that we can test by new observations. We are also beginning to realize what types of experiments should be performed to obtain the most useful information. One purpose of this book is an attempt to judge the significance of certain types of studies in relation to major questions about aging.

Previous books on aging have, almost without exception, been written for the committed gerontologist, or have been aimed at the practicing biologist or physician who would like to know something about aging. This book is written for the biologist, early in his career, who wants to learn the essentials of this subject.

Considering the massive accumulation of journals each week, it could be argued that no single author knows enough to write an up-to-date and thorough book about anything. Such an argument would be particularly valid in the case of aging, which deals with almost all biological subjects, and in addition is concerned with rates of change and progression of processes in all living systems. Therefore an attempt has been made to minimize the hazards of a one-author effort by focusing on mammalian systems. Every type of aging process can be found in a mammal. References to aging in lower forms are made when these are relevant to certain important concepts, questions, or theses. The emphasis on mammalian systems, however, negates the responsibility for attempting critical evaluations of studies on such forms as plants, bacteria, bryozoans, insects, or amphibians, although concepts arising from consideration of mammalian systems will apply to these organisms as well.

Furthermore, in dealing with mammalian systems, no attempt has been made to achieve encyclopedic coverage. The intent has been to write a concise book dealing with principles, one that would be read all the way through, in addition to serving as a reference source. Access to the literature is provided in the selected references at ends of chapters. The lists that appear at the end of most chapters contain references to material in the text judged to be of special significance, as well as additional reports and reviews that will be useful for general background reading. References have been selected because they appear to bear on important questions and on concepts about mechanisms of aging, or because they are representative of the types of studies undertaken in certain areas. In many cases equally appropriate investigations by other workers could have been cited.

In approaching aging as a branch of biology, it would be appropriate to start the book at the beginning and read it through. However, the reader who is anxious to come to grips with the question of why we age might read the sequence of Chapters One, Six, and Seven, and then decide what other sections would be of interest.

This book contains both facts and hypotheses—hopefully, distinguished from each other. Very few of the explanations of biological phenomena that we accept as proved could actually survive a rigorously logical criticism. Mechanisms are often considered proved if there is agreement that a cause-and-effect sequence exists, that such mechanisms are not contradicted by any facts, and that they are capable of explaining major manifestations of the phenomenon in question. These criteria have been used here in advancing and criticizing hypotheses about aging. In a developing field it is often almost as useful to know what is trivial, or false, and to be ignored, as it is to know important truths. For example, physicists who were trying to understand the laws of mechanics judged that they should ignore the effects of friction and air resistance. If they had not excluded these effects from their thinking, they could not have deduced the laws. Thus the aging field has many equivalents of friction and air resistance that must be identified and discarded to open the way to meaningful lines of work. This approach is attempted in the book. One item of new information can demolish a hypothesis constructed over decades and based on hundreds of observations. It is hoped that this book will stimulate thinking about aging processes as well as encourage the search for new items of information.

REFERENCES

Belt, E. 1952. Leonardo da Vinci's studies of the aging process. Geriatrics. 7:205–210.

Child, C. M. 1915. Senescence and Rejuvenescence. Chicago: University of Chicago Press.

Griffin, J. J. 1950. Aristotle's observations on gerontology. Geriatrics. 5:222–226.

Metchnikoff, E. 1907. The Prolongation of Life—Optimistic Studies. London: Heinemann.

Minot, C. S. 1908. The problem of age, growth, and death; a study of cytomorphosis, based on lectures at the Lowell Institute, March 1907, London.

Shock, N. W. 1957. A Classified Bibliography of Gerontology and Geriatrics. Stanford: Stanford University Press.

Strong, L. C. 1952. Observations on gerontology in the 17th century, J. Gerontol. 7:618–619.

Weismann, A. 1882. Über die Dauer des Lebens. Jena.

ONE

Characteristics

of Aging Processes

A property that all aging systems share is that of progressive and irreversible change. Nonaging systems are those that appear the same to us as we examine them from time to time, even though dynamic processes may comprise such a system. For example, if two chemicals A and B interact to give products C and D by a reversible reaction, the reaction will proceed until certain amounts of the four components are present, the amounts depending on starting concentrations and how much free energy is released or absorbed in the reaction. Similarly, starting with C and D, the reaction will yield A and B, and will proceed until certain amounts of the four components are obtained. The reaction at thermodynamic equilibrium is represented in Figure 1.1. If no work is done on the system and environmental conditions are kept constant, the same amount of each component in the same physical state will be present next week and next year. We can observe no change in the system with time. Such a system does not age because the reaction is reversible. It is unlikely that many such equilibria occur outside of chemistry laboratories, which is why it is difficult to find examples of nonaging systems in nature. In nature, environmental conditions change, systems do work or have work done on them by other systems, and components are removed from or added to reactions.

The type of nonaging system that we usually observe in nature,

$$A + B \; \rightleftharpoons \; C + D$$ Fig. 1.1 A chemical reaction at equilibrium.

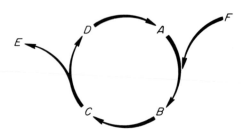

Fig. 1.2   A steady-state process.

particularly in living systems, is a steady-state process (Figure 1.2). This process consists of several different reactions, each of which may be reversible. However, the reaction is driven in one direction by the continuous addition of component *F* and removal of *E*. A steady state is attained when the amount of *F* added is balanced by the amount of *E* removed. The amount of each component will not change with time, although we can tell nothing about the rates of the various reactions by determining the amounts of the components present at any instant. If the rates do not change, the steady state represents a nonaging system. A progressive and irreversible change in rate of utilization of *F* and production of *E* would make this an aging system, even though amounts of components *A, B, C,* and *D* remained constant.

It may not appear to make sense to talk about aging or nonaging of a steady-state process, because the process contains different populations at different times. For example, the molecules of compounds in the Krebs cycle proceed through the cycle and are replaced by new molecules. Since the system is continually being renewed, what is there to age or not age? This is a conceptual problem that is frequently encountered when one is considering the aging of a cell whose components are turning over, or the aging of an organism whose cells are being replaced. The problem serves to point out that aging can be most readily perceived and appreciated when it occurs in a substance or structure that remains present and can be observed as it undergoes change. However, as will be dealt with in later sections, a system or organization has an identity and properties of its own, somewhat independent of the turnover of its components, and progressive changes can occur in the function and efficiency of such systems. In some cases, perhaps eventually in all cases, aging of such a system can be traced to changes in some nonrenewable component in a second system that has some regulatory influence on the first.

A physiological counterpart of the steady state is seen in the maintenance of homeostasis. Here, various processes counteract each other to maintain some factor or activity at a steady optimal level. The factor

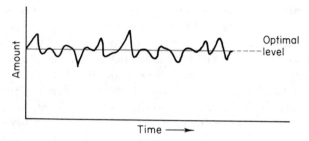

Fig. 1.3 The maintenance of homeostasis.

to be maintained may be body temperature, blood sugar, intracellular calcium, blood cell concentration, or any of the thousands of other structures and metabolites that cannot vary beyond certain limits without being incompatible with life. Processes that raise the level of some factor are opposed by reactions that diminish the level. Figure 1.3 indicates the fluctuations of some property or substance around an optimal level with the passage of time. This represents a nonaging system as long as the level around which the deviations occur remains constant, and as long as the deviations occur at the same rates. Many such mechanisms appear not to age when examined over short time intervals. However, long-term observations may reveal a progressive alteration in the mean level or increasing sluggishness in the reestablishment of the level following displacements.

Aging versus developmental and abnormal processes

Aging, then, can be represented by a single arrow, while nonaging processes are at equilibrium or in a steady state. Although all aging processes are progressive and irreversible under usual conditions, it will be apparent that there are systems that undergo progressive change that are not generally thought of as aging. Growth and development of living systems must be considered in this connection. The borderline between development and aging is frequently indistinct. One is free to use any definition that is convenient and can be made clear to others. Development can be considered as a form of aging, or aging can be thought of as a continuation of development. It is often useful, however, to attempt a distinction between the two. Developmental processes are usually not steadily progressive but slow down or stop, the state of maturity being defined by the cessation or slowing of such processes; whereas aging processes tend to begin or accelerate at maturity, although they may be in evidence at earlier stages. By teleological criteria, development can be viewed as consisting of early processes that enhance the functional capacities of a system, whereas aging consists of later processes that diminish or have no effect on ability to function. Essentially all processes that are steadily progressive turn out to be harmful to the system involved.

Other steadily progressing processes, which are not usually considered to represent aging, are certain diseases. These are referred to as "diseases" because they occur in only a fraction of a population. If they occurred in all members of a population, they would be called "aging processes." This brings us to another important criterion of the aging process: It is a normal process in that it occurs in all members of the population under consideration.

We can now define an aging process as one that occurs in all members of a population, that is progressive and irreversible under usual conditions, and that begins or accelerates at maturity in those systems that undergo growth and development.

End points

As a system ages, changes occur in its properties, organization, and composition. These changes can be observed from time to time, and rates of aging can be determined. Frequently, however, progressive alterations result in a very abrupt change or end point in the state of a system. Such end points are often used in the study of aging processes. Examples would be the burning out of a light bulb or the death of a cell or animal.

If aging processes are proceeding in all members of a rather homogeneous population, and if they are responsible for attainment of an end point, the amount of time required (or age) for end points in the population should give an approximately normal frequency distribution (Figure 1.4). If the end point is death, whether of a light bulb, storage battery, insect, or human being, the modal value in Figure 1.4 can be considered as the mean life span of the population.

Using the ages at the end point from Figure 1.4, we can plot the percentage of the population at each age that has not reached the end point. If the end point is death, the percentage of those surviving can be plotted as a function of age (Figure 1.5). A rather rectangular curve is obtained, which indicates the mean life span by the 50 percent survival point.

By dividing the total life span into a number of short intervals, the

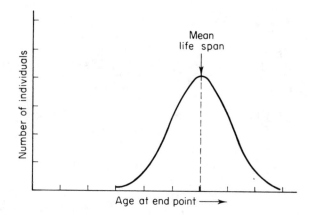

Fig. 1.4 Number of individuals in an aging population reaching an end point as a function of time.

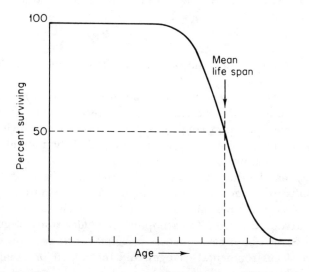

Fig. 1.5 Percent survival as a function of time for an aging population.

data of Figure 1.5 can be used to calculate how many are surviving at the beginning of each interval, and what percentage of these attain the end point, or die, during the interval. These values plotted against age give the age-specific death rate. Figure 1.6 shows both the rate and probability of dying of members of an aging population as a function of age. The log of the age-specific death rate is included in Figure 1.6. The log curve becomes approximately linear after the mean

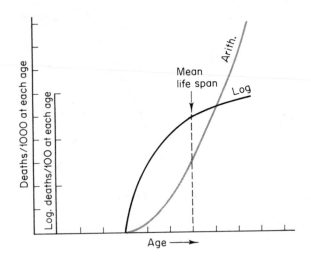

Fig. 1.6   Rate and probability of attaining end points for an aging population as a function of time.

life span, indicating that the rate and probability of dying double at regular intervals during this period.

These curves would be obtained only in the case of a homogeneous population, one in which the same aging processes were occurring in all the members at approximately equal rates, and in which the end points were the result of the same processes in all the individuals. Few populations in nature are so homogeneous. In particular, end points, or deaths, may be due to different processes in different individuals. This results in a skewing of the frequency distribution and in variations in the shapes of percent survival and age-specific death-rate curves. If such curves are plotted for a population under study, a great deal can be inferred about consequences of aging processes, rates of aging, the effect of environmental changes, and the role of programming or genetics in the dying out of populations.

End points may have no relationship to aging processes. An example might be drinking glasses. A large number of these could exist at a given time, and, with the passage of time, the probability of their being broken would have nothing to do with how old the individual glasses were. Similarly, a population of organisms may die out by an infection, and the susceptibility to infection or its severity may have nothing to do with the age of the affected organisms. In such cases the same percentage of those present at the beginning of every time interval would be expected to attain the end point during that interval. This would

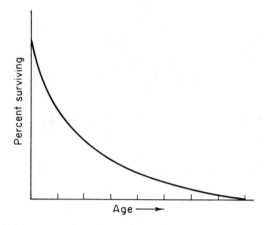

Fig. 1.7   Percent surviving as a function of time for a population in which the probability of reaching end points remains constant with time. End points are not caused by aging processes.

hold for all intervals. There would be no increase with increasing age, as seen in populations where end points are due to aging processes. The age-specific death rate would then be a horizontal line. The percent survival curve would take the form of Figure 1.7. This is the same curve as that for the velocity of a first-order chemical reaction as a function of time. It tells us that the number of individuals dying at each interval is proportional to those present, and that the proportionality is constant with the passage of time.

As mentioned above, few populations in nature will give a percent survival curve as rectangular as Figure 1.5. In even fewer populations, perhaps none, is the end point completely accidental—that is, having no relationship to age. It turns out that most populations yield percent survival curves that fall somewhere between the curve of Figure 1.5 for age-caused end points and the curve of Figure 1.7 for accidental, non-age-related end points. By inspecting such curves for real populations, much can be learned about the relative importance of accidental and age-related processes in causing death or other end points.

TWO

Chemical Aging

Understanding the mechanisms of biological aging must ultimately depend on knowing the changes that occur with time to molecules that comprise living systems. Furthermore, it is most likely that these chemical changes are of types that have been studied and about which quite a bit is known. That is, there would appear to be little justification at this point for looking for a new type of chemistry to explain aging at higher levels of organization. The ways in which substances can change with time are quite limited. The problems are in knowing exactly which biologically important ions and molecules undergo these changes, in knowing the specific reactions involved, and in relating the chemical changes to alterations in function of the living systems.

It would be difficult to avoid the conclusion that primary, or most fundamental, changes most likely occur in nondynamic or nonrenewable substances. Or, more simply, for something to age, it must remain present—or at least the rate of aging must be greater than the rate of replacement. The only exception might be the accumulation of alterations in a self-replicating molecule or structure.

Molecular turnover, as will be dealt with in later sections, is widespread in living systems. We would not expect a population of continuously replaced non-self-replicating molecules to be the fundamental site of aging. On the other hand, such a population could demonstrate age changes as a consequence of primary changes in other molecules. Such secondary changes would usually be in terms of concentrations. For example, an enzyme that participates in the synthesis of some molecule might become inactive with time. This would result in a decreased concentration of the molecule, even though it is turning over.

Similarly, if a system responsible for degradation became inactive, the substance being degraded would increase in concentration.

It is also apparent that there is a relationship between complexity and progressive change, both in chemical systems and in living organisms. There are more ways in which complex substances and systems than simple systems can change; the ease with which aging processes can be discerned is frequently related to the level of organization of a substance or system. Thus, we do not observe age changes in subatomic particles, atoms, or ions. Radioactive decay represents change in a population of atoms and could be considered an aging process. However, the end point of atomic disintegration is random; the probability of its occurrence has no relationship to how long the atom has been in existence. If the number of atoms that have not disintegrated (i.e., the percentage surviving) is plotted against time, a first-order reaction curve of the type shown in Figure 1.7 in the previous chapter is obtained. This indicates end points that are not age-dependent.

Also in the preceding chapter a distinction was made between a reaction at equilibrium and an aging process. This distinction holds only for those reactions that have attained equilibrium, and in which constant amounts of reactants and products can be identified. In the strictest sense there are probably no completely irreversible chemical reactions. Reactions usually considered to be irreversible are those in which we can observe the disappearance of reactants and the accumulation of products, to the point where the reactants are present in very small amounts or cannot be measured. The arrow indicating a reversal of the reaction is very short. Aging processes at the molecular level are generally of this type.

Crystals

Perhaps the simplest example of aging involves the progressive formation of ionic crystals. Ions in solution become arranged so that each ion is surrounded by the largest possible number of oppositely charged ions, and all charges are neutralized in the resulting lattice. Such a lattice will demonstrate a periodicity in arrangement of ions, and the composition of the repeat units will depend on the size of the ions involved. In sodium chloride crystals each ion is surrounded by six ions of opposite charge. A crystal may be composed of a large number of different types of ions, as well as water molecules (water of hydration), and may have other types of ions absorbed to the surface, where reversible reactions frequently occur. Hydroxyapatite is a widespread inorganic crystal in animals. Its lattice is composed of four different ions, and additional ions are adsorbed to the surface, where exchange with ions in solution takes place. Organic molecules also form crystals in which molecules are held together by both covalent and noncovalent bonds.

Movement of ions and molecules is restricted in crystals. Ions from solution will enter a crystal, and the latter will grow as long as the concentration of ions in solution is above a certain level. Although exchange may take place at the suface of the crystal, ions and molecules deeper in the lattice are inaccessible and will persist. Whether or not crystal formation is an aging process depends on persistence of components and on progression, or growth, of the lattice. If ions in solution are maintained at steady-state concentrations and environmental conditions are stable, the system will age by crystal growth. Reversal of such a process would require the addition of new regulatory mechanisms.

Macromolecular aggregations

Similar crystallization processes occur with molecules of greater complexity. Large and complex molecules—protein, nucleic acid, lipid, and carbohydrate—comprise the bulk of biological chemicals. Many of these exist as high polymers, that is, in arrays of repeating units. Such polymers frequently contain segments with the configuration, reactive groups, and charges that enable them to form crystals with corresponding segments of other polymer chains. As shown in Figure 2.1, individual polymers will exist early in solution or in an amorphous state. With the passage of time, crystalline regions will appear where the polymer molecules are held together. Finally, the entire structure may become oriented, with periodic crystalline zones.

As in the case of inorganic crystals, polymers become increasingly insoluble with crystallization. Bonds holding the subunits together in the

Fig. 2.1 Amorphous polymer forming oriented crystalline polymer.

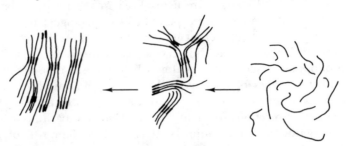

crystalline zones may be covalent, hydrogen, ionic, van der Waals' forces, or a combination of these. Formation of such crystals is facilitated by exertion of tensile stress on the system. Once an ordered structure is attained, there is an opportunity for more bonds or cross-links to form between the linear polymers. Consequently, aging is manifested by an increasing crystallinity, decreasing solubility, and alterations in other properties that depend on the number and location of cross-links that tend to maintain the structure in a given configuration. Again, as with inorganic crystals, such an aggregation of subunits will occur naturally in accord with thermodynamic principles, unless additional factors are imposed on the system.

Aggregation of molecules with the formation of cross-links is a particularly widespread aging process. It is responsible for the aging of rubber, plastics, leather, paper, and paint. Attempts are often made to inhibit aging of such nonliving systems by slowing or controlling interactions by various treatments. Since animals contain high concentrations of molecules that can undergo these aggregations, they are faced with the same molecular aging problems.

The formation and growth of polymer chains themselves represent an example of chemical aging. Molecules with functional groups, particularly unsaturated hydrocarbons, will frequently react with each other to yield chains of increasing length and decreasing solubility. The resulting polymer may consist of different molecules, as is seen in polyester and polyamide, polymerized by ester and amide bonds, respectively. Or the polymer may be composed of a single type of molecule, as is often the case when polymerization of molecules containing the vinyl group ($CH_2=CH-$) occurs. Polymerization of unsaturated hydrocarbons may be accelerated by oxidation or light. Control of aging processes of these types is the basis of the synthetic rubber, resin, and plastic industries.

Closely related to the processes of polymer formation and crystallization is the formation of insoluble complex compounds. Such compounds may not have the ordered structure of polymers and crystals, although their formation would occur by the same types of reactions and would have the same consequences in regard to solubility and other properties. Insolubility of products would tend to characterize those reactions as aging processes since reversal would be minimized. The products formed could be quite heterogeneous. Proteins, inorganic ions, and nucleic acids could aggregate. Or carbohydrates and lipids would be expected to react with each other. Because of the variety of functional groups and potential bonds available in biological molecules and ions, it would be possible for very large aggregates to form. These could contain ionic crystals, polymers, and complex macromolecules.

Denaturation

Complex macromolecules may be characterized by their chemical composition, or primary structure. In addition, however, such molecules may contain chains with zones of highly ordered coiling (secondary structure), and the chains themselves may be folded or twisted into specific configurations (tertiary structure). Such complex configurations have been studied most thoroughly in proteins, where they are essential for biological activity. Specific configurations are maintained by a variety of chemical bonds. These molecules are susceptible to alterations of configuration with time, such that they lose biological activity and demonstrate different physical properties. The altered, or "denatured," molecules are generally less soluble, more symmetrical, more easily degraded, and they demonstrate reactive groups that were previously masked or inaccessible.

Denaturation is believed to be due to the rupture of bonds that hold components of the molecule in specific folded configurations, with a consequent unfolding to a more random state. Change from the native to the denatured state is associated with a marked increase in entropy. Denaturation will thus tend to occur naturally with the passage of time. Some proteins can remain undenatured and at thermodynamic equilibrium for indefinite periods if environmental conditions are held constant within narrow limits. Such environmental control probably does not exist outside of laboratories. Denaturation can be greatly accelerated by such agents as heat, light, increased pressure, surface tension, dehydration, and chemicals that rupture hydrogen bonds.

Mechanical wear and tear

Structures of macromolecules subjected to repeated and prolonged stresses may be damaged. Membranes and fibers may become fragmented or split, or may develop perforations.

Mutations

The concept of mutation is a familiar one because of the growth of modern genetics. It denotes an alteration in a macromolecule that persists and causes a change in biological function. Mutations have been studied most extensively in nucleic acids, but there is no good reason why similar changes could not occur in other macromolecules. A mutation may take place at the time of synthesis of a molecule. A bond may rupture in a large molecule or may form at an abnormal site. Chemical groups may be cleaved off, or oxidized or reduced. A large number of mutations is theoretically possible in the case of any large molecule, and would be expected to occur as accidents. In addition, the rate of mutation can be greatly accelerated by ionizing radiation and by certain chemical agents. A population of macromolecules would thus contain an increasing percentage of altered molecules with the passage of time.

Concentration changes

When a system contains two or more components or populations of molecules, it may age not by changes in individual molecules but by changes in relative concentrations. Aging of this type may occur in nonrenewable populations or in systems in which molecular turnover occurs. As mentioned earlier, primary age changes occurring would result in changing concentrations of that molecule. Even in the absence of any primary changes, differential rates of synthesis and/or degradation of different components would cause a progressive change in proportions of components within the system. The system would thus be considered an aging one. In a system of any complexity, it is clear that for aging of this type not to occur, rates of synthesis and degradation must be balanced for each component. Even a very slight imbalance in turnover of one component will, with the passage of time, cause an increasingly conspicuous aging of the system.

An extreme example of aging of this type, and one related to crystallization, or aggregation of subunits, is merely the accumulation of a substance. This occurs when one of the components in a mixed population can be formed but cannot be degraded at the rate of other components.

Time

In discussing aging processes, we often talk about the passage of time as though time were a river that could act on things. This is a useful convention, but we should realize there is no such thing as absolute time. There are only clocks and laws of thermodynamics that give sequences to events. A human being could serve as a clock, albeit an imprecise one. The earth would rotate 29,000 times and orbit the sun 80 times, more or less, during a human life span.

Some additional generalities

It is apparent that some of the characterizations of an aging system discussed in Chapter One lose precision when applied at the molecular level. It should be emphasized that these criteria and definitions hold best for complex systems and, like most attempts at categorization, are not entirely satisfactory in all cases. Crystal formation, the accumulation of substances, changes in concentrations, and macromolecular aggregations—when progressive and irreversible—constitute aging processes by earlier definitions. Some forms of denaturation, in which the rupture of many bonds is required, may represent aging end points in that the probability of occurrence increases with time. On the other hand, mutations and other denaturations may be instantaneous rather than progressive. Further, the reaction may be a random-hit process, with a probability of occurrence unrelated to the age of the molecule. In such cases, it is useful to consider the system, or population of molecules, as aging. Aging end points, if they occur, would then be apparent at higher levels of organization than that of individual molecules.

The relevance to aging of the types of chemical reactions decribed here is that living systems contain many molecules that can undergo these changes. Essentially all biological chemicals can participate in such molecular aging. Furthermore, these reactions tend to occur naturally or spontaneously with the passage of time. Thus, the question is not how a living system can age chemically, but rather which aging processes are permitted to occur and which are inhibited or have their consequences reversed by additional processes. If such chemical processes did not occur, there would be no reason why a complex living system could not persist in a steady state indefinitely. The eventual goal of much aging research is to gain understanding of these chemical processes that are intrinsic to cell and tissue components.

THREE

Extracellular Aging

The extracellular compartment

Large amounts of body components are outside of cells. The size of this extracellular compartment is difficult to measure. However, an approximation can be arrived at on the basis of water determinations. In a mammal, body water is about 70 percent of the body weight. Of this, about 50 percent of the body weight is intracellular water. The remaining 20 percent, the extracellular water, is in two compartments—5 percent in the blood plasma and 15 percent that is extracellular and extravascular. Our interest in aging will concern us with this tissue extracellular compartment. Assuming values obtained from tendon measurements of 65 percent water and 35 percent solids in this compartment (Kohn and Rollerson, 1959), and considering the extracellular water to be 15 percent of the body weight, we arrive at a figure of about 23 percent of the body for the weight or volume of this extracellular tissue compartment.

The fractions of tissues and organs that are extracellular vary enormously from one site to another. Perhaps 80 percent or more of skin, bone, tendon, ligaments, and fascia is extracellular. At the other extreme, organs such as the liver, kidney, and muscle have extracellular values at or considerably below the mean value of 23 percent. The physical state of this compartment also varies a great deal, depending on the components present and their organization. Extracellular material may be semisolid or colloidal, and elastic, tough, fibrous, or hard. Extracellular components fall into two classes: those that are passing through, and those that are structural constituents and characterize this compartment. Among the substances passing through are all of the inorganic ions from the blood, particularly sodium, chloride, and bicarbonate in high concentrations. Plasma proteins, notably albumin, also filter into the extracellular compartment. Substances that pass between cells and blood or lymphatic vessels must travel through an extracellular compartment. These would include metabolites, nutrients, hormones, and gases.

The characteristic structural components of the extracellular compartment comprise the connective tissue. At the junction between epithelial or endothelial cells and the connective tissue, there is usually a basement membrane. This membrane is rich in glycoprotein, and is probably important in regulating the passage of materials to and from cells. The connective tissue itself contains inorganic ions and additional poorly characterized proteins and glycoproteins in low concentrations. The major components of connective tissue have been well studied. These are the fibrous proteins—collagen, reticulin, and elastin—and the glycosaminoglycans. All of these substances are probably synthesized by mesodermal cells, the fibroblasts, and all are high polymers.

Glycosaminoglycans

The polysaccharides present in the highest concentrations— and those studied most thoroughly—are polymers of disaccharides. The most prevalent ones are listed with the composition of repeating units and distribution in Table 3.1. The highly polymerized particles vary considerably in molecular configuration and molecular weight, as well as in concentrations in different tissue. Particle weights as high as 8×10^6 have been described for hyaluronic acid. Molecular weights and configuration determine physical properties of the polymers. The polysaccharides exist as greatly hydrated gels, such that the space they fill is enormous compared to what would be expected for the unhydrated molecules. Hyaluronic acid is highly viscous and is found in high concentrations in mobile tissues and wherever lubrication is required. On the other hand, the hydrated chondroitin sulfates are turgid, and provide tissues with a combination of firmness and some flexibility.

The glycans appear to be synthesized and degraded quite rapidly. Half-lives of from a couple of days to a month have been described for various polysaccharides at different sites. Turnover studies have been carried out almost entirely with tissues such as cartilage, dermis, tendon, and bone. Essentially nothing is known about turnover rates of glycans in parenchymatous organs.

TABLE 3.1

Repeating Polymeric Units and Sites of Major Deposition of Glycosaminoglycans of Connective Tissue. (From Sobel, 1967.)

Substance		Site
Hyaluronic acid	(→ 4 glucuronic acid β1-3 acetyl glucosamine β1 →)	Ubiquitous in connective tissue (?), skin, tendon, synovial fluid, vitreous humor, ligamentus nuchae, heart valve, aorta
Chondroitin sulfate A	(→ 4 glucuronic acid β1-3 acetyl galactosamine-4 sulfate β1 →)	Cartilage, bone, cornea, aorta, ligamentum nuchae
Chondroitin sulfate B	(→ 4 L-iduronic acid β1-3 acetyl galactosamine-4 sulfate β1 →)	Skin, heart valves, cartilage, tendon, cornea, aorta, lung, ligamentum nuchae
Chondroitin sulfate C	(→ 4 glucuronic acid β1-3 acetyl galactosamine-6 sulfate β1 →)	Cartilage, sclera, bone, tendon, heart valve
Keratosulfate	(→ 3 galactose β1-4 acetyl glucosamine-6 sulfate β1 →)	Cornea, rib cartilage, bone, nucleus pulposus
Heparitin sulfate	[glucuronic acid, iduronic acid 1 → 4, glucosamine, N-acetyl, N-sulfate, α-linkages(?), variable composition]	Aorta, lung, liver

Fibrous proteins of connective tissue

The major proteins of mammalian connective tissue are collagen, reticulin, and elastin. Reticulin may be considered a variety of collagen, as its most significant difference from typical collagen is that it is bound to appreciable amounts of lipid and carbohydrate. A discussion of collagen will probably apply to reticulin as well. We shall consider collagen in some detail because it may be very important in its own right in mammalian aging, and because it can serve as a model for the types of age changes that can occur in polymerized, relatively inert macromolecules.

A great deal is known about the chemistry of collagen. This is because collagen is the source of leather, gelatin, and, in previous years, of glue. Scientists in these industries were carrying out extensive studies of collagen, while biologists considered the extracellular proteins as merely inert packing that must be gotten rid of to facilitate the study of isolated cellular systems. In recent decades, however, biologists have come to realize that collagen comprises 25 to 30 percent of the total body protein and is of importance in organ function as well as in many pathological processes. Extensive studies of collagen chemistry, synthesis, and biology have been reported (Traub and Piez, 1971; Goldberg and Sherr, 1973; Vogel, 1973).

Collagen is an unusual protein in that about one-third, by weight, of its amino acid residues consists of proline plus hydroxyproline, and another third is glycine. It is poor in sulfur-containing amino acids. Tropocollagen, the basic collagen molecule, is rod-shaped, approximately 3000 Å long, and 15 Å in diameter. It has a molecular weight of about 300,000. The molecule is composed of three polypeptide chains, each with a molecular weight of approximately 95,000; these chains are arranged in a left-handed helix. Shortly after synthesis as high-molecular-weight procollagan, nonhelical peptides are split off, and, the molecules undergo a side-to-side aggregation. Most of this aggregation occurs in the extracellular compartment after procollagen molecules are extruded from fibroblasts. The lateral aggregation occurs with adjacent molecules one-quarter of their length out of phase with each other in a staggered arrangement. This results in a periodicity of about 640 Å in dried fibrils, which can be seen by electron microscopy (Figure 3.1). The building up of subunits proceeds to the formation of fibrils. Fibril bundles are then formed to the point where gross fibers may be identified in many organs and tissues. At the ultrastructural level, zones of crystallinity alternate with amorphous regions. This arrangement is frequently observed in oriented polymers, as noted in Chapter Two.

When collagen is first synthesized, there is very little cross-linking between peptide chains within tropocollagen molecules, and no covalent bonds between molecules that have aggregated. As the collagen matures, additional intra- and intermolecular cross-links form. There is evidence that links in both locations form by a single continuous process. If young or growing tissue is extracted with a neutral salt solution, appreciable amounts of collagen go into solution. This represents tropocollagen, or poorly cross-linked aggregates. As the tissue

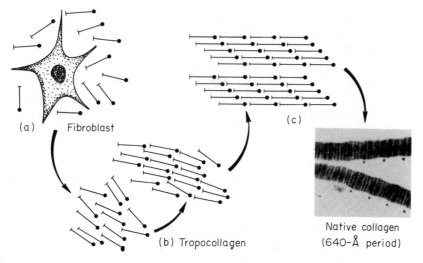

(a) Fibroblast

(c)

(b) Tropocollagen

Native collagen
(640-Å period)

Fig. 3.1 The formation of collagen fibers. (Modified from Seifter and Gallop, 1966.)

becomes more mature, less and less of the collagen is extractable. Finally, in the mature tissue, collagen subunits are firmly bound into fibrils, and only traces may be extracted.

The types of cross-links that form in collagen have received a great deal of attention because of their role in determining the properties of fibrils. It has been shown that hydrogen bonds and short-range forces dependent on steric factors are of importance. In addition, many different types of covalent bonds, some involving hexose derivatives, have been implicated in the cross-linking of collagen subunits. It appears that two types of covalent bond may be of particular significance. One type results from an aldol condensation between two aldehydes on adjacent peptide chains, the other comes from a Schiff base formation between an aldehyde and an amino group on an adjacent chain. The aldehydes are formed by the oxidative deamination of lysine and hydroxylysine.

When it was first appreciated that most body proteins were in a dynamic state—that is, continually turning over—collagen was listed as one of the inert, or nonrenewable, proteins. Experiments in which proteins were labeled with an isotope at birth (isotope content was determined with the passage of time) suggested that once collagen was synthesized, it was not broken down and replaced. In accord with this view, investigators could not find an enzyme in tissues of higher animals that was capable of degrading undenatured collagen at physiologic pH. More recent studies have shown, however, that collagen may turn over quite rapidly at some sites, such as in the postpartum uterus.

Turnover at slower rates has also been detected in other organs. By the use of very sensitive methods, collagen-degrading enzymes have been identified in resorbing tadpole tails, leukocytes, uteri, and bone cells. Accumulated data suggest that collagen exists in at least two metabolic pools. The collagen that is most recently synthesized has an appreciable turnover rate that varies from site to site as a function of physiological alterations (Heikkinen and Vuori, 1972) and tissue stresses. Most of the body collagen, comprising the second pool, is mature and insoluble, and either is nonrenewable or has an exceedingly low rate of turnover. It would appear that a significant fraction of insoluble collagen remains present for the life of the animal, and should be an excellent candidate for age-related changes.

Understanding the chemistry of elastin has been hindered by its extreme insolubility. It cannot be extracted from tissues by mild extraction procedures, as in the case of tropocollagen. Preliminary isolation is usually by extraction of tissue with hot alkali. The insoluble residue is then used for further purification. Elastin is also an unusual protein in that about 95 percent of its amino acids are nonpolar, and 80 percent of the residues are glycine, alanine, valine, and proline (Seifter and Gallop, 1966). Elastin fibers appear amorphous by electron microscopy, and are believed to exist as three-dimensional networks of coiled or kinked polypeptide chains held together by covalent bonds. Elastin is probably synthesized in the form of soluble subunits, or so-called proelastin. Proelastin is a hypothetical substance that has not been isolated and probably becomes polymerized immediately. Cross-links responsible for maturation of elastin include two amino acids: desmosine and isodesmosine. These are formed by the condensation of four lysine residues, three of which have been oxidatively deaminated. Another amino acid implicated in cross-links is lysinonorleucine. Recent studies have indicated that aldehyde groups of the type found in collagen also play a role in the cross-linking of elastin.

Little data is available on elastin turnover, but elastin is probably at least as inert as collagen (Walford, Carter, and Schneider, 1964). As would be expected, elastin has the highest concentrations in those tissues that show elastic behavior (Table 3.2).

Gels and fibers in tissues

Synthesis of the polysaccharides and protein fibers of connective tissue does not occur at rates that insure constant amounts of the various components in a given tissue. Rates of disappearance are also different for the different components. It has frequently been observed that

TABLE 3.2

Elastin Content of Various Tissues. (Modified from Seifter and Gallop, 1966.)

Tissue	*Species*	*Elastin (%)* [a]
Aorta	Ox	40
Aorta	Pig	57
Aorta	Rat	48
Aorta (thoracic)	Dog	29–32
Aorta (abdominal)	Dog	11–16
Pulmonary arteries	Dog	16–20
Spleen	Ox	5
Spleen	Pig	1.2
Spleen	Rat	0.6
Lung (10–30 years)	Human	4
Lung (45–58 years)	Human	7
Lung (64–70 years)	Human	10
Lung (78–94 years)	Human	14
Lung	Human	19
Yellow ligaments (lumbar tract) (25–37 years)	Human	70
Yellow ligaments (lumbar tract) (45–68 years)	Human	56

[a] On dry weight basis.

early in connective tissue development, polysaccharides are found in high concentration. Later, fibrous proteins appear in greater amounts as the concentration of polysaccharides falls. This has led to the view that mucopolysaccharides may play a role in orientation and organization of the fibrous proteins.

As noted above, there is great variation in content and composition of connective tissue at different sites. Connective tissue constitutes the bulk of bone, cartilage, skin, tendon, and ligaments. It is present in very high concentrations in lung and blood vessels. If sections of parenchymatous organs are stained for mucopolysaccharides and fibrous proteins, it is found that thin zones of connective tissue occur around cells and blood vessels of all sizes. An exception is the brain, where the neurones and glial cells are not surrounded by connective tissue, but where the usual pattern of connective tissue in the walls of vessels and in perivascular location is observed.

The amounts of collagen and elastin present depend on the function of the tissue. Collagen maintains form, provides strength, and limits deformations, and is present in high concentrations where these

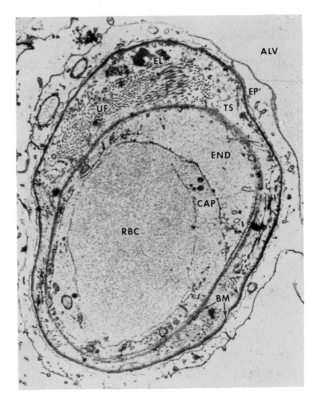

Fig. 3.2 Human lung by electron microscopy. ALV—alveolus, EP—epithelium, TS—tissue extracellular space, BM—basement membranes, EL—elastin, UF—unit fiber (collagen), END—endothelium, CAP—capillary lumen, RBC—red blood cell. (From Low, 1961.)

factors are required (Vogel, 1974). Elastin is a prominent component of mobile and distensible tissues. The extracellular space of the lung and its relationships are shown in Figure 3.2. Polysaccharide is not demonstrated by this technique, but the elastin and collagen content and the dimensions of this space between two basement membranes can be appreciated. It is clear that muscle contraction and tissue pulsations of all types must occur within a matrix of connective tissue, and that all materials passing between cell and vessel must go through connective tissue. Function of connective tissue will be dealt with again in later sections dealing with mechanisms of mammalian aging.

Several generations ago, students of aging noted that connective tissue in the aged appeared dried out or more fibrillar, and advanced the notion that aging was due to dehydration or syneresis of body colloids. We are now in a position to attempt explanations of these observations in more precise terms.

Quantitative age changes

Composition of the extracellular space is probably never in a steady state. Different substances are synthesized and degraded at varying rates, and the amounts of serum and cellular components diffusing through are undoubtedly not constant. We are concerned with progressive and irreversible changes that satisfy the criteria of aging processes. It may be difficult to identify such changes in the extracellular compartment because of certain pathological processes that are age-influenced and are widespread in mammals. The late stage of all inflammatory reactions is characterized by the synthesis of connective tissue polysaccharides and proteins. When such reactions occur in all members of a population, and are progressive, we may consider them as true aging processes.

Fig. 3.3 Extracellular body water (thiocyanate diffusion space) as a function of age in human beings. (From Dittmer, 1961.)

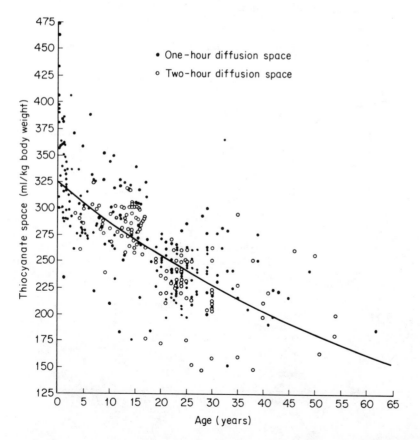

If total extracellular water is measured by thiocyanate diffusion space, it is found that there is a general decrease with age in human beings (Figure 3.3). The scatter of points is quite typical in such measurements of human populations. Since the plasma volume does not change significantly with age, there appears to be a conspicuous decline in tissue extracellular water. The question that arises is whether this represents a shrinkage of the extracellular compartment, or whether the compartment becomes dehydrated. Measurements of inorganic ion concentrations in a variety of human organs have shown increased concentrations of sodium, calcium, and chloride in organs of older individuals. Since these ions are predominantly extracellular, it seems reasonable to conclude that the extracellular compartment increases in size with age. Decreases have been found in the concentration of the intracellular ions potassium (Novak, 1972), magnesium, and phosphate. Figure 3.4 shows changes in body potassium with age and the calculated values for cell mass. Approximately 70 percent of the body potassium is in muscle cells. Such data might be explained on the basis of a moderate muscle atrophy with age.

Fig. 3.4 Total body potassium and cell mass as a function of age in human beings. (Drawn from data of Novak, 1972.)

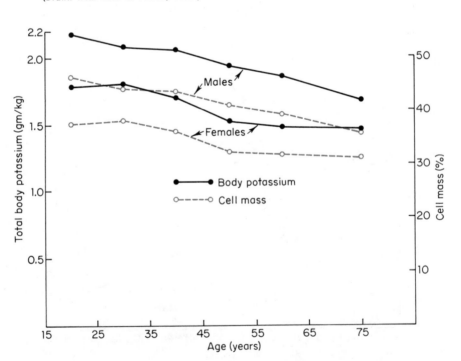

Other studies of wasting or atrophying muscle, as occurs in several diseases as well as with age, have shown relative increases in extracellular substances. It should be noted that such increases do not necessarily denote increased syntheses, or increased absolute amounts, but appear to be consequences of the loss of cellular volume. Such data do not help explain the apparent loss of extracellular water demonstrated by whole-body measurements, and are actually in conflict with these measurements. Changes in the extracellular compartment may vary in different organs, it having been observed that this space decreases from around 21 percent of the brain in 3-month-old rats to 10 percent in 26-month-old animals (Bondareff and Narotzky, 1972).

Human tendon is almost all extracellular. Its changes with age can be recognized by gross examination. In the young, the tendon appears turgid and seems to consist of homogeneous bundles or meshworks. In the aged, it appears much more fibrous and dried out. However, when water content is measured, no significant differences between young and old are found (Kohn and Rollerson, 1959). This suggests that the changes in appearance must be related to how organic substances are hydrated, and to the distribution of water within the tissues, rather than to simple water content. Only a limited number of measurements have been made on water content of fibrous connective tissue, and it is possible that some sites will show a conspicuous loss of water with age. However, with currently available data, we cannot explain apparent whole-body water loss on the basis of loss from such tissue.

Bone comprises a large fraction of the extracellular compartment in mammals. Developing bone is about 60 percent water, whereas very old cortical bone contains about 10 percent water. The mechanism for loss of water has not been studied extensively. It may be that water is simply replaced by collagen and polysaccharides and by inorganic crystal growth during maturation. It is not known if water loss occurs at greatest rates during maturation or during aging.

We must conclude at this point that although significant amounts of extracellular water appear to be lost with age, we do not know where the losses occur. Bone is a possibility. A possibility also exists that the apparent loss of water is, in part, an artifact. Thiocyanate and other agents used to measure extracellular space may diffuse less efficiently with increasing age, and may give misleadingly low values. There are reasons, to be brought out in later sections, for suspecting that this might be the case. We may also conclude that the extracellular compartment does not age by a generalized shrinkage, but that at most sites it increases in size or remains constant.

Much of what we know about age-related changes in the extracellular compartment comes from studies of human blood vessels. These studies

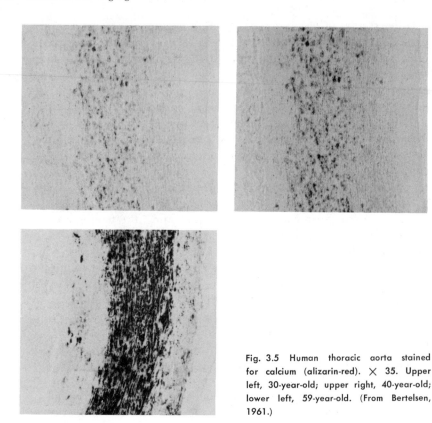

Fig. 3.5 Human thoracic aorta stained for calcium (alizarin-red). × 35. Upper left, 30-year-old; upper right, 40-year-old; lower left, 59-year-old. (From Bertelsen, 1961.)

were undertaken to gain information about arteriosclerosis but have yielded important data about normal aging as well. Several substances that pass through the extracellular compartment become bound or trapped and increase in concentration with increasing age. Calcium salts increase conspicuously. If sections of aorta are stained for calcium, a very striking increase in calcification of the media is observed (Figure 3.5). The pulmonary artery shows the same type of age-related increase in calcium, but absolute values are much lower (Bertelsen, 1961). A large proportion of this salt is probably bound to elastin, as partially purified aortic elastin contains increased calcium as a function of age (Figure 3.6). The increased mineralization of elastin with age may represent progressive deposition, or there may be an age-dependent alteration in elastin that causes increased mineral binding. When isolated human aortic elastin is incubated with calcium, increased binding with increasing elastin age is observed (Figure 3.7).

The accumulation of calcium salts may be a generalized phenom-

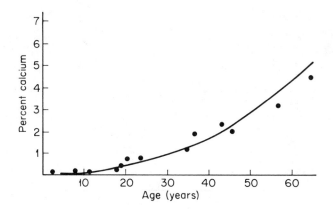

Fig. 3.6 Calcium content of human aortic elastin as a function of age. (Redrawn from Lansing, 1959.)

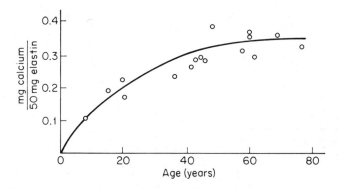

Fig. 3.7 Calcium bound in vitro by elastin from human aortas of different ages. (Redrawn from Eisenstein et al., © 1964, U.S.–Canadian Division of the International Academy of Pathology.)

enon. Crystals of hydroxyapatite form on connective tissue fibrils in the development of bone, and present evidence suggests that calcium in aging, as well as in diseased tissues, may be in the form of apatite. Mineralization of the extracellular matrix of cartilage is a part of mammalian aging. This may occur to the extent that cartilage is converted to bone. It is not known if mineral deposition occurs with age in the extracellular compartment of parenchymatous organs.

Lipids have been found to accumulate in connective tissues with age. Figure 3.8 shows total lipid in human sclera, a dense collagenous connective tissue, as a function of age. Most of the increase is due to cholesterol esters and sphingomyelin. Such lipid deposition may occur

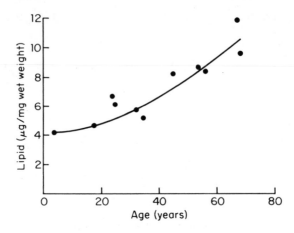

Fig. 3.8   Total lipids in human sclera as a function of age. (Modified from Broekhuyse, 1972.)

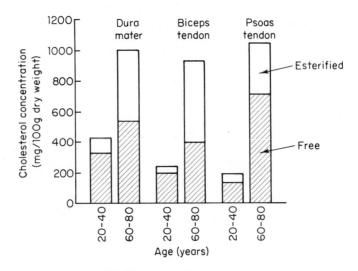

Fig. 3.9   Cholesterol, free and esterified, in human connective tissue as a function of age. (Redrawn from Crouse, Grundy, and Ahrens, 1972.)

in connective tissues throughout the body. Age-related increases in both free and esterified cholesterol have been found in three additional collagen-rich extracellular tissues (Figure 3.9). Because of the low cell concentration in such tissues, it is unlikely that these lipids are synthesized locally. It is more probable that they are trapped or bound as they diffuse through the extracellular compartment. Such lipid accumulation in connective tissue is very similar to characteristic changes in arteries in the age-related disease atherosclerosis and may have a similar basis. This question will be discussed in a later chapter.

The interpretation of quantitative changes in glycosaminoglycans and collagen with age is complicated by the role of these substances in pathologic processes. They are synthesized in inflammation and healing and at sites of prolonged, severe tissue stresses, and they tend to accumulate where there is a loss of cells or cell atrophy. Such accumulation may occur only at certain sites and with great variability. These pathologic processes are particularly widespread in arteries, which are frequently studied with regard to aging. Arteries are also rich in elastin, which may be altered by disease. Some disease processes, particularly those involving blood vessels, are so universal that perhaps they should be considered normal aging processes. This difficulty in distinguishing between disease and aging processes will be a recurring theme.

With regard to polysaccharides of the extracellular compartment, it can be stated that many quantitative changes occur with age. However, it is difficult to generalize about these changes. The six acid mucopolysaccharides and neutral glycoproteins have been studied in different tissues of different animals, where different patterns of age-related changes have been discovered (Hjertquist and Lemperg, 1972; Fleischmajer, Perlish, and Bashey, 1972; Sames, Stegmann, and Rebel, 1974; Sobel, Hewlett, and Hrubant, 1970). A sample of analytical studies in this area reveals the following: The human aorta, in different studies, shows no change or a decrease in total amount of mucopolysaccharide with age. Hyaluronic acid and chondroitin sulfate decrease, while chondroitin sulfate B and heparitin sulfate increase, and the glucosamine/galactosamine ratio increases. An age-related hybridization between chondroitin sulfate and keratan sulfate has been described in human aorta. In the rat aorta the hexosamine content increases. Hexosamine decreases in human and male rat skin, but remains constant in female rat skin and rat buccal mucosa. Rat tendon shows a decrease in hexosamine, while that of the human shows an increase after 50 years of age. Human cartilage shows an increased keratan sulfate plus glycoprotein/chondroitin sulfate ratio with age, and decreased glycosaminoglycan solubility and enzymatic release of glycans. In the case of rat cartilage, sulfur-containing polysaccharides decrease with age while other polysaccharides remain constant. Total acid mucopolysaccharides decrease with age in human heart valves.

Sobel (1967) has extensively reviewed data of the above type and concludes that although different tissues demonstrate individual aging characteristics, there is a recognizable pattern in age changes in polysaccharide content, which is a normal component of aging and independent of pathologic processes. It is generally accepted that poly-saccharide content is high in newly synthesized connective tissue and that the concentration falls with maturity. Sobel suggests that after maturity there is a continuing loss of hyaluronic acid. This molecule is hydrated to the extent of 200 to 500 ml of water per gram, and its loss should result in a decrease in the water-holding capacity of the tissue. Since actual water content of tissues has not been shown to change, there may be a redistribution of water such that less is bound to macromolecules. Sobel further suggests that there is an absolute or relative increase in chondroitin sulfate B and heparitin sulfate. He postulates that with maturity, polysaccharide synthesis subsides, but that hyaluronic acid degradation continues to occur because it is not bound to other components. Degradation and loss of sulfated poly-saccharides might be inhibited because they are bound to protein.

A useful working hypothesis might be that in the absence of patho-logical processes, quantitative changes in polysaccharides represent a continuation of developmental processes. There is a decrease in the amount of polysaccharide, possibly reflecting hyaluronic acid content, and a redistribution of water such that it is not bound and uniform through the connective tissue but aggregated outside of structural units with a consequent reduction in hydrated gel to fibrous protein ratio. The gel/fiber ratio decrease has been emphasized by Sobel, and may explain in part the age-related difference in appearance of connective tissue, as well as having important functional consequences, which will be discussed in later chapters.

The amount of collagen present in some organs is due to processes that occur at the borderline between normal aging and pathological change. As noted above, collagen fibers are synthesized in response to severe or prolonged tissue stresses and are oriented in tissues parallel to lines of stress. Collagen is also formed as part of the healing phase of inflammation. Thus, wherever indolent inflammatory processes or prolonged stresses occur, a scarring, resulting from collagen synthesis, will be observed. This fibrosis occurs at some sites, particularly in arteries, arterioles, and regions of the heart, in all members of mam-malian populations, and should therefore be considered an aging process as well as a disease. Analyses of collagen content at these sites have led to the concept that tissue fibrosis is a generalized aspect of aging. However, a variety of collagen determinations in tendon and other organs have shown that, in the absence of tissue injury, collagen concentration remains quite constant with age. It appears that col-lagen production is regulated by feedback mechanisms that insure that when sufficient collagen is synthesized to maintain form and pro-vide strength in an organ, further production is inhibited, and the amount present remains constant. When more strength is required in damaged or stressed tissue, collagen synthesis is initiated (Tomanek, Taunton, and Liskop, 1972). The most significant age-changes in collagen are in properties, rather than amount, as will be discussed below.

Very little is known about elastin concentration or content as a function of age. Several studies are in agreement that elastin concentration increases in human lung, primarily in the pleura, and an apparent decrease has been described in ligament (Table 3.2). Both a decrease and increase with age and a redistribution of elastin have been described in human aorta (Feldman and Glagov, 1971; John and Thomas, 1972). It is not clear whether such changes are due to gain or loss of other tissue components. Analyses of elastin in old tissue are complicated by the fact that very old collagen and some glycoproteins appear to have the same solubility characteristics as elastin and are difficult to separate from the latter. Glycoprotein, closely associated with elastin, has been shown to increase with age in human lung and aorta (John and Thomas, 1972).

Aging of collagen

As mentioned earlier, collagen is synthesized as soluble procollagen molecules. These are converted to tropocollagen molecules that aggregate to form insoluble collagen fibrils. While an animal is growing, its tissues contain large amounts of neutral salt-soluble collagen. With maturation or growth cessation, the soluble collagen drops to very low levels as it is incorporated into mature collagen. This disappearance of soluble collagen has been frequently demonstrated in animals that have attained their species-specific size as well as in animals whose growth has been inhibited.

With the cessation of growth, then, almost all collagen is in the form of mature insoluble fibrils. In the absence of severe tissue stresses or inflammation, the amount of collagen remains constant and demonstrates very little turnover. Since cross-linking of collagen subunits occurs in the course of collagen maturation, it might be suspected that some cross-linking could continue to occur after the formation of insoluble collagen.

The extent of collagen cross-linking can be measured in several ways. By determining the amount of soluble collagen, the earliest stages of cross-linking can be determined. However, for measurements of cross-linking in insoluble collagen, more indirect methods are required. It has long been known that if collagen fibers are heated to around 62°C, they rapidly contract to a fraction of their original length and take on elasticlike behavior. The contraction is not completely understood, but is thought to depend on melting of crystalline zones in the collagen and on the rupture of hydrogen bonds. A similar contraction when fibers are immersed in a KI solution supports the view that rupture of hydrogen bonds is important. Force of contraction appears to be dependent on the amount of stable cross-links. Verzár (1956) applied this technique to the study of rat tail tendon properties as a function of age. Solids of such tendon consist of over 90 percent collagen, arranged in parallel fibers. He found that the force required to inhibit thermal contraction showed a clear-cut increase with increasing age (Figure 3.10). These data are generally interpreted as indicating an increased cross-linking. As might be anticipated, the most rapid rate of change takes place during growth, but change at slower rates occurs throughout the life span.

Other studies have been based on a phenomenon well-known to polymer chemists: that highly cross-linked polymers will imbibe water and swell under certain conditions. One form of swelling is the so-called osmotic, or Donnan equilibrium, type. Such swelling occurs maximally at certain pH levels. In the case of collagen in HCl solutions, H^+ and Cl^- ions diffuse into the tissue, where H^+ ions neutralize carboxyl ions in the protein. At pH 2.5 there is a Donnan equilibrium established such that there is a maximal excess of diffusible Cl^- ions inside the tissue over Cl^- ions in the external medium. Ions inside will tend to diffuse out and will exert an osmotic pressure,

Fig. 3.10 Weight required to inhibit thermal contraction of rat tail tendon as a function of age. (Redrawn from Verzár, 1956.)

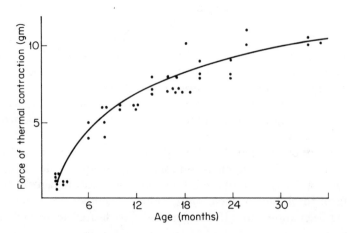

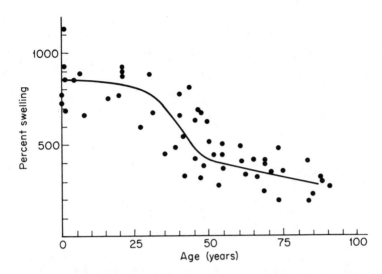

Fig. 3.11 Osmotic swelling of human tendon collagen as a function of age. (From Kohn and Rollerson, 1958.)

causing the tissue to expand by separation of fibrils and subunits. In expanding, the tissue will imbibe water. The amount of swelling is actually a measure of the bulk modulus. Since swelling is restricted by stable cross-links, the amount of swelling would be inversely related to the amount of such links.

Osmotic swelling at pH 2.5 probably involves only mature insoluble collagen since tropocollagen and small aggregates would tend to be extracted by the medium. Figure 3.11 shows swelling data for human tendon as a function of age. There is essentially no change before maturity. Between the ages of 30 and 50 years there is a rather abrupt decline in swelling ability. After 50 years of age, swelling ability continues to decrease at a slower rate.

Swelling of collagenous tissue is also caused by thermal denaturation below the temperature at which contraction occurs. This is probably due to an unfolding of coiled chains. With increasing age of tissues there is an increase in the amount of time required for swelling and a decrease in extent of swelling. By combining thermal denaturation and osmotic swelling data for human tissue, four different stages of increasing cross-linking can be identified as occurring over the life span (Kohn and Rollerson, 1959).

A very large number of studies of aging collagen have been carried out with various tissues of different animals, utilizing different tech-

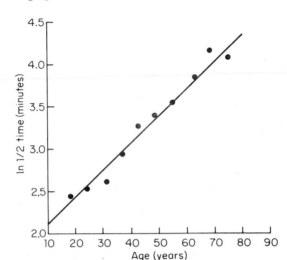

Fig. 3.12 Collagenase digestion of human tendon collagen as a function of age, expressed as the time required for 50% digestion. (Redrawn from Hamlin and Kohn, 1972.)

niques. All properties of collagen that depend on cross-linking or on the degree of aggregation have been found to change with age in ways that would indicate greater cross-linking (Butzow and Eichhorn, 1968). For example, old collagen is less susceptible to digestion by collagenase, presumably because it is stabilized by cross-links. Figure 3.12 shows digestion of purified human tendon collagen as a function of age. It is possible to determine the age of unknown samples with considerable precision by studying such properties of collagen. Age changes in collagen comprise some of the most definitive aging processes at molecular and tissue levels.

Most of these studies have been undertaken with collagen-rich tissues such as skin, tendon, and bone. In parenchymatous organs that contain smaller amounts of collagen and high concentrations of other substances, it is more difficult to gain information about aging collagen. However, a number of workers have studied such collagen by determining solubility properties of hydroxyproline-rich fractions and collagenase digestion of purified collagen fractions, and have obtained data indicating progressive cross-linking with age (Schaub, 1963; Zwolinski, Hamlin, and Kohn, 1976).

All present data permit the conclusion that following maturity, insoluble collagen throughout the body continues to undergo intermolecular cross-linking, and that in human beings the most rapid and extensive cross-linking occurs between the ages of approximately 30 and 50 years.

The types of bonds that form in aging collagen are not known. Most studies of collagen cross-linking have been undertaken with soluble collagen. These have demonstrated some of the earliest cross-links that form during maturation. Traditional analytical methods are applied to molecules in solution. Old collagen is one of the most insoluble of biological substances, and small numbers of additional bonds may cause very marked changes in properties. In degrading old collagen for analysis, it is very likely that age-related cross-links would be ruptured or altered.

One possibility is that aging of collagen is caused by the same types of cross-linking that form during maturation—i.e., aging is a continuation of a developmental process. A number of different types of covalent bonds, as well as short-range forces associated with crystallization, have been described in maturing collagen, but there is no evidence that they increase during aging (Robins, Shimokomaki, and Bailey, 1973). A second possibility is that the aggregation of subunits that occurs in maturation allows new types of specific aging bonds to form. In one of the few studies of cross-linking in insoluble human collagen as a function of age, LaBella and Paul (1965), working with acid hydrolysates, described a decrease in tyrosine and an increase in a substance that fluoresces at 405 nm. The decrease in tyrosine, measured by fluorescence at 305 nm, and the increase in material fluorescing at 405 nm appear to occur linearly with age (Figure 3.13). These workers suggest that tyrosine in collagen becomes oxidized to quinoids, which form covalent bonds with functional groups on adjacent molecules.

Finally, aging of collagen may be by rupture of some bonds that form during maturation, with the exposure of functional groups that can then form new types of bonds. Since our knowledge of cross-linking during maturation is incomplete, and we know even less about bonds forming with age, this possibility cannot be argued very extensively. However, there are some theoretical reasons for not rejecting such a mechanism. It has been pointed out that proteins that do not turn over are incubated at body temperature, 37 to 38°C, for many decades in the case of human beings. Such prolonged incubation would be expected to result in denaturation. It follows that if 37°C could cause denaturation over 30 or 40 years, higher temperatures should cause the same type of denaturation in vitro over a shorter time interval.

Samples of human collagen have been heated at 56°C for various periods, and their osmotic swelling ability was then determined (Kohn and Rollerson, 1959). Elevated temperature caused collagen to show agelike changes in swelling capacity. Furthermore, by measuring rate of change at 56°C, using the energy of activation for thermal denatur-

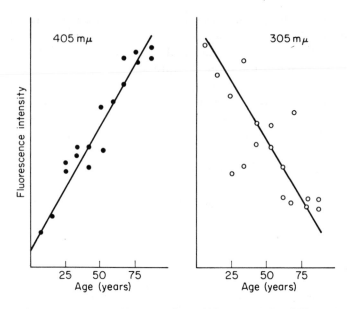

Fig. 3.13   Fluorescence intensity of human tendon at 305 nm (tyrosine) and 405 nm (presumed cross-link) as a function of age. (Redrawn from LaBella and Paul, 1965.)

ation of collagen, and applying the Arrhenius equation, the length of time required at 37°C for loss of osmotic swelling ability, if such loss were due to thermal denaturation, could be calculated. Values obtained were from about 9 to 109 years and, in view of the extrapolations required, were considered consistent with the view that collagen aging could be caused by thermal denaturation. However, thermal denaturation at 56°C did not reproduce the age-related change in susceptibility to digestion by collagenase. Therefore, denaturation cannot be invoked as the sole cause of aging. It is possible that denaturation plays a role in causing rupture of some bonds with an altered molecular configuration, but additional factors, formation of new bonds for example, are required for all of the manifestations of natural aging. Although it is difficult to conceive of no denaturation occurring with decades of incubation, we cannot decide on the basis of current information if such a process is of any importance in the aging of collagen.

Cross-linking of collagen has been described as a physical-chemical process, which would appear to depend only on concentration, time, and temperature. Evidence in support of this view was obtained by experiments in which purified soluble collagen incubated for long periods in vitro gave rise to mature insoluble collagen fibrils. No enzyme system or extraneous agents appeared to be required. However, some studies of collagen synthesis and of collagen defects causd by the administration of certain nitriles to animals indicate that an amine oxidase is probably required for normal cross-linking in vivo. This fits with data showing that cross-links involving aldehyde groups from the oxidative deamination of lysine and hydroxylysine form in maturing collagen (Traub and Piez, 1971).

It is also known that all of the age-related changes in collagen can be reproduced by treatment with a tanning agent, or cross-linker, such as formaldehyde. Since the mammalian body contains many aldehydes that can function as cross-linking agents, some workers have postulated that aging is caused by a generalized tanning of collagen and other proteins by extraneous small molecules. This seems a reasonable suggestion, and if such tanning does not occur, an explanation for its absence must be sought. It can only be stated that cross-linking in vitro does not depend on such an agent, and that extensive analyses of collagen have not revealed the participation of such extraneous small molecules in cross-linking. It may be that functional groups of collagen molecules and polypeptide chains form cross-links before small molecules have a chance to participate, or that steric relationships exclude molecules from cross-linking sites.

Sugars are founds in all samples of purified collagen, generally linked to hydroxylysine. These might play a role in cross-linking associated with aging. Glycosaminoglycans have similarly been suggested as playing a role in age-related changes in collagen properties, but there is no evidence on this point.

Extrinsic factors in collagen cross-linking must be considered because of certain questions arising from comparative aspects of animal life span and rate of change in collagen. The rat lives about $2\frac{1}{2}$ years, and its collagen becomes progressively cross-linked. Human beings live 70 or more years and also show a progressive cross-linking of collagen. If cross-linking depends only on time and temperature, it is not clear why the oldest rat collagen should be any more cross-linked than infantile human collagen. Because of different methods of measurement in different studies, and the measurement of maturation rather than aging, it is not known if collagen at a given site in a $2\frac{1}{2}$-year-old rat is cross-linked to the same extent as that in a 70-year-old human being. However, on the basis of solubility and collagenase digestibility data, the old rat collagen would appear to be much more densely cross-linked than that of a $2\frac{1}{2}$-year-old human. If old rat collagen and human collagen are cross-linked to a similar degree, such cross-linking may depend in part on metabolic factors. Smaller animals with shorter life spans have higher metabolic rates than larger animals with long life spans. A higher metabolic rate may result in the more rapid synthesis of enzymes or tanning agents that accelerate crosslinking.

A role for metabolism in collagen cross-linking has been suggested by the work of Rigby (1964). He subjected collagen fibers to periodic stresses in vitro and found that X-ray diffraction patterns and physical measurements indicated that there was an apparent increase in crystallinity and cross-linking of the fibers. Animals with higher metabolic rates have greater frequencies of tissue stresses. Such stresses might cause accelerated rates of cross-linking in short-lived mammals. It is well-known, incidentally, that tensile stress facilitates the formation of crystalline regions in synthetic polymers, presumably by bringing charged and functional groups close enough together for interactions to occur.

The synthesis and metabolism of collagen are affected by factors that influence synthesis and metabolism of proteins in general, in addition to being affected by local tissue factors. Hypophysectomy causes decreased amine oxidase activity and decreased collagen aldehyde content. These are restored by growth hormone and cortisone (Howarth and Everitt, 1974). Cortisone increases both collagen content and strength of tissue. Collagen metabolism is increased by exercise (Tomanek, Taunton, and Liskop, 1972). It is quite possible that such factors affect rate of collagen aging in different species.

Aging of elastin

Examination of elastin in tissues reveals rather conspicuous changes with age in that old elastin appears frayed, fragmented, more brittle, and more yellow in color. The concept has arisen that elastin suffers from wear and tear, and that some profound chemical changes must be occurring. But because of the difficulty in obtaining pure undegraded elastin, there is considerable confusion about the nature of such changes.

The increasing yellow color of elastin is due to the accumulation of one or more substances that fluoresce. Two fluorescent substances have been identified in human aortic elastin. One, an X substance, increases with age, while the other, a Y substance, remains constant (Figure 3.14). The significance of the increase in X is not known, but this substance could represent a cross-link. A fluorescent material that increases with age in collagen (Figure 3.13) has been postulated to be such a cross-link.

Several analytic studies have indicated that aging of elastin was

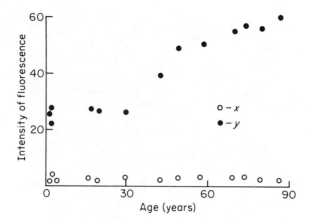

Fig. 3.14 Fluorescence of two substances in human aortic elastin as a function of age. (Redrawn from John and Thomas, 1972.)

associated with a change in amino acid composition. Old elastin, thought to be reasonably pure, was found to contain increased amounts of dicarboxylic amino acids. However, from recent studies it would appear that the amino acid composition probably does not change significantly, and that the dicarboxylic acids are from contamination by collagen or contamination by glycoprotein. The latter increases with age, is bound to elastin, and is rich in dicarboxylic amino acids.

As elastin ages it is found to contain more calcium salts, as noted earlier (Blumenthal, Lansing, and Gray, 1950; Lansing, 1959). This may represent simply a progressive deposition of minerals on elastin, or there may be an age-related molecular change in elastin that increases mineral binding. The latter possibility is suggested by studies in which human aortic elastin of various ages was incubated with calcium salts. An age-dependent increase in mineral binding was observed (Eisenstein et al., 1964). However, since the question of elastin purity has not been resolved, the possibility remains that calcium content and binding capacity may depend on contaminating glycoprotein.

An increased cross-linking would be anticipated on the basis of experience with collagen. The two amino acids involved in cross-linking, desmosine and isodesmosine, have been shown to increase in maturation of elastin, but appear to decrease quite significantly during aging (John and Thomas, 1972). Another molecule involved in elastin cross-links has been identified as lysinonorleucine, and is believed to form by the deamination of an ε-amino group of lysine, followed by a Schiff base formation between the resulting aldehyde group and another

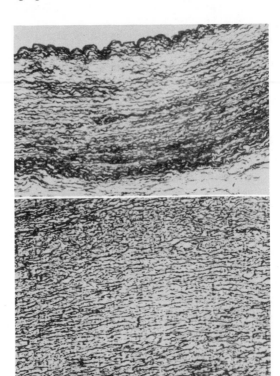

Fig. 3.15 Human iliac arteries stained for elastin. × 90. Top, 18-year-old artery, showing wavy lamellae; bottom, 58-year-old artery, showing fragmentation of elastin. (From Blumenthal, Lansing, and Gray, 1950.)

ε-amino group in a lysine residue on an adjacent chain. One study has indicated that this cross-link increases with age. The possible cross-link role of the fluorescent X has been mentioned. It should be noted that only cross-links that resist strong acid hydrolysis can be identified in these analytic studies. It is very likely that several different kinds of bonds that form during aging are destroyed in preparing samples for analyses.

One of the most prominent changes in elastin is what could be interpreted as a sign of wear and tear. As has been noted, elastin fibers in old blood vessels appear frayed, split, and fragmented (Figure 3.15). We do not know if these changes are due simply to prolonged mechanical damage or to chemical changes, or whether chemical changes occur that facilitate mechanical damage.

Amyloid

Amyloid is a rather mysterious substance that accumulates primarily in the extracellular compartment. Its deposition is associated with several chronic inflammatory diseases, where it usually is found in the liver, spleen, kidney, and adrenal gland. Another distribution in the tongue, heart and blood vessels, gastrointestinal tract, and skeletal and smooth muscle is associated with aging and immunologic disorders. Amyloid deposits can be caused in some mouse strains by a variety of treatments.

Histologically, amyloid is recognized as hyalin, eosinophilic material in extracellular masses, often causing atrophy of adjacent cells (Figure 3.16). It gives characteristic green birefringence with the dye Congo Red, and by electron microscopy is seen to consist of beaded fibrils.

Amyloid is synthesized by reticuloendothelial cells and perhaps by other cells of mesodermal origin. It is a protein distinct from collagen and other well-characterized proteins of connective tissue. Immuno-

Fig. 3.16 Amyloid (arrows) in human heart muscle. × 80.

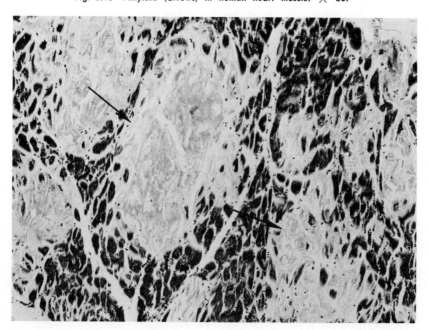

globulin light chains and antibody fragments have been identified in some amyloid preparations, but it is not clear at this time to what extent amyloid consists of such substances. A protein very similar to amyloid, present in low concentrations, has been identified in normal connective tissue, raising the possibility that amyloid is a normal tissue component but is recognized only when it reaches abnormally high concentrations.

The diagnosis of amyloidosis is made by the relatively crude method of histological examination. In aging human populations it has been found, in different studies, to be present in heart and blood vessels in 12 to 70 percent of the individuals (Wright et al., 1969). It is not known if amyloid accumulation is a true aging process, occurring in all members of a population. It is possible that it occurs in everyone, but with marked individual variability, and is recognized only in those who have the very large amounts required for histological identification. This possibility cannot be evaluated until more sensitive methods of analysis become available.

Basement membranes

Basement membranes are structural components of the extracellular compartment. They underlie epithelial and endothelial cell layers and are thought to be of great physiological significance in that all substances passing in and out of blood vessels and the lumens of organs must pass through these structures. Any membrane alteration could result in altered transport. The major protein in these membranes is a form of collagen. These membranes also contain carbohydrate and glycoproteins.

Most studies related to aging have dealt with capillary basement membranes and membranes of renal glomeruli. It has generally been found, both in man and laboratory animals, that there is a thickening of basement membranes with age along with increased variability in membrane thickness in older populations. Table 3.3 shows measurements of membrane thickness in spiny mice and rats as a function of age. It is not known if the increased thickness is caused by increased amounts of the same materials, in the same proportions, that are present in young animals, or if other substances are deposited in the membranes. Although this thickening very likely occurs in all basement membranes with increasing age, we cannot be sure of this on the basis of current information.

TABLE 3.3

Retinal Capillary Basement Membrane Width; Å ± SEM. (Data from Leuenberger, 1973)

Spiny Mice		Rats	
Age, months	*Width*	*Age, months*	*Width*
3	656 ± 13	2	773 ± 82
6	925 ± 19	8	1325 ± 136
12	1098 ± 24	16	1687 ± 152
36	1772 ± 44		

Some generalities

Although there are large gaps in our knowledge, we have enough information to provide us with some general impressions about aging of the extracellular compartment. There appears to be some loss of acid mucopolysaccharide and some changes in relative amounts of certain types of polysaccharide. These changes may cause less water-binding in tissues and a redistribution of water. Collagen, the major fibrous protein, undergoes vary characteristic changes that appear to represent progressive cross-linking. Similar changes probably occur in elastin. The latter appears damaged and less elastic. There is an accumulation of calcium salts, lipids, and amyloid, at least in many cases, and possibly of other materials in or on extracellular components. Basement membranes thicken.

We have not considered the significance or consequences of these age changes. Consequences will be apparent only when we ask specific questions based on aging at higher levels of organization. That is, key aging processes occur at the level of molecules, but we cannot appreciate their significance until we ask questions about aging at the level of cell, organ, or intact animal. Later we will return to aging of extracellular components in attempting to explain aging at higher levels.

Major questions for future work

1. *Mucopolysaccharide content and turnover.* Much more information is required about the effect of age on the concentration of various polysaccharides and their turnover rates, particularly in par-

enchymatous organs. Although some data are available on turnover, the rate of turnover has received little attention as a function of age; it is of interest because differences in turnover rate have been invoked to explain differences in concentration. Age changes in polysaccharides may be of great significance in tissue hydration and in physiologic processes.

2. *Water distribution*. Loss of hyaluronic acid and cross-linking of proteins would be expected to result in a redistribution of water so that instead of being uniformly distributed through connective tissue, the tissue would be compartmentalized into water-rich and water-poor phases. Such a change would be important in physiologic processes, but this possibility has not been adequately investigated. Studies of hydration by such techniques as interference microscopy and by the isolation of hydrated components would be useful.

3. *Basement membranes*. Essentially nothing is known about aging of basement membranes structures other than that they have been reported to thicken. Because they are in key positions to regulate the passage of materials, any age-related change would be likely to cause alteration in diffusion processes. Ultrastructural studies might reveal morphological, organizational, or chemical changes with age, and might be used to discover differences in transport of certain particles.

4. *Accumulation of amyloid and other materials*. Most studies dealing with the subject of accumulation of amyloid and other materials have been carried out with relatively pure collagenous tissue or blood vessels. Connective tissue of parenchymatous organs should be analyzed to discover if minerals, lipids, and amyloid accumulate with age. The development of more sensitive methods for amyloid estimation is necessary. Fractionation of tissue to remove cells might be accomplished with the aid of enzymes that degrade cellular components.

5. *Cross-linking of proteins*. The chemical nature of collagen cross-links must be determined, and it must be ascertained whether or not progressive cross-linking occurs in elastin. This will involve sophisticated methods of purifying and degrading proteins, techniques of organic analysis, and possibly nondestructive analytical procedures.

6. *Cross-linking in different animals*. Identical methods applied to collagen at a given site in old short-lived and old long-lived animals should indicate whether the two collagens are cross-linked to the same extent. Additional studies of the role of enzymes, tanning agents,

stresses, nutrition, and hormones in cross-linking of collagen are required in order to explain probable differences in rates of cross-linking.

REFERENCES

Bertelsen, Sv. 1961. Alterations in human aorta and pulmonary artery with age. Acta Path. and Bact. Scand. **51**:206–228.

Blumenthal, H. T., A. I. Lansing, and S. H. Gray. 1950. The interrelation of elastic tissue and calcium in the genesis of atherosclerosis. Am. J. Pathol. **26**:989–1009.

Bondareff, William, and Robert Narotzky. 1972. Age changes in the neuronal microenvironment. Science (Wash.). **176**:1135–1136.

Broekhuyse, R. M. 1972. Lipids in tissues of the eye: VII. Changes in concentration and composition of sphingomyelins, cholesterol esters and other lipids in aging sclera. Biochim. Biophys. Acta. (Elsevier/North-Holland Biomedical Press). **280**:637–645.

Butzow, J. J., and G. L. Eichhorn. 1968. Physical chemical studies on the age change in rat tail tendon collagen. Biochim. Biophys. Acta. **154**:208–219.

Crouse, J. R., S. M. Grundy, and E. H. Ahrens, Jr. 1972. Cholesterol distribution in the bulk tissues of man: Variation with age. J. Clin. Invest. **51**:1292–1296.

Dittmer, D. S. (ed.) 1961. Blood and Other Body Fluids. Washington: Federation of American Societies for Experimental Biology.

Eisenstein, Reuben, et al. 1964. Mineral binding by human arterial elastic tissue. Lab. Invest. **13**:1198–1204.

Feldman, S. A., and C. Glagov. 1971. Transmedial collagen and elastin gradients in human aortas: Reversal with age. Atherosclerosis. **13**:385–394.

Fleischmajer, Raul, Jerome S. Perlish, and Reza I. Bashey. 1972. Human dermal glycosaminoglycans and aging. Biochim. Biophys. Acta. **279**:265–275.

Goldberg, B., and C. J. Sherr. 1973. Secretion and extracellular processing of procollagen by cultured human fibroblasts. Proc. Nat. Acad. Sci. USA. **70**:361–365.

Hamlin, C. R., and R. R. Kohn. 1972. Determination of human chronological age by study of a collagen sample. Exptl. Gerontol. **7**:377–379.

Heikkinen, Eino, and Ilkka Vuori. 1972. Effect of physical activity on the metabolism of collagen in aged mice. Acta. Physiol. Scand. **84:**543–549.

Hjertquist, Sven-Olof, and Rudolf Lemperg. 1972. Identification and concentration of the glycosaminoglycans of human articular cartilage in relation to age and osteoarthritis. Calcif. Tissue Res. **10:**223–237.

Howarth, D., and A. V. Everitt. 1974. Effect of age, hypophysectomy, cortisone and growth hormone on amine (lysyl) oxidase activity in rat aorta. Gerontologia (Basel). **20:**27–32.

John, R., and J. Thomas. 1972. Chemical compositions of elastins isolated from aortas and pulmonary tissues of humans of different ages. Biochem. J. **127:**261–269.

Kohn, R. R., and E. Rollerson. 1958. Relationship of age to swelling properties of human diaphragm tendon in acid and alkaline solutions. J. Gerontol. **13:**241–247.

———. 1959. Studies on the effect of heat and age in decreasing ability of human collagen to swell in acid. J. Gerontol. **14:**11–15.

LaBella, Frank S., and Gerald Paul. 1965. Structure of collagen from human tendon as influenced by age and sex. J. Gerontol. **20:**54–59.

Lansing, Albert I. 1959. Elastic tissue in atherosclerosis. *In* Irvine H. Page (ed.). Connective-tissue, Thrombosis, and Atherosclerosis. New York: Academic Press, Inc. Pp. 167–179.

Leuenberger, P. M. 1973. Ultrastructure of the ageing retinal vascular system, with special reference to quantitative and qualitative changes of capillary basement membranes. Gerontologia (Basel: S. Karger AG). **19:**1–15.

Low, Frank N. 1961. The extracellular portion of human blood-air barrier and its relation to tissue space. Anat. Rec. **139:**105–111.

Novak, Ladislav P. 1972. Aging, total body potassium, fat-free mass, and cell mass in males and females between ages 18 and 85 years. J. Gerontol. **27:**438–443.

Rigby, B. J. 1964. Effect of cyclic extension on the physical properties of tendon collagen and its possible relation to biological ageing of collagen. Nature. **202:**1072–1074.

Robins, Simon P., Massami Shimokomaki, and Allen J. Bailey. 1973. The chemistry of the collagen cross-links: Age-related changes in the reducible components of intact bovine collagen fibres. Biochem. J. **131:**771–780.

Sames, Klaus, Thomas Stegmann, and Wolfgang Rebel. 1974. Age-related changes in concentrations of acid mucopolysaccharides in human heart valves. Gerontologia. **20:**69–82.

Schaub, M. C. 1963. Qualitative and quantitative changes of collagen in parenchymatous organs of the rat during ageing. Gerontologia. 8:114–122.

Seifter, S., and P. M. Gallop. 1966. The structure proteins. *In* H. Neurath (ed.). The Proteins. New York: Academic Press, Inc.

Sobel, H. 1967. Aging of ground substance in connective tissue. Adv. in Gerontol. Res. 2:205–283.

———, Martinez J. Hewlett, and H. Everett Hrubant. 1970. Collagen and glycosaminoglycans in skin of aging mice. J. Gerontol. 25:102–104.

Tomanek, Robert J., Cheryl A. Taunton, and Karen S. Liskop. 1972. Relationship between age, chronic exercise, and connective tissue of the heart. J. Gerontol. 27:33–38.

Traub, W. and K. A. Piez. 1971. The chemistry and structure of collagen. Adv. in Protein Chem. 25:243–352.

Van der Korst, J. K., A. G. W. Lansvik, and A. E. M. A. Van Hooft-Aarnoutse. 1971. Amylase resistance and insolubility of ageing costal cartilage in man. Ann. Rheum. Dis. 30:290–293.

Verzár, F. 1956. Ageing of collagen fibres. *In* F. Verzár (ed.). Experimental Research on Aging. Experientia Supplementum IV. Basel: Birkhäuser Verlag. Pp. 35–43.

Vogel, H. G. (ed.). 1973. Connective Tissue and Aging. Excerpta Medica, Amsterdam.

———. 1974. Correlation between tensile strength and collagen content in rat skin: Effect of age and cortisol treatment. Connect. Tissue Res. 2:177–182.

Walford, R. L., P. K. Carter, and R. B. Schneider. 1964. Stability of labeled aortic elastic tissue with age and pregnancy in the rat. Arch. Pathol. 78:43–45.

Wright, J. R., et al. 1969. Relationship of amyloid to aging. Medicine. 48:39–60.

Zwolinski, R. C., R. Hamlin, and R. R. Kohn. 1976. Age related alteration in human heart collagen. Proc. Soc. Expt. Biol. Med. 152:362–365.

FOUR

Intracellular Aging

In considering the aging of intracellular components, we are
immediately faced with the problems of categorizing information and
acquiring frames of reference. We shall be interested in components
that turn over in stable cells, and in cells that are themselves turning
over, as well as in nonrenewable materials in both stable and turning-over cells. Interpretation of data is further complicated by such
factors as growth and function, which may cause or reverse certain
alterations. In this chapter we shall consider aging of intracellular
components as an extension of chemical aging. That is, we shall discuss those changes occurring inside of cells that appear to satisfy the
criteria of aging processes in starting or accelerating at maturity and
in being progressive and irreversible. At this point we shall not deal
extensively with the types of cells in which these changes are occurring. The significance of aging of intracellular components in different
kinds of cells will be considered in the next chapter.

Aging of components that turn over

When radioisotopes were first used widely as tracers in metabolic studies, the impression was gained that most proteins and
organelles were in a dynamic state. It appeared that these substances
and structures throughout the mammalian body were being continuously synthesized and degraded or lost, many at very rapid rates. When
some of these systems were studied in more detail, however, it was
found that many turnover rates did not reflect synthesis and degradation of intracellular components. In some cases, what had been mea-

sured was turnover of entire cells rather than of their constituents. Proteins in cells of the gastrointestinal tract appear to have a high rate of turnover because the cells that contain them are continuously being shed and replaced. Periodic sampling of the mucosa for determination of isotope content will not reveal the basis of protein turnover.

Some organs such as liver produce large amounts of protein that leave the cells and are utilized elsewhere. Many serum proteins, for example, are produced in the liver. Since these serum proteins are released from cells shortly after synthesis, analyses of pooled liver cell proteins would give erroneous high values for protein turnover. Furthermore, certain assumptions about protein pools have been found untenable. For example, a fraction of myosin, the major structural protein of muscle, can be extracted in high ionic strength buffers. Isotope incorporation into this fraction indicated that myosin turned over quite rapidly. However, this fraction of myosin is probably not representative of the total myosin and appears to exist in a pool that is metabolically different from that of the less easily extracted myosin. At present we do not know the turnover rate of this important protein.

Although the question of turnover requires extensive reexamination, certain conclusions are justified on the basis of current information. All of the soluble enzymes and other soluble proteins such as those in serum turn over continuously. Turnover rates for these molecules are quite high. Times required for one-half of the molecules to disappear and to be replaced by newly synthesized molecules usually vary between several hours and several weeks, depending on the protein. Half-lives of some soluble enzymes are measured in hours, or less; the half-life of liver tyrosineaminotransferase, for example, is about 1.5 hours. In some cases there appear to be feedback mechanisms working to control synthetic and degradative processes. When one process accelerates or slows down, the other does likewise in apparent attempts to maintain constant protein concentrations.

Insoluble or structural proteins turn over at slower rates, and some may be metabolically inert. These are the proteins we know least about. Some proteolipid protein of the central nervous system is not turned over, and this may be typical of proteins in structures such as cell membranes and nerve sheaths. The turnover of histones, the basic proteins associated with DNA, has not been studied very extensively. However, the few studies available suggest that different fractions of histone turn over at different rates, that turnover of some fractions may accompany RNA synthesis, and that there is considerable variation between different organs in rates of turnover.

Although DNA is synthesized in populations of dividing cells, once formed, it is not degraded. Such complex molecules, just sitting there as it were for prolonged periods, would be likely candidates for age changes. RNA, on the other hand, exists in a number of different populations, some of which have half-lives measured in hours or less.

Turnover of organelles appears to be quite rapid, and may have little or no relationship to the division of cells that contain them. Liver mitochondria have a half-life of around ten days, which indicates that they are turning over within cells that are not dividing. Since different components of the mitochondria have approximately the same turnover rates, it has been concluded that these organelles are synthesized and degraded as units. The half-life of ribosomal proteins has been determined from in vitro studies of rat liver to be slightly over a day.

Thus, many cell components, notably the soluble proteins and organelles, demonstrate rather high rates of turnover that appear to represent programmed, or normal, ongoing metabolic processes. The possible role of aging in these processes has generally not been appreciated, and experimental work bearing on this question has not yet been undertaken. We may, however, postulate that aging processes are of significance in normal turnover. The question is whether or not populations of molecules and organelles undergo progressive changes before they are degraded. A related question is: Do degradative enzymes recognize age-altered molecules and structures and selectively degrade them as they are replaced by young, newly synthesized populations?

The fact that we describe turnover rates in terms of half-lives denotes that loss of molecules is a logarithmic function or a random-hit process in which there is no selection of the molecules that are lost. Exponential die-away curves have been obtained for several highly purified molecules and organelles. Frequently, however, the curves appear to represent composites of fast and slow reactions, some of which may be first-order. An exponential curve could be obtained for the loss of aged molecules if the rate of aging were very fast compared to the rate of loss or degradation—that is, if the molecules were aged in the sense of being unstable shortly after synthesis. The population of aged molecules would then be a large percentage of the total molecules, and their loss could be first-order.

A number of unrelated observations suggest that aging may play a role in turnover. If a solution of protein molecules or a suspension of organelles such as mitochondria or ribosomes is maintained under physiological conditions of pH, ionic strength, and temperature, the populations invariably deteriorate. In the case of proteins, the deterioration is in the form of denaturation with loss of enzyme activities. Some proteins may be kept at equilibrium indefinitely under special conditions of pH and ionic environment, but such conditions would not be likely to persist for long in vivo. Organelles similarly show a loss in biological activity, associated wth protein denaturation, and loss of morphological integrity manifested by fragmentation and vacuolization. It has long been known that denatured proteins are more susceptible to degradation by proteolytic enzymes than are native proteins. A useful hypothesis might be that complex molecules and organelles do age, primarily by denaturation, and that age-altered molecules are selectively degraded in the course of normal turnover. Indeed, if such aging and degradation were found not to occur, additional mechanisms would have to be invoked to explain why they did not.

Teleological reasoning also tends to support this notion. If intracellular components did not become altered with time, there would be no obvious reason for turnover to take place. A complement of enzymes and organelles, once synthesized, would remain present indefinitely, carrying out their respective functions. One can argue the possibility that turnover mechanisms evolved to circumvent the consequences of aging of certain labile intracellular components. It could also be argued teleologically that turnover occurs so that concentrations of components can vary in response to varying functional demands. These questions are amenable to experimental studies, and should constitute a fruitful area for investigation.

Previous studies on the aging of dynamic intracellular components have been hindered by at least two major obstacles. The first is that it has not been feasible to follow properties of a given population of molecules or organelles over their life spans. The second major problem is in the interpretation of observations of age-related changes in both concentration and structure of components that turn over. These components are exceedingly labile and are responsive to physiological changes. The concentration of pancreatic enzymes changes rapidly in response to food intake. Animals that have undergone physical training show increased concentrations of lactate dehydrogenase in the heart and decreases in skeletal muscle. Similarly, exercise may cause an increase of up to 80 percent in muscle myoglobin. Rapid variations in enzyme concentration during development and in response to hormones and vitamins have been frequently documented. Such lability would be assumed to extend to the protein-synthesizing machinery, where it would be manifested by changes in RNA, ribosomes, and endoplasmic reticulum. Relatively short periods of exercise cause a marked increase in the size of heart mitochondria, whereas cold acclimatization causes increased fragility of liver mitochondria.

Such subcellular alterations in response to changing functional demands, presumably associated with a variety of feedback mechanisms, are of great interest and constitute major challenges in biology. However, these alterations tend to confuse the picture when questions dealing with aging are asked. As will be discussed in Chapter 6, aging animals show many debilities. We shall try to describe underlying causes for these debilities in Chapters 6 and 7. Whatever the causes might be, in the presence of altered function we would expect many changes in dynamic intracellular components. In other words, we may not be able to distinguish cause from effect; age-related changes observed in components that turn over may not represent fundamental aging of these components but, rather, trivial consequences of age changes at higher levels of organization.

The question posed in this section was whether or not components that normally turn over demonstrate aging changes before loss or degradation. It must be concluded that although a priori reasoning suggests that such aging does occur, more direct experimental data are required. We will now consider aging of dynamic intracellular components in aging cells and organisms.

Long-term changes in renewable intracellular components

Changes would not be anticipated over long periods of time in the structure or function of individual molecules or of organelles that are turning over rapidly. Any truly intrinsic changes observed would be most readily explained on the basis of age-related alterations in rates of synthesis or degradation such that older cells, for example, turned over components at slower rates so that altered or partially degraded molecules or organelles accumulated. Alternatively, altered molecules could be explained on the basis of accumulation of mutations with time. No qualitative age changes in newly synthesized renewable soluble proteins have been proved, nor have they been sought with any enthusiasm. Several studies of altered enzyme molecules in aging animals have been undertaken and will be described later in this chapter. Early ultrastructural studies described mitochondria of cells from older animals as showing fragmentation. Similar fragmentation was shown in the golgi apparatus, as was a loss of chromidial substance in neurones. More recent data suggest that such changes may have been due to physiological differences between young and old animals or to variations in susceptibility to damage by procedures used.

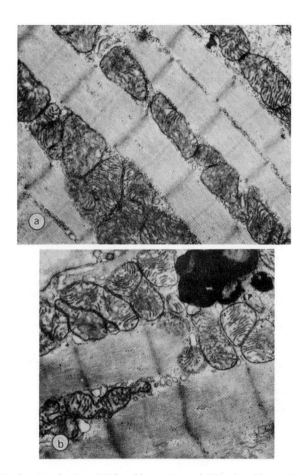

Fig. 4.1 Cardiac muscle from 90-day-old rat (a) and 1004-day-old rat (b). $\times$ 21,000. (From Sulkin and Sulkin, 1967.)

The latter could represent an intrinsic age difference and requires more study.

Studies of the ultrastructure of cardiac muscles and of autonomic ganglion cells from young and old rats have revealed no differences in mitochondria, sarcoplasmic reticulum, or golgi apparatus. As shown in Figure 4.1, the morphology of mitochondria and myofibrils is remarkably similar in rats of very different ages. When young and old animals were exposed to low oxygen tension for long periods, mitochondria from old rats were more severely affected. These mitochondria become swollen and fragmented, while mitochondria from young

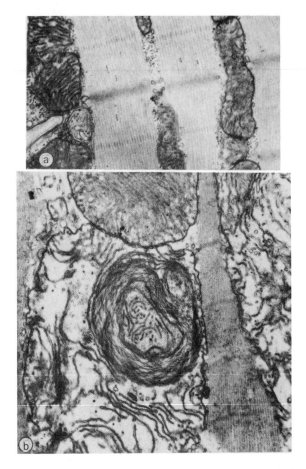

Fig. 4.2 Cardiac muscle from 118-day-old rat (a) and 1032-day-old rat (b) after 28 days in 5.5% O₂ chamber. × 32,600. (From Sulkin and Sulkin, 1967.)

animals showed little change (Figure 4.2.). The mitochondria of the autonomic ganglion cells from old rats also showed marked swelling with loss of cristae and matrix as a response to low oxygen tension, while the organelles from young animals were relatively unaffected (Sulkin and Sulkin, 1967). These studies support the view that qualitative changes in dynamic components over long periods may represent more the effects of environment than of intrinsic aging. In other words, old debilitated animals cannot handle stresses for reasons that will be suggested in later sections, and this continuing inadequacy, or borderline function, may result in subcellular alterations.

A more direct approach to the study of dynamic cellular constituents is to measure their functional capacities in vitro. Metabolic reactions are generally the function of soluble enzymes and organelles that demonstrate rapid turnover, and these reactions can be measured in the laboratory. Some reservations in interpretation are required because, as noted above, the amount and state of these components may reflect the recent history of animals from which they are obtained.

Homogenates of rat brain and liver have been found to show no age-related variation in oxygen consumption. Nor have changes with age been observed in oxidative phosphorylation in brain homogenates and in glycolytic phosphorylation. Succinoxidase activity is approximately the same in mitochondria from young and old rat kidney. Similarly, oxidative phosphorylation of mitochondria from rat liver, heart, and kidney has been reported not to change with age (Gold, Gee, and Strehler, 1968). Rat liver mitochondria, in a more detailed study, showed no change in oxidative phosphorylation (P/O ratio) as a function of age when α-ketoglutarate, malate, and succinate were used as substrates. However, with β-hydroxybutarate as substrate, a significant decline with age in phosphorylation with a constant P/O ratio was described.

Malate dehydrogenase is inhibited by citrate, and it was observed that inhibition was greater in the case of cytoplasmic enzyme from 96-week-old rat brain than 22-week-old samples, but no age differences were apparent in the case of heart cytoplasmic or heart and brain mitochondrial malate dehydrogenase (Singh, 1973). ADP stimulated respiration of myocardial and skeletal muscle mitochondria decreases in the rat after 2 months of age with some substrates but not with others, suggesting that any age changes might not be primary in mitochondrial enzymes (Chen, Warshaw, and Sanadi, 1972). Changes in rates of mitochondrial succinate oxidation in response to thyroid hormone were found to be similar in livers from 12 to 13- and 27 to 29-month-old rats, from which it was concluded that the machinery of respiratory control in response to stress was not impaired with age (Bulos, Shukla, and Saktor, 1972b). Mitochondria from aged animals have been shown to be more sensitive to such treatments as freezing and thawing and incubation, as well as to a toxic agent. These measurements of enzyme activity fail to reveal any generalized changes with age that are likely to be intrinsic to the intracellular components, and to be progressive and irreversible. The age-related phenomena that have been noted may turn out to be caused by changes at higher levels of organization.

There is a theory of aging—the "error theory," that proposes an accumulation of errors in protein synthesis. Attempts have been made to discover if altered protein molecules accumulate with age. One

TABLE 4.1

Aldolase Activity As Units per Mg Protein, in Mouse Skeletal Muscle and Liver As a Function of Age. (From data in papers of Gershon and Gershon, 1973a and b.)

	2 to 2.5 months	31 months
muscle	0.39*	0.32*
liver	0.058	0.029

* Difference not statistically significant.

method has been to prepare an antibody against a purified enzyme, and then compare the amount of active enzyme with the amount of antigenic material (Gershon and Gershon, 1973a and b). In the case of mouse aldolase, there was no change in the amount present in muscle with age, and there was a decrease with age in the amount present in liver. (Table 4.1). An increased amount of inactive enzyme in muscle from old mice was equivocal, but the old liver contained about two times as much antigenic material as liver from young mice. It is of interest that the liver, which can effectively replace altered and dead cells by regeneration, showed a significant change with age, while muscle, which is a stable tissue without effective regenerative capacity, showed little evidence of an accumulation of altered molecules. An altered protein can result from a number of causes, including errors in synthesis, interaction with other molecules, denaturation, and partial degradation. It should further be noted that this study compares growing mice, rather than adult animals, with aging mice. Body weight increased approximately 50 percent between 2.5 and 31 months of age. When differences are observed between mice of these ages, it is not known if the changes occur during growth, aging, or both.

Another attempt to discover if errors in protein synthesis accumulate with age was undertaken with human salivary gland alpha amylase (Helfman and Price, 1974). This protein comprises around 30 percent of the protein secreted, and is secreted in packets, unexposed to cytoplasmic enzymes. No age differences were found in the amount of enzyme per ml of saliva, in enzyme activity per unit protein, or in fractions denatured by heat. It was concluded that no errors in the synthesis of this protein accumulate with age. It has also been observed that the biological activity of insulin per immunoreactive unit does not change between 2 and 24 months of age in the rat (Adelman, 1975).

It can be concluded at this point that when renewable components are examined over long periods, no pattern of qualitative changes can be detected. The changes that have been described might be due to extrinsic causes. The accumulation of errors in synthesis has not been proved in the case of any cell components. It should be noted that we have been discussing properties of renewable cell components and have not considered concentration changes, or changes in dynamic components in short-lived cells that are themselves aging or dying. In addition, a very large number of renewable macromolecules has not been studied in terms of changes in structure or activity as a function of age.

Long-term quantitative changes in renewable components

The amount of a soluble enzyme that is present or the concentration of organelles within a tissue is usually determined by sampling the tissue, preparing a fraction that contains the substance in question, and determining the amount of activity present by chemical methods. In most studies of this type, activity is used as a measure of quantity, although no information is obtained on inactive or masked enzymes present, or on the presence of inhibitors. Also, the nutritional or physiological state of the animal is frequently overlooked. Growing and active animals generally have tissues with higher metabolic rates, higher concentrations of enzymes, and faster protein synthesis than mature animals. Thus, tissues from young animals differ significantly from those of old animals in terms of these components. Adhering to earlier definitions, we are interested in differences between mature and old animals rather than between old and young. Or at the level of cells, we shall be concerned more with differences between mature or differentiated cells and old cells than with variations between rapidly dividing stem cells and differentiated cells.

The only way a population of molecules can change quantitatively is by a change in the rate at which the molecules are synthesized or degraded. Rates of protein synthesis have been of great theoretical interest in aging. It has frequently been postulated, as noted in the previous section, that defects accumulate in DNA or in translation or transcription, and that inadequate protein synthesis is a major cause of both cell and animal aging. Before attempting to evaluate the role of such defects in aging at higher levels of organization, as will be done in later chapters, it is necessary to determine if, in fact, there are alterations in the capacity for protein synthesis or degradation associated with aging. Because of the extreme lability of enzyme and organelle concentration with variation in function, the capacity or potential of a cell to synthesize or degrade a constituent when stimulated is probably of more significance than the amount of that constituent that might be determined at any instant. The rate of protein synthesis in isolated, perfused mouse heart was observed to decrease with age (Geary and Florini, 1972). However, the specific activity of labeled intracellular precursors was highest in the youngest and oldest mice. On the other hand, the synthesis in slices of mouse brain of tubulin, a protein of neurotubules, was found to be constant over the age range of 5 to 25 months, as was the amount of tubulin present (McMartin and Schedlbauer, 1975).

In a large number of studies, the content of different enzymes in different tissues has been determined as a function of age. Barrows and Roeder (1961) determined the concentrations of a variety of enzymes in liver, kidney, and heart of young, mature, and old rats. The most striking differences were between immature and adult animals. No significant differences in enzyme per cell were found with aging between 12 and 24 months of age, except for an increase in the case of cathepsin. These workers also depleted the level of enzymes in animals of different ages by a protein-deficient diet and then determined how fast the enzymes could be synthesized when the rats were given adequate diets. They found no age-related differences in rate of protein synthesis, and concluded that the evidence did not favor impairment in protein synthesis with aging. This conclusion was supported by subsequent studies of lactate dehydrogenase and malate dehydrogenase in five rat organs. Between the ages of 12 and 24 months, the only change was an equivocal decline in skeletal muscle lactate dehydrogenase (Table 4.2). Additional studies of the rat central nervous system

TABLE 4.2

Effect of Age on Lactate Dehydrogenase Activity of Various Tissues of Rats. (From Schmuckler and Barrows, 1966.)

Tissue	Age (months)			
	1	*3*	*12*	*24*
Liver	170.2± 9.5 [a]	150.4± 8.1	163.7±13.6	173.9± 8.5
Kidney	120.3± 3.9	129.6± 5.8	125.1± 7.2	122.9± 5.5
Brain	126.1± 8.4	120.5± 9.4	113.7± 5.9	113.6± 4.0
Muscle	255.6±11.8	324 ±18.7	344.7±18.2	284.2±13.7
Heart	229.6±15.2	280.8±13.4	288.3± 9.5	273.9±10.8

[a] Moles DPN per Gm. protein/hr. $\times$ $10^{-3} \pm SE_M$.

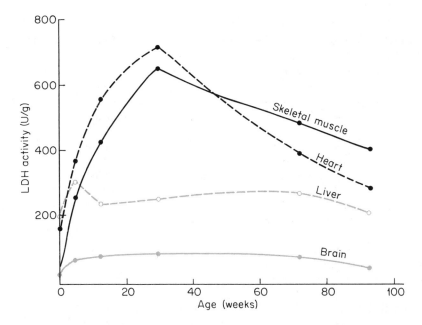

Fig. 4.3 Effect of age on lactate dehydrogenase activity of various tissues of rats. (Drawn from data of Singh and Kanungo, 1968. Used with permission of copyright holder, The American Society of Biological Chemists.)

and the human aorta have also failed to support the view that the synthesis of intracellular protein is impaired with age.

Contradictory results have been obtained in other studies. Lactate dehydrogenase has been found to increase during growth of rats, and then to decline significantly in skeletal muscle and heart with age, while showing equivocal changes in brain and liver (Figure 4.3). Fumarase activity has been reported to remain constant during adult life in mouse intestinal mucosa and liver, while declining in diaphragm and kidney (Zorzoli, 1968).

In a study of 12 enzymes in mouse liver and lung, some were found to decrease with age, while others increased or did not change. The pattern was different in the two tissues, and sex differences were also apparent (Wilson, 1972). A study of three enzymes in mouse brain showed that two decreased with age, and one increased. The almost random-appearing differences in enzyme content of tissues with age can be appreciated in a summary of what happens to myocardial enzymes (Table 4.3).

Thus, studies based on sampling of tissues and determining contents of enzyme activity have revealed no pattern of change with age. The

TABLE 4.3

Changes in Myocardial Enzymes Associated with Aging. (Modified from Limas, 1971.)

Enzyme	Change
Monoamine oxidase	Increase
Dopamine-β-oxidase	Decrease
Dopa-decarboxylase	Decrease
Catechol-0-methyl-transferase	No change
Dopa/α-ketogluterate transaminase	No change
Lactate dehydrogenase	Decrease
Cytochrome oxidase	Decrease
Succinate oxidase	No change
Glucose-6-phosphate dehydrogenase	Decrease
Malate dehydrogenase	Increase
β-hydroxyacyl CoA dehydrogenase	No change

conclusion reached is that when different enzymes in different tissues are studied as a function of age, amounts present are found to either increase, decrease, or stay the same. Because of the extreme lability of enzyme concentration, best appreciated by changes during growth, one wonders if some of the reported changes with age and conflicting observations are due to differences in diets or to the physiological state of the animals.

Information on the metabolism of molecules and organelles represents surveys of the complex systems of enzymes and transport processes responsible for the synthesis and degradation of the components, and also indicates the role of feedback mechanisms that respond to variations in activity and nutrition. A number of studies of metabolism as a function of age have been carried out. The uptake of labeled palmitic acid by mouse brain tissue was found to decrease with age, but the time of maximum incorporation into brain lipids, turnover rate, and the distribution of label into various brain lipids did not vary with age (Sun, 1972). Reduced levels of catecholamine metabolism have also been reported in brains of senescent mice (Finch, 1973). On the other hand, cyclic-AMP levels are constant between 6 months and 2 years of age in rat brain (Zimmerman and Berg, 1974).

In what would appear to be a very significant study, mitochondria turnover was determined in a variety of organs in 12- and 24-month-old rats. Few differences in turnover with age were noted, and in some cases, turnover was greater in tissues from older animals (Table 4.4). Thus, the very complex cellular machinery involved in mitochondrial turnover does not appear to be significantly influenced by age.

TABLE 4.4

Turnover of Mitochondria, as Half-life in Days, in Organs of the Rat. (From Menzies and Gold, 1971.)

	Age	
	12 months	*24 months*
Liver	9.0	9.5
Testes	11.0	13.4
Heart	16.3	18.4
Brain	26.8	23.5
Intestinal mucosa	23.5	16.7
Lung	13.6	17.3
Kidney	11.6	10.8

The resting or baseline state of enzymes and organelles may represent the immediate past history of animals rather than any intrinsic and irreversible changes with age. When cells are stressed to produce enzymes, the synthetic capacity, which is probably a more meaningful indicator of intrinsic change, can be determined. The synthesis of enzymes following starvation, showing no age differences, was mentioned earlier. Synthesis can also be stimulated by causing tissues to grow or regenerate, or by inducing enzymes with drugs, substrates, or hormones.

Gutman, Hanzlikova, and Vyskocil (1971) studied protein synthesis in nerves following nerve section and observed that 24 to 28-month-old rats did not contain as much newly synthesized protein as 1 to 3-month-old rats. Since the young rats were growing rapidly, this information is not very useful with regard to animal aging for the reasons noted above. A comparison between 12- and 24-month-old animals would be more meaningful. However, since nerve cells do not turn over, this can probably be accepted as an example of intracellular aging. Questions posed by this study are: (1) To what extent is metabolism of long-lived stable cells such as neurones influenced by extrinsic factors depending on the age of the animal that contains them? (2) When a smaller amount of protein is identified at a given time, does this result from decreased synthesis or increased degradation?

A very large number of studies of enzyme induction as a function of age have now been carried out and have been reviewed by Roth and Adelman (1975) and Adelman (1975). These have failed to reveal any generalized decrease in synthetic capacity with age, although some variations in response to inducing agents have been observed in animals of different ages. DNA synthesis in rat salivary gland in response to isoproterenol is reduced with age with high doses of the agent, but is greater in old animals with low doses. The same phenomenon has been reported in the case of rat liver tyrosine aminotransferase induced by tyrosine and cortisol. Insulin-induced glucose oxidation and lipid synthesis by human adipose tissue decrease with age. Lipolysis in human fat cells induced by norepinephrine decreases with age, except in cells from obese subjects, where an age effect is not apparent.

In stimulation of rat liver mitochondrial alpha-glycerol-phosphate dehydrogenase by thyroid hormone, no age differences were observed in rate of induction or maximum levels of enzyme attained (Bulos, Shukla, and Sacktor, 1972a). The resting level of kidney catalase is decreased in aging mice. However, treatment with the drug clofibrate, an agent that stimulates enzyme levels in liver and kidney, caused enzyme activity to increase and reach approximately the same levels

Fig. 4.4 Catalase activity in mouse liver following clofibrate treatment, as a function of age. (Drawn from data of Baird, et al., 1974.)

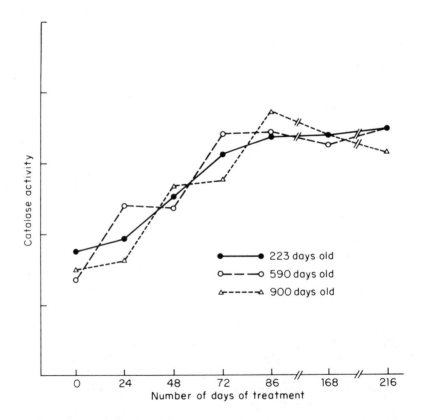

independently of age. Data for the liver enzyme are shown in Figure 4.4.

Mouse liver tyrosine aminotransferase induction shows little or no age difference when stimulated by a variety of hormones (Figure 4.5).

Fig. 4.5 Induction of tyrosine aminotransferase, by several hormones, in livers of 2-month- and 2-year-old rats. (Redrawn from Adelman and Freeman, 1972.)

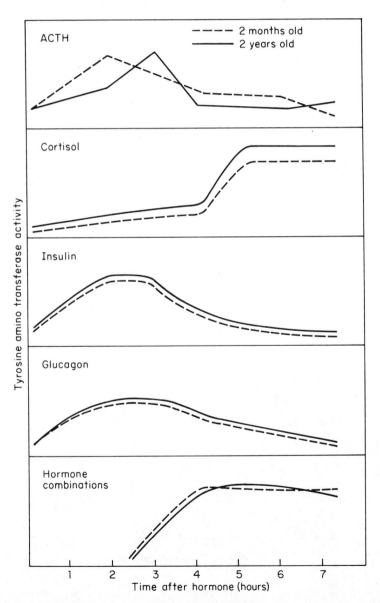

Some induced enzymes show no age differences in final level of enzyme, but do indicate an age dependence in the initiation of induction. In the case of rat liver NADH: cytochrome c reductase induced by phenobarbitol, the initial rate of induction is greater in young animals, but later the rate is higher in the old rats, and the final levels attained are independent of age (Figure 4.6). The same phenomenon occurs in the case of glucokinase induced by glucose, where a linear relationship is seen between age and duration of the initial lag in induction (Figure 4.7). It is possible that steady-state levels of enzyme

Fig. 4.6 Time course of NADH: cytochrome reductase in liver of rats of two ages, induced by phenobarbitol. (Redrawn from Adelman, 1971.)

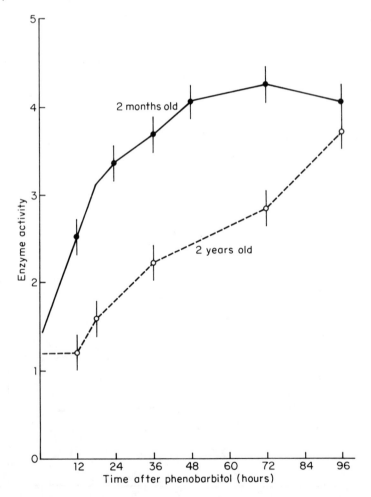

synthesis are lower in older animals, secondary to the lower level of physiological function—an age change to be discussed in later sections. The lag period in older animals might represent the time required for the protein-synthesizing machinery to compensate for the lower initial level of activity. This possibility is amenable to investigation by repeated induction in the same animal.

The proteins discussed in this section are within cells that have long life spans in relation to animal life spans. Nerve cells and heart and skeletal muscle cells do not normally divide or turn over, and are generally present and viable throughout the animal life span. Liver cells and, to a lesser extent, kidney cells have the capacity to divide, and may do so rapidly under certain circumstances. However, both types of cells normally have a very low rate of division and replacement. It appears clear that in these cells there is no widespread or generalized quantitative change associated with age in dynamic components. There also appears to be no significant or generalized loss of capacity to

Fig. 4.7 Lag period in liver glucokinase induction by glucose, as a function of rat age. (Redrawn from Adelman, 1971.)

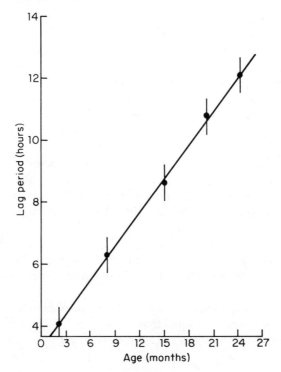

synthesize proteins in these long-lived cells, as a function of the age of the animal. It may be argued that there is suggestive evidence that some proteins are less rapidly synthesized with age, that some studies have shown lower enzyme concentrations, and that since only a small number of proteins have been studied, the possibility remains that there is a decline in the ability to synthesize certain key molecules that have not yet been studied. Perhaps, however, the burden of proof should be on the view that aging is associated with an inability to synthesize proteins. To represent an intrinsic aging change, such a decline in synthetic ability would have to accelerate after maturity of the system involved, and would have to occur independently of growth, activity, and systemic physiological alterations.

Aging of dynamic components in individual short-lived cells

Changes in neurones and in muscle cells occurring over the animal's life span should be considered examples of intracellular aging since these cells do not normally divide and are not replaced. Investigations of tissues such as epithelia, liver, or kidney cannot in all cases be viewed as intracellular studies because it is not known whether any changes noted occur within a given cell during its life span. Over very long periods, it is likely that different cells are being studied as a result of cell turnover. Cells that are stable and turn over very slowly comprise the majority of cells in mammals.

There are many populations of cells in mammals, however, that have short life spans in relationship to the animal's life span. These cells are born and die quite independently of the animal that contains them. They appear to have rates of turnover that are rapid and programmed. Typically, there is a zone or focus where stem cells divide, giving rise to the cell population. The newly formed cells do not divide but undergo chemical and morphological specialization. They then deteriorate and die. As they die, they are replaced by new cells. Examples of such cell populations are stratified epithelia of the skin and urinary tract, glandular epithelia of the gastrointestinal tract, red blood cells, and granulocytic leukocytes. Between the last cell division and death, each cell in these populations represents an aging system.

In many cases the entire cell life span can be observed in one micoscopic field. In a stratified squamous epithelium, division occurs in the basal cell layer. In the superficial layers, division does not occur, but the cells become flattened and synthesize large amounts of keratin. Dynamic cell populations usually synthesize some special product such as mucin, glycogen, enzymes, hemoglobin, or keratin. In the case of squamous epithelium we know that the basal cells synthesize little or no keratin, whereas the superficial cells synthesize large amounts. Because of this difference in synthesis and the marked changes in appearance with aging, we can assume that very profound changes occur with age in the enzyme complement of such cells. However, essentially no systematic work has been done on changing enzyme patterns in cells of this type with special reference to cell aging.

Some studies carried out on special populations of dynamic cells suggest that quantitative changes do occur in cell components that turn over, and also suggest an answer to the question posed earlier about the possibility that molecules that turn over become aged before they are lost or degraded. Rat neutrophils have life spans measured in hours, and they do not divide. When such cells are maintained in vitro, under what appear to be ideal conditions, there is a rapid loss in the activity of at least two enzymes, succinic dehydrogenase and an enzyme, or enzymes, responsible for lactic acid production (Figure 4.8). There are many possible explanations for this observation. However, it is likely that degradation, denaturation, or loss through diffusion proceeds faster than synthesis of enzymes, which may decrease with age in vitro.

Red blood cells have received a lot of attention because of their use in medicine and because they can be isolated in large amounts. The mature cell in mammals has lost its nucleus and has a life span in the circulation of dogs and human beings of about 110 days. Without the nucleus, the cell cannot synthesize new messenger RNA, and protein synthesis is essentially cut off, although hypothetically some synthesis could occur because of persisting RNA. Thus, although the red cell is far from a typical cell, it is of use in the study of intracellular aging because aging processes are not complicated by growth and syntheses. In the absence of aging processes there would be no reason for the red cell not remaining at equilibrium or in a steady state indefinitely.

Red cells can be obtained from an individual, and mature cells can be separated from old ones by utilizing specific gravity differences. A number of studies are in agreement that there is a generalized loss in the activity of many enzymes with cell aging, or after loss of nuclei. This would be anticipated, and is presumably on the basis of either enzyme denaturation or loss by diffusion. The loss, however, is not uniform; the ratio of aldolase *A* to *C* varies in aging rabbit red cells (Weber, Hatzfeld, and Schapira, 1973). One enzyme, catalase, appears

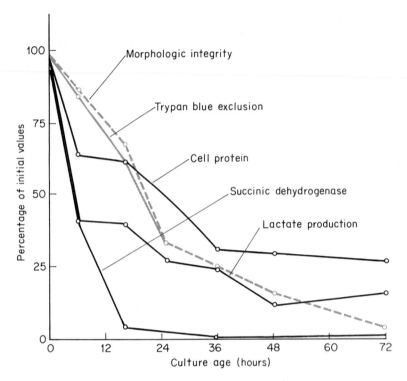

Fig. 4.8 Properties of rat leukocytes aging in vitro. (From Kohn and Fitzgerald, 1964.)

to be maintained at a constant level of activity with age. However, this enzyme exists in at least three forms, and, with age, there is a decrease in one form and an increase in a second (Thorup, Carpenter, and Howard, 1964). This may represent molecular aggregation with age if the three catalases are isozymes formed by interactions of small numbers of subunits. A structural change with age, manifested by alteration in electrical charge, has also been demonstrated in the β-chain of hemoglobin. In the normal nucleated cell such soluble proteins would probably be turning over, and changes of the type described would be very hard to detect. These data suggest that in the absence or slowing of protein synthesis, losses or alterations in some proteins would be expected, and these could proceed to a point incompatible with cell life. The catalase and hemoglobin data also hint that soluble proteins in nucleated cells might be altered before being lost and replaced.

On the other hand, a study of mouse red blood cells aged in vivo, in which new cell formation was inhibited by actinomycin D treatment, showed no loss of glucose-6-phosphate dehydrogenase and 6-

phospho-gluconate dehydrogenase during 35 days (Van Gastel and Bishop, 1968). If this finding is confirmed, it would be a demonstration of remarkable enzyme stability.

The protein-synthesizing machinery and age

In previous sections, indirect studies on the question of errors in protein synthesis were cited. The most direct approach to the problem of protein synthesis as a function of age would be to study the macromolecules, organelles, and co-factors responsible for the synthesis of proteins. A number of such studies have been undertaken, frequently with the assumption that there is a generalized age-related decrease in the ability to synthesize proteins, even though this is a tenuous notion, as discussed above. Few studies have been carried out, unfortunately, on what happens within an individual cell with the passage of time, and most investigations of this type have been done with tissues obtained from animals of different ages.

The DNA content of bovine thymus and of rat brain, muscle, kidney, and liver cells does not change significantly over the animal's life span. Although molecular weights of rat liver DNA were observed to decrease during maturation, little change was found between 400 and 1000 days of age (Massie et al., 1973). In a study of chromatins from dog heart, no differences in protein/DNA and RNA/DNA ratios, or in salt extractability, or percentage DNA transcribed were found as a function of age (Shirey and Sobel, 1972).

Histones in bovine thymus similarly remain constant in total concentration. No age-related variation in proportions of mouse and rat liver histones could be detected (Carter and Chae, 1975).

It has been postulated by von Hahn that there is an increased binding of histones to DNA with age. He isolated fractions containing various histone-DNA aggregates from bovine thymus and found equivocal changes with age in concentrations of the fractions. Extending these studies to rat liver, von Hahn and Fritz (1966) isolated fractions with similar histone/DNA concentration ratios from animals of different ages and determined their melting temperatures, on the assumption that melting temperature was a measure of the strength of DNA-histone binding. Although there was a marked scatter of values, results were consistent with the view that binding increased with age (Figure 4.9).

At a higher level of organization, that of the chromosome, some in-

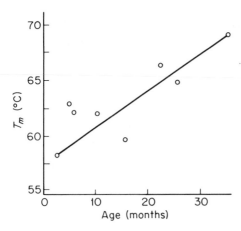

Fig. 4.9 Melting temperature (Tm) for DNA preparation with 1–2% histone from rat liver of different ages. (Redrawn from von Hahn and Fritz, 1966.)

teresting observations have been made. The unfertilized egg is a useful example of an aging cell. It has been observed that chromosomes of aging rabbit eggs become either pycnotic or scattered (Austin, 1967). Oocytes from mice show an age-related increase in univalents, and a decrease in chiasma frequencies (Luthardt, Palmer, and Yu, 1973). An increased incidence of trisomy 21 (Down's syndrome) in the offspring of human females of increasing age has been frequently documented. Also, increased numbers of aneuploid lymphocytes in human females, and lymphocytes lacking Y chromosomes in males have been reported in the aged. These chromosomal abnormalities represent more the accumulation of accidents in cell populations than progressive aging processes.

The question of age and abnormal chromosomes has also been studied by Curtis (1963), who treated mice with an agent to destroy much of the liver, and then scored gross chromosomal aberrations in dividing cells as a function of age in liver as it regenerated. He found that the percentage of aberrations increased with age, that the increase was greater in a short-lived mouse strain, and that irradiation caused a marked increase in the percentage of altered cells. With the passage of time after irradiation, there was a drop in the percentage of aberrations (Figure 4.10). The significance of these observations will be discussed in later sections dealing with the aging of animals. However, for the time being, it should be noted that the long-lived strain apparently never has as many aberrations as the short-lived strain has at the end of its median life span, that the short-lived strain has about as many abnormal chromosomes at about 250 days of age as the long-lived strain has at the end of its life span, that irradiated animals at 4 months of age have close to twice as many altered chromosomes as

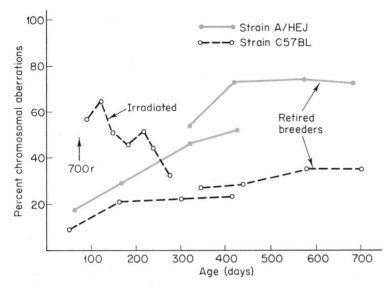

Fig. 4.10 Chromosomal aberrations as a function of age of short- (A/HEJ) and long-(C57BL)-lived strains of mice, and of mice following irradiations. (Redrawn from data of Curtis. Copyright 1963 by the American Association for the Advancement of Science.)

the long-lived mice at the ends of their life spans, and that aberrations do not increase after maturity.

The activity of liver DNA polymerase has been found to decrease with age when two-stranded DNA was used as primer, but to increase with heat-denatured DNA (Mukundan, Devi, and Sarkar, 1963). However, this change is clearly correlated with growth rate rather than aging because the most rapid rate of change is in young growing animals. The change is also reversible, in that regenerating liver polymerase takes on the properties of the enzyme from young liver.

Nuclear RNA synthesis has been determined as a function of age in rat brain, liver, and muscle, and has been found to both increase and decrease with age in various studies (Gibas and Harman, 1970; Britton, Sherman, and Florini, 1972). No age difference in activity of nuclear RNA polymerase has been observed (Britton, Sherman, and Florini, 1972).

By using RNA-DNA hybridization techniques, it has been observed that there is a ribosomal gene loss, or inactivity, as a function of age in heart muscle of human beings and dogs (Johnson, Johnson, and Strehler, 1975). The turnover rate of ribosomes of various tissues was found not to differ in 12- and 24-month-old rats (Menzies, Mishra, and Gold, 1972). Soluble RNA turnover was found to decrease with age in rat spleen. Labeled soluble RNA decayed in a single exponential pattern in young liver and kidney, but yielded a double exponential decay curve in 24-month-old rats. The half-life for the slow second component in old liver was the same as that for decay in the 12-month-old animals. The second component in old kidney indicated a slower decay rate than the rate in younger animals (Menzies, Mishra, and Gold, 1972).

Purified rat liver microsomes from 7 to 11- and 19 to 25-month-old rats have been reported to show decreased amino acid incorporation with age, and evidence was obtained suggesting the presence of an inhibitor of incorporation in the microsomes from the old animal (Hrachovec, 1971). On the other hand, transfer RNA in liver and brain of mature and old mice was studied in terms of acceptance of a number of amino acids, and no significant age differences were observed. This negative finding was viewed as evidence against an age-related accumulation of translation errors (Frazer and Young, 1972).

Thus, the available information on changes with age in RNA, ribosomes, and translation is fragmentary and in some cases contradictory.

It appears that at the chromosome level, gross alterations occur in the aging of short-lived cells—at least in eggs, and probably in the aging of organs such as the liver. At the molecular level, however, we must draw the same conclusions as from the studies of protein synthesis. Although some interesting questions have been raised, no intrinsic age-related defect in function of the protein-synthesizing machinery has been consistently demonstrated.

Degradation of intracellular components

When one is considering how intracellular components might be broken down or gotten rid of, the major problem would appear to be removal of macromolecules and structural complexes. Smaller molecules might diffuse out of cells or might be consumed in a variety of metabolic reactions. Mechanisms by which complex molecules might be degraded bear on problems of aging in several ways. In the normal turnover of macromolecules, discussed earlier as possibly representing aging of a population, synthesis rates must be balanced by degradative rates in order to maintain a stable population size. If the rate of degradation exceeded or was exceeded by the rate of synthesis, the population would diminish or become larger. Any progressive and irreversible change in population size would represent an aging process. Thus, degradative processes could play a role in the aging of a population of molecules of constant size, or could determine concentration changes with age.

If synthesis or accumulation of molecules occurs and there is no mechanism of degradation, the result will be an accumulation of molecules—an aging process. Similarly, if synthesis subsides and degradation does not occur, the result will be a stable population of molecules that could then undergo such age changes as denaturation, polymerization, or crystallization.

As animals age there is frequently a wasting or atrophy of organs. A good example of this is skeletal muscle atrophy, which is probably secondary to generalized debility and lack of function rather than due to intrinsic cellular aging processes. Such consequences of aging are associated with losses of large amounts of structural proteins, enzymes, and organelles. The end point of cell aging is cell death. In some cases, particularly when such cells are at epithelial surfaces, they are sloughed off. In other instances all of the components of dead and dying cells are degraded and removed by various mechanisms.

Although degradative processes are of great significance in many biologic processes, we are unable to describe mechanisms in any detail. For the present, we can only define the problems and indulge in some speculation. The remarkable progress in understanding protein synthesis has not been balanced by an understanding of what happens at the other end, where the proteins are lost. This ignorance leads to some perplexing questions about systems where we know proteins or organelles are being rapidly lost. For example, when a nerve to rat muscle is cut, the muscle loses about 50 percent of its total substance in 12 days. Although structural proteins such as myosin are lost at a rapid rate, no enzymes capable of degrading myosin have been found in muscle. It would appear that either the isolated myosin has been altered so that it is not susceptible to degradation, or that very special conditions are required for digestion, or that the macromolecule is lost intact without digestion to small molecules.

A very large number of hydrolytic enzymes have been identified in various organs and cells. These include the cathepsins, which are the intracellular counterparts of pepsin, trypsin, and chymotrypsin. Many peptidases with different specificities, as well as glycosidases, esterases, and nucleases, have also been identified and characterized. These hydrolytic enzymes are usually studied by extracting them from tissues and reacting them with synthetic substrates, or in the case of proteolytic enzymes, with well-characterized substrates such as denatured hemoglobin or casein. It is often assumed that these enzymes are responsible for the degradation of intracellular components, although such components have rarely been tested as substrates.

A great deal of interest has been directed toward lysosomes, the intracellular organelles, which contain these hydrolytic enzymes in high concentration (de Duve, 1963; Novikoff, 1963). Lysosomes are

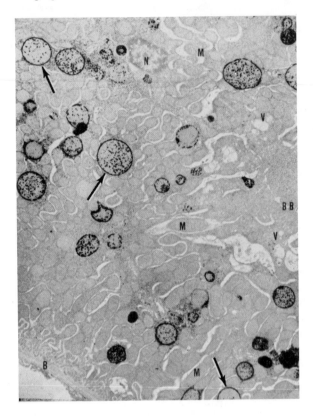

Fig. 4.11   Rat kidney lysosomes (arrows) demonstrated by acid phosphatase stain. × 7,600. V—apical vacuoles, M—mitochondria, N—nucleus, B—basement membrane, BB—brush border. (From Novikoff, 1963.)

bounded by a single membrane and are about the size of mitochondria (Figure 4.11). They can be localized histochemically, usually by testing for acid phosphatase, and can be obtained in quite pure form by density gradient centrifugation. A large number of studies have been carried out on factors that stabilize these organelles and on factors that cause activation of their enzymes and rupture of membranes with passage of active enzymes into the cytoplasm. It has been found, for example, that steroid hormone treatment of animals stabilizes lysosomes, while enzymes are released when lysosomes are exposed to such factors as vitamin A, osmotic shock, detergents, freezing and thawing, and mechanical stresses. Morphologic studies have given rise to the concept that lysosomes bring about intracellular digestion, in many cases by combining with organelles that contain the materials to be digested. Figure 4.12 diagrams the organelles involved and the se-

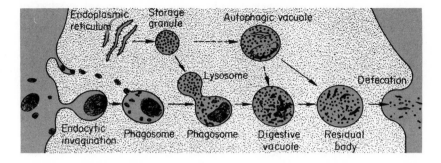

Fig. 4.12 Proposed sequences in intracellular digestion. Storage granules, digestive vacuoles, residual bodies, and autophagic vacuoles are viewed as forms of lysosomes. (From duDuve, The Lysosomes. Copyright © 1963 by Scientific American, Inc. All rights reserved.)

quence of events that is believed to occur in intracellular digestion when lysosomes are intact.

Lysosomes are present in high concentration in liver, kidney, and spleen but are low in muscle. Although more systematic analyses of organs are required, it appears that the concentration may be proportional to rates of protein or organelle turnover.

Lysosomes have been implicated in several pathologic processes, where they may participate in inflammatory reactions and in the events leading to antibody synthesis. Circumstantial evidence and a priori considerations also suggest a role for lysosomes and hydrolytic enzymes in aging processes, although contradictory findings indicate that the relationship between these enzymes and organelles and loss of macromolecules is not very straightforward.

In almost all cases where it is known that intracellular degradation is increased, there are increased concentrations of lysosomes and hydrolytic enzymes. These increases are noted in such instances as skeletal muscle wasting, loss of uterine muscle mass following birth, resorption of tadpole tails, and in degenerating and dying cells. Lysosomal enzymes are also increased, however, in regenerating tissue, specifically in regenerating liver following partial hepatectomy, and in regenerating amphibian tails. It has been suggested on the basis of such data that hydrolytic enzymes may play a role in the synthesis of macromolecules. A simple view of intracellular degradation is also made untenable by observations that lysosomal cathepsins appear to be inactivated during kidney necrosis, and that lysosomal enzyme activity is increased only very late in liver cell degeneration. These data have indicated to some workers that lysosomes play a late and somewhat trivial role in scavenging cell debris rather than bringing about generalized loss of cellular constituents.

Very few studies have been carried out on cell components that might serve as substrates for intracellular hydrolytic enzymes. In one study, liver lysosomes were isolated, and enzymes were freed by freezing and thawing. Enzymes were then incubated with various fractions of liver cells. The lysosomal preparations actively degraded the liver homogenate, mitochondria, and microsomes, but not nuclei. It has also been observed, however, that muscle lysosomal cathepsins have no detectable activity against actin or myosin, the major structural proteins of muscle.

No definitive pattern has been detected in lysosomal enzymes of different nondiseased tissues as a function of age. Some have been reported to increase, while others remain more or less constant (Comolli, 1971).

It would be difficult to avoid the conclusion that cellular enzymes must be responsible for the degradation of most of the components that are known to disappear from cells, although conceivably some components might be lost intact through cell membranes, and then degraded at distant sites or excreted. It is clear, however, that intracellular degradation does not consist of simple enzyme-substrate interactions. Very likely, multiple enzymes must act on a single substrate or organelle to cause extensive degradation, substrates must be altered in some way to be recognized by the enzymes, and unusual environmental conditions must be required for activation of the degradative enzymes. We would also assume the existence of feedback mechanisms regulating the synthesis and activation of hydrolytic enzymes, since concentrations of these enzymes and rates of intracellular degradation are highly labile.

Accumulations—functional

If synthesis of an intracellular substance proceeds and there is no effective mechanism of removal or degradation, the substance will accumulate. This accumulation will constitute an aging process. Some accumulations may be functional in the sense that they are useful to tissue or organism, although they may be harmful to the individual cell involved. In these cases, there has presumably been selection favoring evolution of certain intracellular accumulations. These cases perhaps demonstrate how evolution may result in cellular debility and death for the benefit of the intact organism.

Keratin, a structural protein produced by cells of stratified squamous epithelium, forms a horny impervious layer that protects the epithelium and underlying structures. Steps in the formation and maturation of keratin are analogous to those of collagen. It is first synthesized as a soluble prekeratin, which forms filaments. In mature keratin the filaments are organized into fibrils that are insoluble and resistant to proteolytic enzymes. Chemical inertness is due to a dense cross-linking by disulfide bonds. Epithelial cells continue to synthesize keratin until the cell is completely filled, after which no other cellular functions occur. At that stage the cell is essentially a scale of keratin, and is sloughed from the surface. A similar accumulation occurs in cells of the eye lens. In these cells a series of proteins with unusual optical properties, the crystallins and albuminoid, accumulate. Cells containing these proteins lose their nuclei and are converted to fibers, which persist as major components of the lens. Over long periods of time the accumulated lens proteins undergo an additional form of molecular aging, which will be touched on in a later section.

Additional examples of functional accumulation are the cells of holocrine glands. These cells continue to synthesize specialized products until they become filled. They then rupture and release the products. In a sebaceous gland, cells move from the deeper layers, where cell division occurs, toward the gland surface, synthesizing increasing amounts of sebum. By the time the cells have reached the surface, they consist of bags of sebum.

Other cells have mechanisms for getting rid of cell products, but discrepancies between rate of synthesis and rate of removal may be so out of balance that over the cell's life span a very conspicuous accumulation of products occurs. An example of this is the mucin-producing cell, or goblet cell, of the gastrointestinal tract. There is some evidence that accumulation of mucin is cyclical, in which case the criterion of irreversibility required for an aging process would not be satisfied.

Accumulation of pigment

Investigators of histology, using the light microscope, very early observed aggregations of golden brown granules in long-lived cells such as skeletal and cardiac muscle cells and neurones. These granules were usually in a perinuclear position. In cardiac muscle the aggregates characteristically extend from both ends of the nuclei (Figure 4.13). It was apparent that these accumulations increased with age and that similar pigmented granules could be observed in cases of long-standing tissue hypoxia and vitamin E deficiency. The granules have

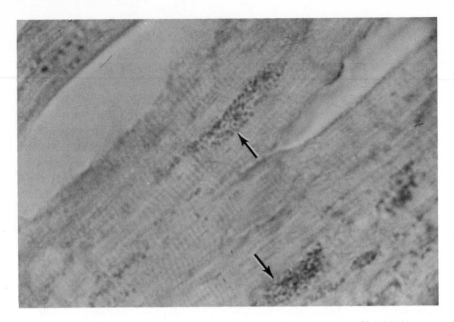

Fig. 4.13   Lipofuscin granules in cardiac muscle. × 600. (From Strehler, 1964.)

been given a variety of names, such as wear-and-tear, aging, ceroid, and lipofuscin pigments. Lipofuscin appears to be the current designation of choice.

Lipofuscin granules have been studied most extensively in muscle and neurones but have been identified in many organs, notably the adrenal cortex, ovarian cells, and interstitial cells of the testis. There is considerable variation between individual cells in concentration, but it is clear that with age both the concentration per cell and the number of cells containing lipofuscin increase (Strehler, 1964). In the dog the percentage of myocardium taken up by lipofuscin pigment increases steadily with age (Figure 4.14). Similar measurements have been made of human myocardial lipofuscin, and it is of interest that the rate of accumulation in the dog is about 5.5 times as fast as in the human, whereas human beings have a life span about 5.5 times that of the dog. That is, old dogs and old humans have approximately the same amount of lipofuscin. This indicates that pigment formation is not the consequence of simple reactions that are only time and temperature dependent, but that accumulation results from metabolic reactions that occur at different rates in mammals with different life spans.

Ultrastructure of the granules is quite variable. They may occur as

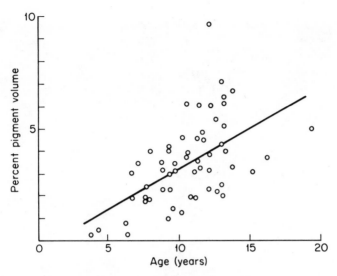

Fig. 4.14 Percentage of myocardial volume occupied by lipofuscin pigment as a function of age in dogs. (From Munnell and Getty, 1968.)

dense aggregates of very small granules or as organelles containing vacuoles of varying size (Figure 4.15). Peripheral membranes are present in some cases. The granules are very heterogeneous structures by chemical analysis. They contain many lipids of known composition, including lecithin, cephalin, sphingomyelin, and cholesterol esters. Also, many glycerides and saturated and unsaturated hydrocarbons have been identified in the granules. It is generally believed that a large component of lipofuscin consists of macromolecules formed by oxidative polymerization of unsaturated lipids. Protein also constitutes a significant fraction of the granules, and a number of enzyme activities have been identified. These include hydrolytic enzymes of the type found in lysosomes, as well as respiratory enzymes. The granules contain acidic groups, and it has been suggested that some of these components may be adsorbed to their surface.

The genesis of lipofuscin granules is not known. It has been postulated by various investigators that they represent degenerated mitochondria or lysosomes, that they are unique orangelles that sequester harmful intracellular garbage, or that they are formed by cross-linking of elements of the endoplasmic reticulum. Their increase represents a true aging process in which aggregation and polymerization appear to occur, resulting in the accumulation of substances for which there is no adequate mechanism of removal.

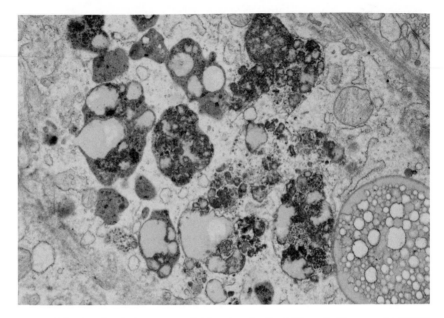

Fig. 4.15 Vacuolated pigment granules in adrenal cell of 20-month-old mouse. X 18,000. (From Samorajski and Ordy, 1967.)

Accumulation of minerals

The accumulation of minerals, particularly calcium salts, in connective tissue with age was mentioned in an earlier chapter. Similar accumulations might be expected in cells, in view of the fact that crystal formation and growth represent aging processes that should take place wherever ions are present in significant concentrations for long periods.

Several decades ago a number of observations gave rise to the concept that rapidly dividing cells such as those in neoplasms had very low concentrations of calcium, while cells that were stable or slowly dividing had high concentrations. It was reported that calcium ions increased with age in the cortex of cells from plants, rotifers, planarians, and amphibians. An age-related increase in cellular binding of calcium was claimed on the basis of experiments in which increased calcium was found in the livers of mature mice compared to young mice, after the injection of a calcium isotope. Contradictory results were obtained when a variety of organs from rats of different ages were homogenized and incubated with calcium. No difference in calcium binding with age was noted.

Although data on calcium binding are equivocal, it has been suggested that such binding may be harmful to cells on the basis of experiments in which longevity of unfertilized invertebrate eggs and rotifers was achieved by decreasing calcium in the media, and by citrate treatment to remove calcium.

Whereas calcium is predominantly extracellular, magnesium has a higher concentration within cells. One study has indicated that the latter ion increases in concentration with age in human smooth and skeletal muscle.

On the basis of current information, one cannot generalize about mineralization of cells with age. Additional systematic studies, employing more modern methods of tissue fractionation and elemental analyses, are required.

Aging of stable and structural cell components

Many cells contain structural macromolecules that have very low rates of turnover. Contractile proteins of muscle, which comprise a large fraction of the total body protein, are examples. Other structural components of cells such as membranes would be expected to have low rates of turnover because of their insolubility and complex organization, although very little is really known about their metabolism. Any macromolecules, structures, or organelles present at a given site for long periods would be good candidates for aging. The possible histone binding to DNA and gross morphological changes in chromosomes with age have been mentioned earlier.

Several ultrastructural changes with age have been reported (Hasan and Glees, 1973; Limas, 1971; Samorajski, Friede, and Ordy, 1971; Vaughan and Peters, 1974). Increased golgi structures and increased numbers of vesicles have been observed in heart cells with increasing age. In axons, microtubules were found to increase, while neurofibrils were reported to both increase and decrease in different studies. A disorganization of the rough endoplasmic reticulum, the invagination of nuclear membranes, and the appearance of membrane-bound inclusion material have been reported in cells from aging animals. It is likely that such changes are secondary and perhaps reversible, rather than true intrinsic cellular aging processes.

In what may be a very significant study, myelin was found to decrease with age in human peripheral nerves (Spritz, Singh, and Geyer,

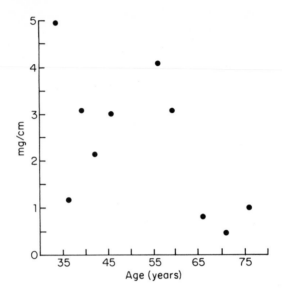

Fig. 4.16 Amount of myelin per cm of femoral nerve, as a function of age in human beings. (Redrawn from Spritz, Singh, and Geyer, 1973.)

1973). Figure 4.16 shows amount of myelin per unit length of the femoral nerve, as a function of age.

Indirect studies of membranes and macromolecules have been undertaken by determining how the binding of substances known to interact with such structures varies with age (Roth and Adelman, 1975). The binding of insulin to rat liver cell membranes does not change significantly after maturity. Glucocorticoid-binding proteins of a variety of rat tissues have been reported to decrease with age. The binding of dexamethasone by cytoplasmic macromolecules of various rat tissues as a function of age is shown in Figure 4.17. There is little or no decline with age in binding by rat liver, while glucocorticoid binding by human liver has been reported to decrease with age.

Splenic leukocytes show a 60 percent reduction in glucocorticoid-binding sites of cytosols in the rat between 12 to 14- and 24 to 26 months of age. However, since spleen leukocytes turn over and migrate in and out of the spleen, there is no reason to believe that the same or comparable cells are being studied in the two age groups.

Slices of rabbit uterus and skeletal muscle take up less estradiol and progesterone with increasing age of the animal. On the other hand, brain cholinoreceptor proteins have been reported to be more sensitive to acetylcholine in 24- than 10-month-old rats.

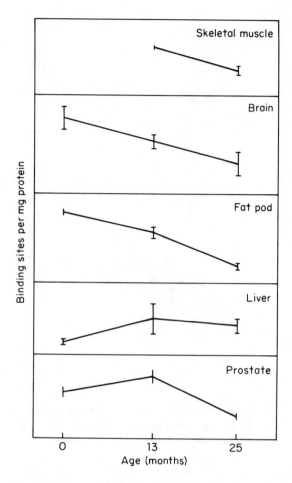

Fig. 4.17 In vitro dexamethasone-binding by cytosols of various tissues of adrenalectomized rats as a function of age. (Redrawn from Roth, 1974.)

Among intracellular macromolecules that would be expected to age are the eye lens proteins. These consist of several populations of soluble molecules, the crystallins, and several insoluble or poorly soluble high molecular-weight proteins. Figure 4.18 shows changes with age in the human lens; the amount of protein increases. The soluble protein is greatest at around 50 years of age, and then decreases as the amount of insoluble protein increases. It has also been shown that the molecular weight of protein in the soluble fraction increases with age, the high molecular weight material increasing most in the central part of the lens (Spector, Li, and Sigelman, 1974).

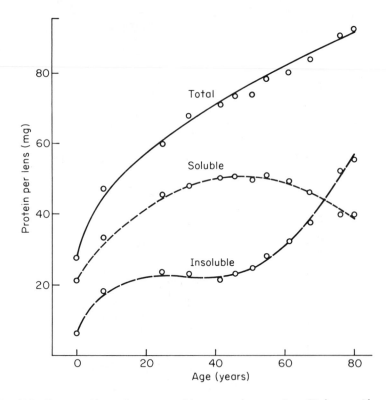

Fig. 4.18 Changes with age in amounts of human eye lens proteins. [Redrawn, with permission, from Satoh, 1972. Age-related changes in the structural proteins of human lens. Exp. Eye Res, 14 : 53–57. Copyright by Academic Press Inc. (London) Ltd.]

These data are consistent with the view that newly synthesized proteins are soluble and that, with age, one or more of the soluble proteins aggregate to form high molecular-weight aggregates and finally the insoluble proteins. Both disulfide and hydrogen bonds have been implicated in the formation of insoluble aggregates. Such an intracellular aggregation bears a close resemblance to the progressive cross-linking and insolubilization of the extracellular protein collagen. It is not known whether insoluble lens protein undergoes a progressive cross-linking with age similar to collagen.

Very conspicuous age changes in collagen were detected by measuring osmotic swelling ability, which is a manifestation of the modulus of elasticity, as discussed in the last chapter. Similar studies have been made of human myocardium to determine if an age-related aggregation or cross-linking of intracellular muscle proteins occurred (Kohn and Rollerson, 1959). After the cessation of growth, there is a marked decrease in the ability of heart muscle to swell (Figure 4.19). This

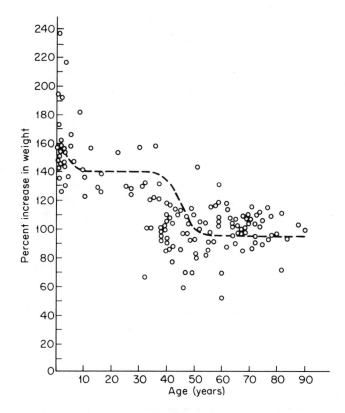

Fig. 4.19 Swelling ability of human myocardium as a function of age. (From Kohn and Rollerson, 1959.)

indicates the appearance with age of a factor that prevents the structural proteins from separating from one another. Subsequent studies showed that the age difference did not persist at the subcellular level and might, therefore, be due to the cell membranes or connective tissue, rather than to the contractile proteins. Solubility studies of the contractile proteins of skeletal muscle have not revealed any changes suggesting a progressive cross-linking with age. However, only preliminary studies have been undertaken of structural proteins of muscle.

Degeneration in vitro

As mentioned earlier, isolated populations of macromolecules and organelles are either unstable so that they deteriorate with time, or require such rigidly controlled environmental conditions that they become unstable as environmental factors undergo slight variations. It is also likely that the chemical stability of these intracellular constituents is dependent on the production of energy in the form of ATP and on the continued participation of these molecules and organelles in physiological processes. Concepts of this type are useful in attempting to understand why cellular components, either isolated or within cells, do not remain as they are indefinitely. In other words, why do these components undergo progressive deteriorations that satisfy the definition of aging processes? Maintaining intracellular constituents—cells and tissues—under artificial conditions that may not be optimal and in which they do not function normally gives some indications of the types of deterioration that may occur more or less spontaneously.

For example, maintaining rat leukocytes under what would appear to be close to ideal conditions results in a rapid loss of enzyme activity, as shown in Figure 4.8. Cell membranes also become altered in that normal membranes exclude the dye Trypan blue, while there is a progressive decrease in the number of cells that can exclude this dye on incubation in vitro. There is also a loss of protein during incubation.

When the intrastructure of these incubated cells is examined by electron microscopy, progressive alterations in all components are observed. As shown in Figure 4.20, the cell and nuclear membranes become very indistinct between 4 and 8 hours. Nuclear material appears to undergo a rearrangement and then to become more uniformly granular and indistinct after 3 hours. Cytoplasmic granules decrease in number and become poorly defined after 3 hours. These changes can be best characterized as a generalized structural deterioration that is not caused by any external injury or insult. Similar widespread degenerations have been described in liver cells in vitro. Mechanisms of these degenerations at the molecular level are unknown but may consist of activation or release of hydrolytic enzymes with cleavage of bonds in structural macromolecules, local changes in pH that solubilize certain components, or a redistribution of inorganic ions that alters the colloidal state of molecular aggregations.

In the case of stored red blood cells, glycolysis proceeds slowly, and the lactate that forms lowers the pH, causing decreased activity of hexokinase and phosphofructokinase. Glycolysis then ceases, and the decrease in high energy phosphate compounds results in widespread structural and functional alterations of cells.

An overview

Both experimental evidence and a priori considerations seem to indicate that macromolecules, organelles, and structural elements such as membranes, myelin, and chromosomes deteriorate or undergo

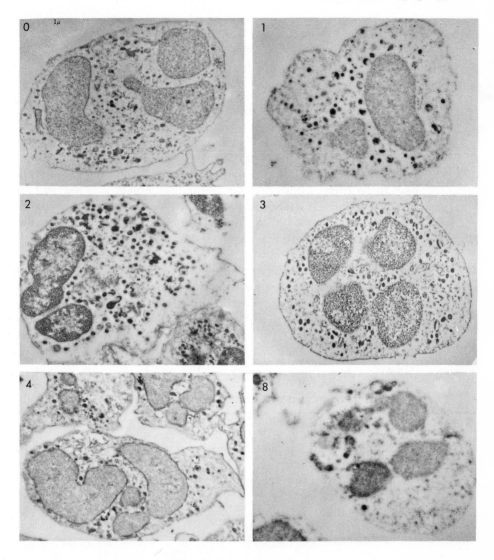

Fig. 4.20 Changes with time in rat neutrophils maintained in vitro. Culture age in hours is indicated for each picture.

morphological aberrations with time. Although it has not been feasible to observe a given intracellular component change *in situ* under normal conditions, it is possible that components that turn over undergo these alterations, and probable that the degenerative changes occur in short-lived cells that degenerate themselves. There is no convincing evidence that renewable components become altered in long-lived cells, that is, that newly synthesized components in old cells are different from similar components of young cells.

It also has not been shown that long-lived cells lose their capacity to synthesize components, although chromosomal aberrations and possible histone-DNA aggregations have been observed with time. Some changes in enzyme content and in properties of organelles in cells and organs of different ages have been reported, but it is not known if these represent irreversible, intrinsic aging processes, or if they are the consequences of altered function at higher levels of organization.

In view of the enormous amount of data on hand, there would appear to be little justification for the indiscriminate measurement of enzymes, proteins, or RNA in different tissues as a function of age, if questions are being asked about intrinsic cellular aging processes. Experiments to test certain hypotheses could be useful if tissues of animals of different ages were stimulated to synthesize at maximal rates. Furthermore, data on muscle and brain, where cells persist, are of more interest than data on liver, an organ that can rid itself of altered and dead cells. In fact, the significance of an observation in liver is in question; the very existence of an age-related alteration in cells of this organ suggest the alteration may not have serious consequences. If cells of liver were made defective, they would very likely have been replaced.

It is clear that insoluble pigmented macromolecular aggregates accumulate in long-lived cells, and that several types of insoluble substances accumulate in specialized cells. It also appears likely that minerals accumulate in certain types of cells.

Finally, many of the most interesting questions we might ask have received little or no attention. A large number of possible intracellular age changes have been neither excluded nor proven.

Some research for the future

1. *Turnover and stability.* Many structures such as cellular and nuclear membranes, fibrils, and tubules may be present for long periods and undergo changes with age. More data are required on the turnover of these structures. Studies utilizing new fractionation techniques in combination with isotope labeling should be informative.

2. *Aging of structural components.* The structures listed in (1) above might be isolated and studied as a function of age in regard to chemical composition, particularly mineral binding, and in regard to enzyme content, cross-linking of subunits, and permeability. Studies

should be extended on the amount of myelin present and its composition and properties, in view of the potential importance of changes of this substance with age.

3. *Aging in normal turnover.* By inhibiting synthesis in cells it might be possible to follow populations of macromolecules and organelles through the degradative phase of the turnover cycle. Studies of their properties should indicate whether they undergo age changes prior to degradation.

4. *Synthetic capacity in short-lived cells.* Populations of rapidly turning-over cells with short life spans could be studied *in situ* by histochemical techniques, or, after the last cell division, by chemical methods to determine whether the ability to synthesize metabolic enzymes is lost as specialized cell products are formed.

5. *Degradative processes.* Intracellular components that are known to be lost or degraded could be isolated and incubated with various cell fractions in an attempt to identify enzyme systems responsible for degradation. Factors that activate or stimulate synthesis of these systems could then be studied.

REFERENCES

Adelman, R. C. 1971. Age-dependent effects in enzyme induction—A biochemical expression of aging. Exptl. Gerontol.(Oxford: Pergamon Press Ltd). 6:75–87.

———. 1975. Impaired hormonal regulation of enzyme activity during aging. Fed. Proc. 34:179–182.

Adelman, R. C., and C. Freeman. 1972. Age-dependent regulation of glucokinase and tyrosine aminotransferase activities of rat liver in vivo by adrenal, pancreatic and pituitary hormones. Endocrinology (Philadelphia: J. B. Lippincott Company). 90:1551–1560.

Austin, C. R. 1967. Chromosome deterioration in ageing eggs of the rabbit. Nature. 213:1018–1019.

Baird, M. B., et al. 1974. Response of liver and kidney catalase to a-p-chlorophenoxyisobutyrate (clofibrate) in C57BL/6J male mice of different ages. Gerontologia (Basel: S. Karger AG). 20:169–178.

Barrows, C. H., Jr., and L. M. Roeder. 1961. Effect of age on protein synthesis in rats. J. Gerontol. 16:321–325.

Britton, V. J., F. G. Sherman, and J. R. Florini. 1972. Effect of age on RNA synthesis by nucleic and soluble RNA polymerases from liver and muscle of C57BL/6J mice. J. Gerontol. 27:188–192.

Bulos, Bernard, Shri Shukla, and Bertram Sacktor. 1972a. The rate of induction of the mitochondrial α-glycerol-phosphate dehydrogenase by the thyroid hormone in adult senescent rats. Mech. Ageing Dev. 1:227–231.

———. 1972b. Effect of thyroid hormone on respiratory control of liver mitochondria from adult and senescent rats. Arch. Biochem. Biophys. 151:387–390.

Carter, Donald B., and Chi-Bom Chae. 1975. Composition of liver histones in aging rat and mouse. J. Gerontol. 30:28–32.

Chen, Jenn C., Joseph B. Warshaw, and D. Rao Sanadi. 1972. Regulation of mitochondrial respiration in senescence. J. Cell Physiol. 80:141–148.

Comolli, R. 1971. Hydrolase activity and intracellular pH in liver, heart, and diaphragm of aging rats. Exptl. Geront. 6:219–225.

Curtis, Howard J. 1963. Biological mechanisms underlying the aging process. Science. 141:686–694.

deDuve, Christian. 1963. The lysosome. Scientific American. 208:64–72.

Detwiler, T. C., and H. H. Draper. 1962. Physiological aspects of aging. IV. Senescent changes in the metabolism and composition of nucleic acids of liver and muscle in the rat. J. Gerontol. 17:138–143.

Finch, Caleb E. 1973. Catecholamine metabolism in the brains of ageing male mice. Brain Res. 52:261–276.

Fonda, Margaret L., Darrell W. Acree, and Sidney B. Auerbach. 1973. The relationship of γ-aminobutyrate levels and its metabolism to age in brains of mice. Arch. Biochem. Biophys. 159:622–628.

Frazer, John M., and Wen-Kuang Yang. 1973. Isoaccepting transfer ribonucleic acids in liver and brain of young and old BC3F$_1$ mice. Arch. Biochem. Biophys. 153:610–618.

Geary, S., and J. R. Florini. 1972. Effect of age on rate of protein synthesis in isolated perfused mouse hearts. J. Gerontol. 27:325–332.

Gershon, Harriet, and David Gershon. 1973a. Inactive enzyme molecules in aging mice: Liver aldolase. Proc. Natl. Acad. Sci. USA. 70:909–913.

———. 1973b. Altered enzyme molecules in senescent organisms; mouse muscle aldolase. Mech. Ageing Dev. 2:33–41.

Gibas, M. A., and D. Harman. 1970. Ribonucleic acid synthesis by nuclei isolated from rats of different ages. J. Gerontol. 25:105–107.

Gold, P. H., M. V. Gee, and B. L. Strehler. 1968. Effect of age on oxidative phosphorylation in the rat. J. Gerontol. 23:509–512.

Intracellular Aging 97

Gutmann, E., V. Hanzlikova, and F. Vyskocil. 1971. Age changes in cross striated muscle of the rat. J. Physiol. (London). 216:331–343.

Hasan, M., and P. Glees. 1973. Ultrastructural age changes in hippocampal neurons, synapses and neuroglia. Exp. Gerontol. 8:75–83.

Helfman, P. M., and P. A. Price. 1974. Human parotid α-amylase—A test of the error theory of aging. Exp. Gerontol. 9:209–214.

Hrachovec, J. P. 1971. The effect of age on tissue protein synthesis: I. Age changes in amino acid incorporation by rat liver purified microsomes. Gerontologia (Basel). 17:75–86.

Johnson, L. K., R. W. Johnson, and B. L. Strehler. 1975. Cardiac hypertrophy and changes in cardiac ribosomal RNA gene dosage in man. J. Molec. Cell. Cardiol. 7:125–133.

Kohn, Robert R., and Roy G. Fitzgerald. 1964. Rat leukocytes aging in vitro: A study of morphologic and metabolic degeneration. Exptl. Molec. Path. 3:51–56.

Kohn, Robert R., and Edward Rollerson. 1959. Age changes in swelling properties of human myocardium. Proc. Soc. Exptl. Biol. Med. 100:253–256.

Limas, C. J. 1971. Aging of the myocardium. Acta Cardiol. 26:249–259.

Luthardt, F. W., Catherine G. Palmer, and P.-L. Yu. 1973. Chiasma and univalent frequencies in aging female mice. Cytogenetic. Cell. Genet. 12:68–79.

McMartin, D. N., and L. M. Schedlbauer. 1975. Incorporation of (^{14}C) leucine into protein and tubulin by brain slices from young and old mice. J. Gerontol. 30:132–136.

Massie, H. R., et al. 1973. Changes in the structure of rat liver DNA in relation to age. Arch. Biochem. Biophys. 153:736–741.

Menzies, R. A., and P. H. Gold. 1971. The turnover of mitochondria in a variety of tissues of young adult and aged rats. J. Biol. Chem. 246:2425–2429.

Menzies, Robert A., Ram K. Mishra, and Philip H. Gold. 1972. The turnover of ribosomes and soluble RNA in a variety of tissues of young adult and aged rats. Mech. Ageing Dev. 1:117–132.

Munnell, John F., and Robert Getty. 1968. Rate of accumulation of cardiac lipofuscin in the aging canine. J. Gerontol. 23:154–158.

Mukundan, M. A., A. Devi, and N. K. Sarkar. 1963. Effect of age on the incorporation of C^{14} thymidine into DNA, catalysed by soluble extract of rat liver. Biochem. Biophys. Res. Comm. 11:353–359.

Novikoff, A. B. 1963. Lysosomes in the physiology and pathology of cells: Contributions of staining methods. _In_ A. V. S. deReuck and

Margaret P. Cameron (eds.). Lysosomes. Ciba Foundation Symposium. London: J. & A. Churchill. Boston: Little, Brown and Company. Pp. 36–77.

Roth, G. S. 1974. Age-related changes in specific glucocorticoid binding by steroid-responsive tissues of rats. Endocrinol. (Philadelphia: J. B. Lippincott Company). 94:82–90.

Roth, G. S., and R. C. Adelman. 1975. Age-related changes in hormone binding by target cells and tissues; possible role in altered adaptive responsiveness. Exptl. Gerontol. 10:1–11.

Samorajski, T., R. L. Friede, and J. M. Ordy. 1971. Age differences in the ultrastructure of axons in the pyramidal tract of the mouse. J. Gerontol. 26:542–551.

Samorajski, Thaddeus, and J. Mark Ordy. 1967. The histochemistry and ultrastructure of lipid pigment in the adrenal glands of aging mice. J. Gerontol. 22:253–267.

Satoh, Kenshi. 1972. Age-related changes in the structural proteins of human lens. Exp. Eye Res. 14:53–57.

Schmukler, Morton, and Charles H. Barrows, Jr. 1966. Age differences in lactic and malic dehydrogenases in the rat. J. Gerontol. 21:109–111.

Shirey, T. L., and H. Sobel. 1972. Compositional and transcriptional properties of chromatins isolated from cardiac muscle of young-mature and old dogs. Expt. Gerontol. 7:15–29.

Singh, S. N. 1973. Effect of age on the activity and citrate inhibition of malate dehydrogenase of the brain and heart of rats. Experientia. 29:42–43.

Singh, S. N., and M. S. Kanungo. 1968. Alterations in lactate dehydrogenase of the brain, heart, skeletal muscle and liver of rats of various ages. J. Biol. Chem. 243:4526–4529.

Spector, Abraham, Suzanne Li, and Jesse Sigelman. 1974. Age-dependent changes in the molecular size of human lens proteins and their relationship to light scatter. Invest. Opthalmol. 13:795–798.

Spritz, Norton, Harbhajan Singh, and Barbara Geyer. 1973. Myelin from human peripheral nerves: Quantitative and qualitative studies in two age groups. J. Clin. Invest. 52:520–523.

Strehler, Bernard L. 1964. On the histochemistry and ultrastructure of age pigment. Adv. in Gerontol. Res. 1:343–384.

Sulkin, Norman M., and Dorothy F. Sulkin. 1967. Age differences in response to chronic hypoxia on the fine structure of cardiac muscle and autonomic ganglion cells. J. Gerontol. 22:485–501.

Sun, Grace Y. 1972. The metabolism of palmitic acid in mouse brain: An age study. Neurobiol. Biochem. Morphol. **1**:232–238.

Thorup, O. A., Jr., J. T. Carpenter, and P. Howard. 1964. Human erythrocyte catalase: Demonstration of heterogeneity and relationship to erythrocyte ageing in vivo. Brit. J. Haemotol. **10**:542–550.

Van Gastel, C., and C. Bishop. 1968. Changes in activities of some enzymes during in vivo aging of mouse erythrocytes. Proc. Soc. Exptl. Biol. Med. **127**:1067–1071.

Vaughan, Deborah W., and Alan Peters. 1974. Neuroglial cells in the cerebral cortex of rats from young adulthood to old age: An electron microscope study. J. Neurocytol. **3**:405–429.

von Hahn, H. P., and Elvira Fritz. 1966. Age-related alterations in the structure of DNA. III. Thermal stability of rat liver DNA, related to age, histone content and ionic strength. Gerontologia (Basil: S. Karger A.G.). **12**:237–250.

Weber, A., A. Hatzfeld, and F. Schapira. 1973. Studies on aldolase isozymes in red cells: Ageing and action of antisera. Enzyme (Basel). **14**:13–24.

Wilson, Patricia D. 1972. Enzyme patterns in young and old mouse livers and lungs. Gerontologia (Basel). **18**:36–54.

Zimmerman, Irwin, and Alan Berg. 1974. Levels of adenosine 3', 5' cyclic monophosphate in the cerebral cortex of aging rats. Mech. Ageing Dev. **3**:33–36.

Zorzoli, A. 1968. Fumarase activity in mouse tissues during development and aging. J. Gerontol. **23**:506–508.

FIVE

Aging of Cells

At the level of complexity of the cell we become concerned for the first time with aging of a living system. Changes of interest will be those that are progressive and that are manifested by alterations in function of the system. At the level of the cell, the end points of death or degeneration are more discernible than they are in the case of subcellular substances or structures. It will also be clear that aging of the cell as a system may proceed independently of the aging of some of its components. In other words, the cell may be in a steady state while populations of macromolecules and organelles are degenerating and are being replaced. Or the cell may degenerate and die while many of its components are not significantly altered.

As systems become more complex, the number of ways in which aging problems can be approached increases. Questions arise concerning the probability of reaching end points as a function of time. Frequently the most obvious changes with age are in functional or gross morphological characteristics. These changes are secondary to more basic changes at the molecular level—that is, they are manifestations of fundamental aging processes. It is important conceptually to distinguish the aging processes that can be observed from the primary molecular changes that might be responsible. We can often describe in general terms the manifestations of cell aging, and we may know about some basic subcellular changes or be able to suggest some reasonable hypotheses. However, it will be apparent that no cause-and-effect sequences relating basic changes to debilities of age have been proved. If no important functional changes occur with age in certain cells, it would indicate that intracellular processes discussed in the previous chapter are of questionable significance. On the other hand, if changes with age in cell function and survival were observed, studies of the causative intracellular processes would be indicated.

Rates at which cells age and ways in which aging is manifested vary from one type of cell population to another. Before we discuss cell aging, a classification of types of cell populations is required.

The different kinds of cell populations

There are many ways of classifying cell populations. The classification scheme most useful in regard to aging is based on cell life span and on the capacity of cells to divide, or on frequency of cell division. No classification is entirely satisfactory. However, most cell types can be fitted into categories described by Cowdry. These categories, with some modifications, are as follows:

Vegetative intermitotic cells

The vegetative intermitotic cells are cells that are continuously or periodically dividing. They are the unspecialized primordial or stem cells that give rise to populations of specialized cells. Examples of these stem cells are the basal cells of epidermis and epithelia, hemocytoblasts of bone marrow, spermatogonia, and primitive crypt cells of intestine. Each cell as an entity exists only between mitoses.

Differentiating intermitotic cells

The differentiative intermitotic cells arise from vegetative intermitotics. They are more highly developed than the stem cells; evidence of specialization is usually apparent. They also divide more or less on schedule, although duration of existence between mitoses varies widely in different populations. Erythroblasts and myeloblasts of the red and white blood cell lines, respectively, and spermatocytes exist between mitoses for very short periods. Other partially differentiated cells, such as those in liver, divide infrequently.

Reverting postmitotic cells

Reverting postmitotic cells are mature, highly specialized cells that do not normally divide, or they divide only rarely, unless they receive stimulation. They retain the capacity to divide, however, and some of them may proliferate very rapidly under certain circumstances. Examples of cells in this category are fibrocytes, chondrocytes, osteocytes, endothelial cells, lymphocytes, and kidney cells. Some liver cells that proliferate rapidly in regeneration and some gland cells might be placed in this group.

Short-lived fixed postmitotic cells

The short-lived postmitotic cells are the mature cells that arise from the differentiating intermitotics. They are the final products of cell populations that are turning over in what appears to be a programmed fashion. As they degenerate, they are replaced by cells from the differentiating intermitotic series. The fixed postmitotics do not divide. Granulocytic leukocytes, red blood cells, keratinizing squamous cells, mucus, acid, and enzyme-producing cells of the gastrointestinal tract are examples.

Long-lived fixed postmitotic cells

The long-lived variety of postmitotic cells also do not divide. However, rather than being members of turning-over populations, they are formed early in the life of the animal and persist rather indefinitely. The best examples are neurones. Muscle cells, although they have a limited capacity to divide, do not normally do so, and are therefore included in this group.

Differences in life span between different mammalian cells are enormous. Certain white blood cells in the human being have life spans measured in hours, whereas neurones and muscle cells are capable of living at least as long as the oldest person. Since these different types of cells presumably started off with the same genetic potential, differences in life span represent a remarkable divergence in gene expression.

Aging of intermitotics

One would not expect that the cells that exist between mitoses would undergo any changes that could be considered aging. At each mitosis two new cells are born. Theoretically, however, progressive alterations could occur in certain components that could be carried on into the next generation. The significance of such changes would then depend on the rate of alteration as compared to the rates of new syntheses and cell division. Some years ago it was claimed that cumulative cellular changes, occurring over many generations, had been demonstrated in rotifers. These findings have not been repeated, however, nor have they been shown to occur in other species. On the other hand, it has been clearly shown that changes occur in proliferating cells in tissue culture. These studies will be discussed below.

It has not been feasible to study the properties of a given cell between mitoses in an animal. If changes occur in intermitotics, they should be inferred from or detected in altered populations of cells studied at different times over the life span of an animal. Such alterations might be in chemical composition, in metabolic activity, in numbers of cells, or in ability to divide. As in the case of intracellular components, discussed in the previous chapter, the number of cells and their activity are frequently the results of extrinsic feedback mechanisms. For that reason we must be conservative in judging an age-related observation; what would appear to be a progressive cellular change might be reversible. It could be due to an extrinsic cause, and be more a measure of the physiological state of the animal than of aging cells. Thus, the capacity of cells to divide would be more significant than the number present.

Rate of cell division as a function of age has been studied in several vegetative intermitotic populations. Crypt cells of the mouse small intestine are stem cells that divide and give rise to more highly specialized cells. If a radioactive component of DNA is injected, it will be rapidly incorporated into cells that are synthesizing DNA. The tissue can then be sampled at various times, and the percentage of cells in mitosis that contain the label can be determined by autoradiography. The time between one cell division and the next (generation time) can be measured, because when the cells that are synthesizing DNA at the time of administration of the label divide, 100 percent of the cells in mitosis will be labeled. Time between highest or lowest percentage values will be the generation time. Duration of the 100 percent peak may also be used as a measure of the time during which DNA was being synthesized when the labeled precursor was present.

From the data in Figure 5.1, it can be seen that there is a definite lengthening of generation time during the animal's growth period, and a probable slight lengthening between maturity and old age. It was calculated that the generation time rose from 10.1 hours at 55 days of age to 14.1 hours at 300 days. It then remained quite constant until 675 days, rising subsequently to 15.7 hours at 1050 days of age. Increases in generation time were in the time during which DNA was synthesized and in the period in the cell cycle immediately before DNA synthesis. There is also some evidence that the population of proliferating crypt cells declines with age. On the basis of numbers of cells labeled, it was calculated that there were 126 proliferating cells per crypt in 100-day-old mice, and 89 in 825-day-old animals.

The number of intestinal epithelial cells does not change with age.

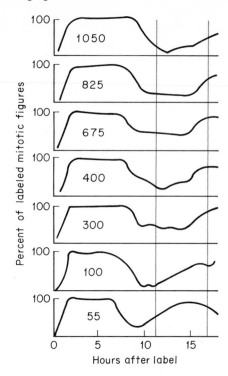

Fig. 5.1 Generation cycle of intestinal epithelium of mice. Age of mice in days indicated for each curve. (Redrawn from Lesher, 1966.)

Since the proliferating crypt cells give rise to short-lived fixed postmitotics, and show both a decrease in number and a lengthened generation time with age, life spans of the fixed postmitotics must be increased with increasing age of the animals.

In terms of intermitotic cell aging, it will be apparent that changes in number of dividing crypt cells and in generation times do not occur linearly as a function of animal age. In the very old animals that are about to die, a large proportion of the crypt cells are seen to be dividing with only a slight prolongation of generation time, compared to the cells of young adult animals. We cannot decide from these data if an individual intermitotic cell in an older animal is different from one in a younger animal. Such factors as alterations in feeding habits and activity and in blood supply to the gut, which might influence the rate at which the isotope is supplied to crypt cells, might influence the experimental results. Since these factors would tend to maximize age differences, the data are consistent with the view that these intermitotics do not change very significantly with age.

Many studies have been undertaken of cell division in epithelia as a function of age. For example, in a stratified squamous epithelium,

TABLE 5.1

Progenitor Population and Synthesis Index of Two Epithelial Cell Populations in Rats of Different Ages. (From Sharov and Massler, 1967.)

	2 mo.	*9 mo.*	*19 mo.*	*27 mo.*
Palate				
No. of progenitor cells				
per mm	231.2	230.6	185.8	149.0
Synthesis index	20.5	11.4	14.1	16.5
Tongue				
No. of progenitor cells				
per mm	255.3	269.9	253.3	185.2
Synthesis index	16.8	12.3	13.5	19.0

individual stem cells and mitoses can be identified histologically, and cells synthesizing DNA can be localized by autoradiography. The effect of animal age on numbers of stem or progenitor cells and on DNA synthesis as a measure of frequency of division has been studied at two sites in the rat. As shown in Table 5.1, in the period from 2 to 9 months of age while animals are maturing, the number of stem cells remains rather constant, while the percentage of cells synthesizing DNA prior to division at a given time (synthesis index) decreases. After 9 months, as animals age, there is a decrease in the number of progenitor cells and an increase in the synthesis index. As a result of these two changes, the actual number of dividing cells does not change with age, and the tissue turnover rate also remains relatively constant.

Many such autoradiographic studies of intermitotic cell division in epithelia have been reviewed by Cameron. Most populations show a decline in number of dividing cells with age. This is not universal however; some basal cell layers, particularly in human tissues, show little change or actually an increase in percentage of dividing cells with increasing age. It is important to note that there is no pattern of decreased cellularity in these epithelial tissues with increasing age. Thus, even where cell division decreases, there is no loss of cells. Cell populations are maintained, presumably by longer life spans of the fixed postmitotics.

Red blood cells arise from intermitotic cells in the bone marrow. They age in the circulation and, as the old cells disappear, they are replaced by young cells arising from division of the bone marrow cells. There is a continuous turnover by which the level of circulating red cells is kept constant (Eadie and Brown, 1953). Turnover of these cells in 6- and 18-month-old rats was studied by labeling circulating red cells with radioactive chromium, and injecting cells from young and old animals into young and old rats (Mende, 1965). It was found that rates of disappearance of labeled cells with time was the same in all four groups. This indicated that rates of red cell formation and destruction were independent of age.

The problem of stem cell division in bone marrow as a function of animal age has been approached in an unusual way. If bone marrow cells are injected into an animal that has been irradiated, individual cells will lodge in the spleen and divide, giving rise to nodules of cells that can easily be observed and counted. When a standard number of bone marrow cells from mice of various ages was injected into standard recipients, it was found that the number of splenic colonies increased with increasing age of donors up to 18 months of age, followed by a rather abrupt decrease by 20 months, and a slightly smaller decline by 24 months. This was interpreted as indicating that the number of stem cells capable of dividing increased to the age of 18 months and then declined. This concept fitted very well with other data showing that maximum resistance to death by radiation damage to marrow was at around 18 months of age (Yuhas and Storer, 1967).

Rate of stem cell division in the marrow is very susceptible to control by a number of factors. Production of red cells is stimulated by any change causing a diminished oxygen supply to tissues, as well as by cobalt in the diet. When weanling, young adult, and old rats were given excessive amounts of cobalt, and a second series was placed daily in a low-pressure chamber for 45 days, all the animals showed a marked increase in hematocrits (number of circulating red cells, as percentage by volume of blood), and no age-related differences between old and adult rats in extent or rate of increase were apparent (Grant and LeGrand, 1964). When the three groups of animals were exposed to low pressure for 94 days, by 40 to 50 days hematocrits of the weanling, young, and old rats were 67, 71, and 63 percent, respectively (Figure 5.2). Thus, with a marked stress, there appeared a rather modest decline in proliferative response with age.

An experiment with marrow proliferative capacity in terms of regeneration was performed. The three groups of rats were bled to remove blood equal to 2 percent of the body weight. Times required for return of hematocrit to normal levels, and numbers of circulating reticulocytes (nucleated red cells from recent cell divisions) as a function of time after bleeding were determined. As shown in Figure 5.3, the only age difference is a slight sluggishness in response in the oldest animals.

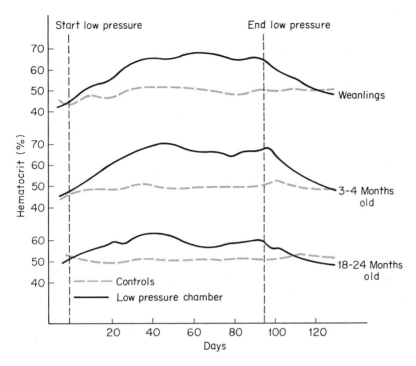

Fig. 5.2 Hematocrits of rats of different ages when exposed to ambient pressure of 380 mm Hg. (Redrawn from Grant and LeGrande, 1964.)

Fig. 5.3 Reticulocyte and hematocrit responses of rats of different ages to acute blood loss. (Redrawn from Grant and LeGrande, 1964.)

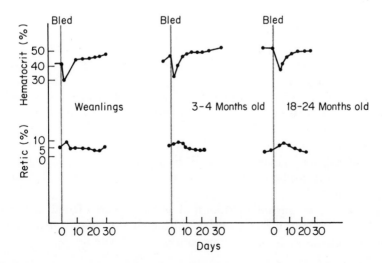

The authors conclude from these studies that changes in the marrow intermitotics with age, if any, are subtle.

An important question about intermitotics is whether or not their capacity to divide is related to the age of the animals that contain them. Or, stated in another way, is increasing age of animals associated with failure of these cell populations? One way to study this is to transplant a population of intermitotic cells from animal to animal, and determine if this population of turning-over cells lives as long as or longer than the host or donor. Studies of this type have been carried out by Krohn (1962), using mouse skin. Skin contains stratified squamous epithelium, hair follicles, and sebaceous glands, all of which consist of turning-over cell populations.

Krohn's procedure is to transplant a piece of skin onto a mouse, and after time has passed to transfer the same graft to another mouse, and so on. As a graft heals into place, there is a scarring around the periphery that diminishes the size of the graft. As the same bit of skin is passed through several graftings, it gets smaller and smaller, until it can no longer be transferred. It was found that skin persisted through transplantations for $4\frac{1}{2}$ to 5 years before it became too small. This is about twice as long as a mouse's mean life span. The maximum recorded life span of a mouse at the time of these studies was $3\frac{1}{2}$ years.

Differences in viability when old and young skin were transplanted to young mice were equivocal. Krohn transplanted parental skin to hybrids so that grafts could be identified by difference in hair color. With one strain combination, skin from old donors did not persist as long as skin from young donors, and appeared to age *in situ*. With another strain combination, however, no differences with regard to age of donor were apparent.

These studies do not tell us whether or not these intermitotics are intrinsically immortal. They do indicate, however, that a population of stem cells is capable of dividing and giving rise to differentiated tissue for a much longer time than the life span of the animal from which it is obtained.

It should be noted that in transplantation of skin, the connective tissue dermis is also transplanted. This is primarily collagenous tissue, which has little or no turnover. Thus, the graft consists, in part, of aging tissue from the original donor. Environmental effects of this aging matrix might eventually limit the viability of cells and might be the cause of transplant deterioration that was seen in some of Krohn's experiments.

Similar serial transplantation studies have been carried out with prostate and bone marrow cells, resulting in the same conclusions— namely, cells in such populations continue to divide for periods much longer than the life spans of the animals from which they are obtained (Franks, 1970). Particularly definitive studies have been undertaken with bone marrow cells. Harrison (1975) made use of a system in which genetically anemic mice can be cured by transplantation of bone marrow cells from a histocompatible strain. Donor hemoglobin can be identified in recipient mice, where it comprises over 90 percent of the hemoglobin in the cured mice. The ability of transplanted cells to function normally in recipient mice can be tested by determining the amount of hemoglobin formed in response to hemorrhage, and in response to erythropoietin, a hormone that stimulates division of red blood cell precursors.

Cure of anemia was just as effective with marrow cells from mice with a mean age of 34 months as it was with cells from mice with a mean age of 6 months, suggesting that this population of cells did not age in any significant way between 6 and 34 months of age. Marrow cells from cured mice were then used, after 10 to 14 months in the recipient, to treat additional anemic mice, and this serial transplantation was repeated through five transplants. Results are shown in Figure 5.4. Cell lines from both old and young original donors eventually declined in efficiency with serial passage, the old showing greater overall decline at some passages. However, the best transplants from the old line did as well as the best young in every transplant, and

Fig. 5.4 Percentage of genetic anemic mice cured at 6 to 9 months (mean ± SE) by transplanted marrow originally from young and old donors. Marrow was serially transplanted to new anemic mice at 10 to 14 month intervals. (From Harrison, 1975.)

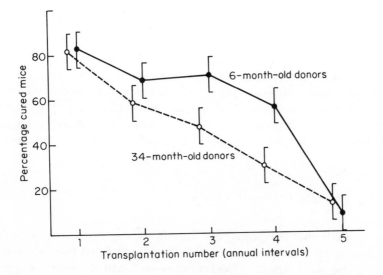

the old line also reacted normally to hemorrhage and erythropoietin. Serially transplanted marrow cells showed normal function for 77 to 84 months. The maximum life span of the mouse is around 36 months. From these and other data, Harrison concluded there was no intrinsic programmed aging of bone marrow cells over the life span of the animal, and that declines in effectiveness of the cells with increasing numbers of transplants were due to the transplantation procedure rather than to the age of the cells, or to the numbers of cell divisions they had experienced.

In reviewing the data on aging of intermitotics in an attempt to answer one of the original questions—whether or not an intermitotic cell from an old animal differs from one in a younger animal—we must conclude that there is no evidence that this is so. In terms of cell division, it appears that in some systems the rates are correlated with rates of growth of the animal. Probably changes of this type that are part of growth should not be considered aging processes. As animals age, one gains the impression that intermitotics continue to maintain tissues in a steady state and are capable of proliferating in response to stimuli to reestablish the normal level of functioning cells. It also appears likely that numbers of stem cells are in great excess in younger animals, and that there is probably some loss with age. When subjected to stress, some systems in older animals appear somewhat sluggish in their response, even though they finally achieve the required results. Such delayed responses could be due to many extracellular factors.

It is clear that there is no generalized loss of stem cells or loss of capacity to divide that is directly related to the life span of animals. There is also no time course for loss of stem cells that is characteristic of all populations. As suggested by the above observations, some populations show no decline, others may decrease slightly very late in life, and others might show a slight decline following maturity.

Death of stem cells could be caused by intracellular accidents, by mutations, or by extrinsic factors such as inadequate nutrition or the accumulation of toxic materials in the environment. Losses have not been sufficiently documented for us to know that they represent aging processes, in that cells die in greater numbers with increasing time.

Aging of cells in tissue culture

Cells that are propagated in culture can be viewed as intermitotics or reverted postmitotics that have been freed from their natural tissue environment. These cells are useful in the study of aging in several ways: effects of environmental factors— which might vary with age—on proliferating cells can be determined, properties of dividing cell populations from animals of different ages can be observed, and intrinsic cellular age changes may become apparent (Hay, 1967).

Tissue culture media are generally enriched with serum or embryo extract. It was discovered early that plasma or serum from old animals inhibited cell proliferation. As shown in Table 5.2, with increasing age of the animals from which plasma is obtained, there is a progressive decline in rate of cell proliferation and in the life span of populations. It was subsequently found that both a protein and lipid fraction from old serum were inhibitory. This suggests that in old animals, some stem cells might be poisoned by toxic factors in blood. As animals age, their homeostatic mechanisms become less efficient, a factor that will be dealt with in some detail later. It is not unlikely that a variety of inhibitory substances that are excreted or metabolized in young animals accumulate in the blood of older animals.

When small bits of tissue are placed in culture, there is a lag period before proliferating cells migrate out from the main mass. This lag period becomes longer, the older the animal from which the explant is obtained (Table 5.3). In the case of liver explants, the older the donor, the less the percentage of explants that show growth and the longer the lag period. If regenerating liver is used, the age differences are no longer apparent. There is some evidence that the increasing lag period with increasing age of donor is due to extracellular factors. Treatment of explants by hydrolytic enzymes such as papain, elastase, and collagenase shortens the lag period. It has been suggested that cell proliferation and movement are hindered by the connective tissue

TABLE 5.2

Effect of Plasma from Chickens of Various Ages on Fibroblast Outgrowth. (From Hay, 1967.)

Donor age	Av. no. of passages before growth cessation	Av. relative rate of outgrowth
6 weeks	20	148
3 months	13	100
3 years	8	51
9 years	2	22

After Carrel and Ebeling (1921).

TABLE 5.3

Latent Period before Cellular Emigration from Various Organ Explants. (Modified from Hay, 1967.)

Tissue	Donor age	Latent period	Source
Chicken spleen	14–16-day embryo	<2 hours	Carrel and
	Adult	12 hours	Burrows (1911)
Chicken heart	4-day embryo	4.9 hours	Cohn and
	8-day embryo	5.5 hours	Murray (1925)
	14-day embryo	9.3 hours	
	18-day embryo	11 hours	
Chicken thoracic aorta	Adult	3–5 days	Simms and Stillman (1936–1937)
Chicken heart	5–7-day embryo	6 hours	Hoffman *et al.*
	20-day embryo	10–12 hours	(1937)
	1 year	28–120 hours	
Rat liver	4–8 weeks	58 hours	Glinos and
	4–8 months	82 hours	Bartlett (1951)
	18–24 months	96 hours	

matrix in which the cells are imbedded. Age changes in components of connective tissue such as cross-linking of proteins and loss of poly-saccharide, discussed in Chapter Three, might cause the variations in explant behavior with aging of donors.

An interesting relationship between animal life span and DNA repair has been brought out in tissue culture studies. If cultured fibro-blasts of different species are radiated with UV (ultraviolet) light, the amount of DNA repaired was proportional to animal life span (Hart and Setlow, 1974). The significance of this observation is not known, but it suggests cells in longer-lived animals may have been selected for repair capacity. Additional studies of this phenomenon are required.

Many studies of cells in culture suggested that the populations were immortal—that they would go on dividing forever if kept in an ideal medium and at optimum cell concentrations. It was discovered, how-ever, that some cell lines would proliferate indefinitely, while other lines would die out after a certain number of generations or sub-cultures, no matter how well they were treated. It appeared that the cultures that died out consisted of normal diploid cells. The cell lines

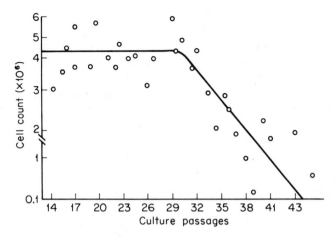

Fig. 5.5 Cell counts at successive passages (2:1 dilution ratio) of cultures of human fetal lung cells. (Redrawn from Hayflick, 1965.)

that appeared immortal often took on some of the characteristics of cancer cells, in showing aneuploidy or chromosomal abnormalities.

The dying out of normal human diploid cells in culture has been studied in detail by Hayflick (1965). Using fetal lung fibroblasts, he found that cultures died out after about 50 passages, or 50 doublings, taking slightly less than one year. As shown in Figure 5.5, the number of viable cells remained high for a long period during subcultures, and then dropped off quite abruptly. Loss of cells was exponential during the dying-out phase. The resulting curve represents the dying out of an aging population in that the probability of dying increases with increasing time. Possibly dying out is more related to the passage of time than to the number of cell divisions, since cultures that were subcultured in different ways varied in numbers of doublings but died out at around the same time.

It is not known why these cultured cells die out. Obvious explanations such as latent viruses, alterations in media, and dying out of necessary "feeder cells" in originally mixed cultures appear to have been excluded. Among the remaining possibilities is an accumulation of accidents or mutations in DNA or other non-turning-over macromolecules, or the slow accumulation of some harmful intracellular substance. Also, cell growth and division occurring rapidly over a long period could result in the diluting out of some cell component that cannot be reproduced at a sufficient rate. During aging in culture and in the dying-out phase, a variety of cellular changes have been observed. These have been reviewed by Cristofalo, and include increased lysosomal enzymes, increased RNA, and increasing heterogeneity in terms of organelles and cell size.

The dying out of cultured cells has often been advanced as a model of animal aging or of an important age-related phenomenon involving mitotic cell populations in animals (Cristofalo, 1972). It is now quite clear that dying out of cell populations after a specific number of doublings does not occur during aging of an animal. As noted in the previous section, populations of dividing cells are maintained, and can continue to divide for much longer periods than the life span of the animal from which they are obtained. Furthermore, it has not been shown that cells from older animals have used up their divisions and therefore go through less divisions in culture. Figure 5.6 shows the number of doublings in vitro of fibroblast cultures obtained from human beings of different ages. Although there may be some drop off in doublings in vitro between birth and maturity, there is no real age difference after maturity, or during aging of human beings. Also, the

Fig. 5.6 Number of in vitro doublings of human skin fibroblasts, as a function of donor age. (Redrawn from Martin, Sprague, and Epstein, © 1970 U.S.—Canadian Division of the International Academy of Pathology.)

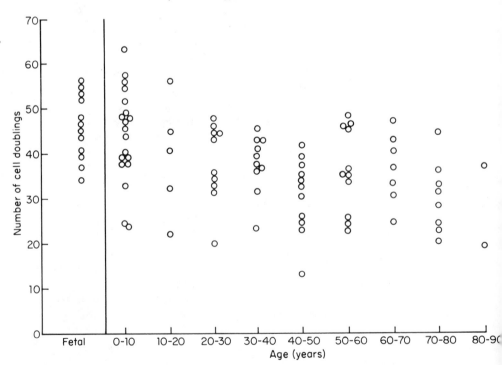

number of doublings of cells in vitro was found by Stanley, Pye, and MacGregor (1975) not to correlate with life spans of various mammalian species. Thus, a human being, cat, and fat-tailed dunnart with maximum life spans of 110, 28, and 3 years, respectively, gave culture doublings respectively of 60, 92, and 170.

A great many calculations have been made to determine if any cell lines in an animal go through more than 50 generations. Different conclusions have been reached, primarily because it is not known whether all stem cells divide regularly, or to what extent a group of stem cells is homogeneous in terms of past number of generations, or whether one cell may be the result of 3 past divisions while the adjacent cell may have had 20 divisions in its past. It would certainly appear that 50 generations per fetal cell is greatly in excess of what would be required during an animal's life span. Starting with two cells, 50 generations would give around 1000 liters of cells. Considering the entire fetus, the volume of cells that could be produced is truly astronomical. Experimental data would suggest, however, that animals would not have to make do with 50 doublings. For example, Cameron, on the basis of chronic labeling studies, has calculated that mouse tongue epithelial cells go through an average of 565 and a minimum of 146 doublings over the life span (Cameron, 1972).

Obviously, the rapid and prolonged proliferation of cells that occurs in tissue culture does not occur in vivo. Also, in vivo, no population of stem cells is known to die out in one year in the adult. Nor do stem cells in an animal continue to give rise only to stem cells. Probably close to half of all cells arising from stem cell division differentiate to fixed postmitotic cells.

Fibroblasts, the cells used in most tissue culture studies, are reverting postmitotic cells. They normally do not divide in an adult animal. When stimulated by tissue injury or stress, they go through several divisions and then become quiescent. A system in which they double every week represents a selection, by artifact, of cells, environment, or both. There is no population of cells in an animal to which such cultures can be rigorously compared. They cannot be compared to fibroblasts because these are not dividing, or to other cell populations because the latter are not fibroblasts.

The question of whether cell populations that regularly undergo division in an animal are potentially immortal and capable of division forever, as it were, or would eventually die out after some number of divisions, has not been answered by studies of tissue cultures or of cells in animals. What has been determined apparently is that there is no intrinsic failure in these cells, manifested by cessation of cell division and death, over the life span of a mammal.

Aging of reverting postmitotics

Aging of reverting postmitotic cells, in a strict sense, has not been studied; that is, nothing is known about what happens to an individual cell with the passage of time. Studies have been undertaken of populations of reverting postmitotics in animals of different ages, and data have been acquired on capacity to revert to the mitotic state as a function of age of the cell population, on various functional properties of these cells in animals of different ages, and on probable sorting-out and redistribution of subgroups of cell populations in animals of different ages.

The liver has been a useful organ to study in regard to proliferation of these cells as a function of age. The cells rarely divide in an adult liver; about one out of 10,000 to 20,000 cells is in mitosis at any time. However, if lobes of the liver are removed, approximating 70 percent of the liver in most experiments, cells in the remaining lobes proliferate rapidly and reconstitute most of the original liver mass in a few days. This is an excellent example of the lability of cell division rates and suggests the extent to which rates might be influenced by control or feedback mechanisms.

Liver regeneration in rats of different ages has been studied. Investigators used young growing rats 4 to 6 weeks old, 4 to 8-month-old adult rats, and 21 to 30-month-old rats. The very young animals regenerated liver more rapidly than did the older animals. There was no difference, however, in rate of regeneration between adult and old rats (Figure 5.7). The actual rate of DNA synthesis early in regeneration was investigated by injecting a radioactive DNA precursor at various times after removal of liver, and measuring specific activity of DNA after 2 hours. As shown in Figure 5.8, liver of weanling rats gave two peaks of maximum DNA labeling. This indicates that cell division of the two cell populations is synchronized. In 4-month-old animals only one population of DNA-synthesizing cells is identified, and the curve is spread out, indicating less synchrony. Still less synchrony is apparent in the case of 12 to 15-month-old rats. The onset of DNA synthesis in the young adults lags about 3 hours after that in the weanling rats, while synthesis in the older animals lags by 8 to 12 hours. By 50 hours, which is still early in regeneration, there is no difference in rate of DNA synthesis between 4- and 12 to 15-month-old animals.

The authors point out that the shapes and time relationships of these curves are valid for comparisons, but that heights of the curves are of

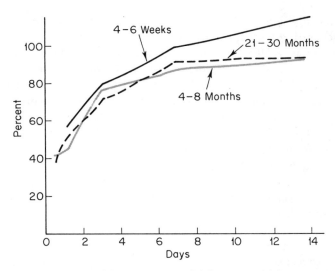

Fig. 5.7 Percentage of original liver mass restored following partial hepatectomy in rats, corrected for changes in body weight. Ages of animals indicated for each curve. (Redrawn from Bucher and Glinos, 1950.)

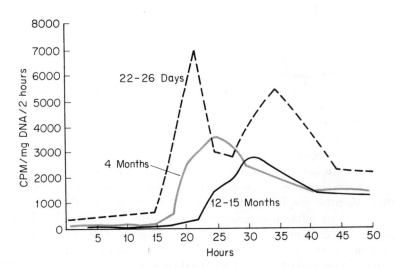

Fig. 5.8 Rates of DNA synthesis in livers from rats of different ages following partial hepatectomy. (Redrawn from Bucher, Swaffield, and DiTroia, 1964.)

questionable value because these depend on specific activity of the isotope at the site of DNA synthesis, which could be altered by a number of uncontrolled or unknown variables. In addition, the normal rate of liver cell division varies with growth rate. If rates of DNA synthesis in regenerating liver are compared to rates in normal liver, it is found that there is a 20-fold increase in weanlings, a 50-fold increase in young adults, and a 125-fold increase in the older animals. It could thus be argued that there is an increased proliferative capacity with age. This might not be so, however, since the DNA precursor pool is larger in younger animals, and this might dilute the isotope, causing newly synthesized DNA to have a lower specific activity.

These arguments serve to demonstrate the difficulties in inferring a basic mechanism from a general observation. As in the case of gut epithelium, it appears that the greatest changes in the proliferative pattern of liver cells are associated with changes in the growth rate of the animal. It is of particular interest that a population of cells that synthesizes DNA in weanling animals may not be able to do so in adults. In terms of aging after slowing of growth in the animals, initial proliferative response to a stimulus is delayed. This delay could be due either to intrinsic cellular aging changes or to environmental causes. Regardless of animal age, however, liver cells are capable of dividing and reconstituting liver tissue that is apparently normal in mass and function. This would suggest that there are no fundamental differences in liver reverting postmitotics as the animal ages.

Cells of the immune system—lymphocytes and macrophages that proliferate in response to foreign substances—represent reverting postmitotic cells. Immunology is a rapidly developing field, and a great deal of interest has been shown in possible age changes in immunological reactions. Immune responses in aging animals will be discussed in the next chapter. Here we will consider only those aspects of the immune response that might indicate aging processes involving identifiable reverting postmitotic cells.

Immune responses are known to vary with strain of animal, and with nutritional and endocrine status, presence of disease, type of antigen and method of administration, and method used for assay. Many immune responses also require the interaction of two or more cell types, are affected by suppressor cells, and are altered by changes in antigen distribution and uptake by tissues. It is not surprising, therefore, that a clear picture of the role of age in cellular immunological phenomena has not been forthcoming.

Humoral antibody production, where a helper T-cell population is required, appears to reach a peak at maturity and then decline, when measured either by amount of serum antibody or by number of antibody-forming spleen cells (plaque-forming cells). Figure 5.9 shows immune response, as a function of age in mice, to sheep red blood cells. This response requires both B and T cells. The peak response to a

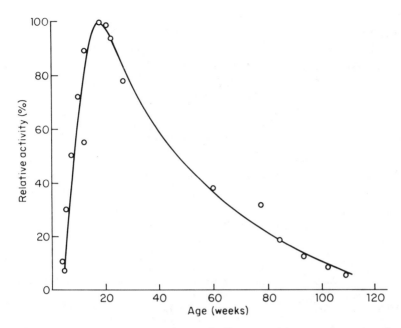

Fig. 5.9 Primary immune responses to sheep red cells, measured by serum titer and number of spleen plaque-forming cells, as a function of age in mice. (Reprinted from Federation Proceedings **33**:2033–2035, 1974. From the article, "Humoral immunity in aging," by A. A. Nordin and T. Makinodan.)

T-cell independent antigen has been reported to occur at a later age (Gerbase-DeLima et al., 1974). By transplanting spleen cells from mice of different ages into irradiated recipients of different ages and then testing the immune response, it is possible to gain information on the relative roles played by an aging environment in the animal and by an aging cell population in changing immune responses with age. In one study of this type it was concluded that about 90 percent of the decreases in antibody response with age had a cellular basis, while about 10 percent was due to age changes in the environment of cells (Makinodan and Adler, 1975).

Macrophages, which are reverting postmitotic cells that are important in processing of antigen, have been studied as a function of age, and no alterations have been detected (Makinodan and Adler, 1975; Nordin and Makinodan, 1974). The number of B cells in mouse spleen does not appear to vary with age. There are conflicting reports on the numbers of T cells in mouse spleens of different ages, some indicating no change, while others report decreases in numbers with age (Makinodan and Adler, 1975; Nordin and Makinodan, 1974). The B-cell immune response in vitro to sheep red blood cells actually shows an increase with increasing age of donors when large numbers of standard helper T cells are added (Farrar, Loughman, and Nordin, 1974). This has suggested to some investigators that decline in the immune response with age is primarily due to an altered T-cell population.

Bone marrow can apparently produce all types of immunocompetent cells. When bone marrow from young and old mice is transplanted to young recipients and the latters' responses to antigen in terms of numbers of plaque-forming cells are determined, it is observed that shortly after transplantation, the response of the old transplant is less than the young, but by 6 months, and with adequate sheep red cell stimulation, the recipients of old bone marrow respond as well as the recipients of young marrow (Figure 5.10). The function of transplanted spleen cells also depends on the length of time after transplantation. After 70 days after transplantation, recipients radiated prior to re-

Fig. 5.10 Immune response (mean ± SE) to increasing doses of sheep red blood cells 6 months after grafting young and old bone marrow into irradiated young recipients. (From Harrison and Doubleday. © 1975 The Williams & Wilkins Co., Baltimore.)

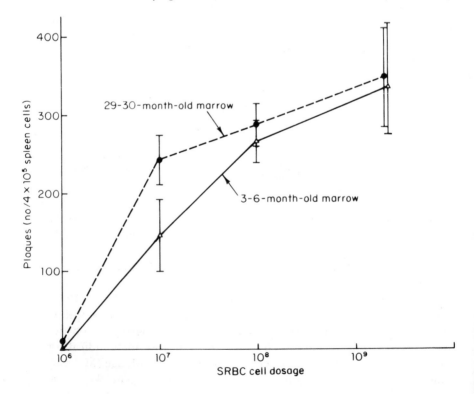

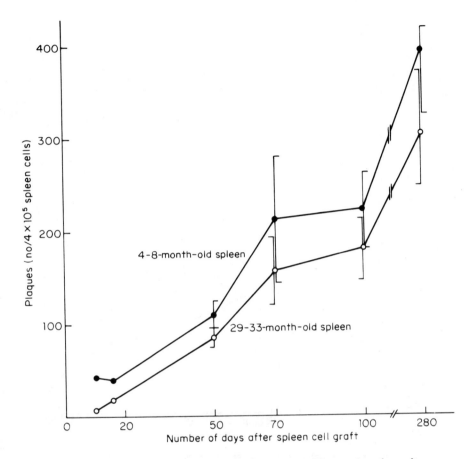

Fig. 5.11 Immune responses to sheep red blood cells (mean ± SE) at various times after transplanting spleen cells from young and old mice into irradiated recipients. (From Harrison and Doubleday. © 1975 The Williams & Wilkins Co., Baltimore.)

ceiving both old and young spleen cells gave plaque-forming cell responses in the normal range for young animals (Figure 5.11). It was concluded from these and subsequent studies that age-related immunological defects are not intrinsic to the lymphoid stem cells or cells that are precursors of the immunocompetent cells (Harrison, Astle, and Doubleday, 1977).

The thymus gland involutes over the life span of an animal. The involution is not related to aging of the animal but occurs most rapidly during a period when the animal is growing. In the mouse, the thymus attains a peak weight at 6 weeks of age and then undergoes rapid atrophy (Figure 5.12). It should be noted that the drop-off

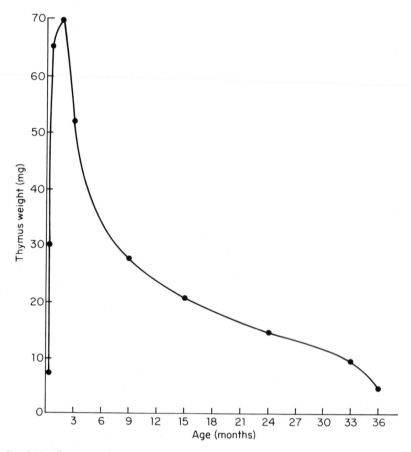

Fig. 5.12 Thymus weight as a function of age in mice. (From Hirokawa and Makinodan. © 1975 The Williams & Wilkins Co., Baltimore.)

in thymus weight occurs before the drop-off in immunological function mentioned above. The atrophy is primarily due to loss of thymocytes in the gland cortex (Hirokawa and Makinodan, 1975). Both cell death and cell migration from the thymus are responsible for atrophy of the gland. The rate of cell division of remaining cells is apparently not diminished in involuted glands (Blau, 1972). It would be expected that some cell mediated immunity and other T-cell functions would decrease in association with the thymic involution.

Mitosis in response to phytohemagglutinin is a T-cell property, and various cell preparations have shown a decreased response with increasing animal age, suggesting a lower proportion of T cells (Mathies et al., 1973; Walters and Clayman, 1975; Weksler and Hütteroth,

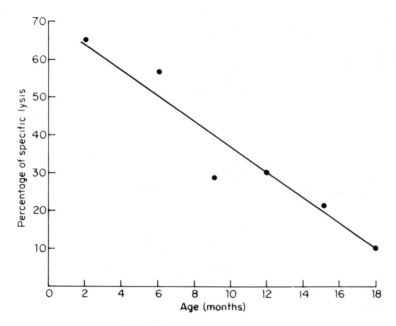

Fig. 5.13 Lysis in vitro of mastocytoma cells by standard numbers of spleen cells from mice of various ages that had been immunized with mastocytoma cells. (From Menon, Jaroslow, and Koesterer, 1974.)

1974). Other studies, however, have shown marked scatter at each age, with little or no change over the life span (Pisciotta et al., 1967). The number of spleen cells that proliferate in response to allogenic cells has been observed to decrease with age (Gerbase-DeLima et al., 1974). The lysis of foreign tumor cells by a fixed number of spleen cells from immunized mice of different ages is shown in Figure 5.13. The age difference in such studies is apparently in the number of immuno-competent cells present as a result of proliferation. The activity of each immunocompetent cell apparently does not change with age (Goodman and Makinodan, 1975; Menon, Jaroslow, and Koesterer, 1974).

It has also been reported that with increasing age of mice, there is a decrease in the ability to repopulate T-cell areas of lymph nodes and spleen, and a decrease in theta-positive (thymus-derived) cells in spleen (Hirokawa and Makinodan, 1975). As noted above, the question of numbers of splenic T cells as a function of age has not been settled. Several studies report a decrease with age in numbers of cells with T-cell functions only in those mouse strains that are susceptible to autoimmune disease late in life (Rodey, Good, and Yunis, 1971; Stutman, 1974).

Data on the mixed lymphocyte reaction employing cells from animals of different ages are inconclusive (Walters and Clayman, 1975; Meredith et al., 1975; Gerbase-DeLima and Walford, 1975). Thymus cells have been reported not to change or to show increased activity with animal age. The activity of lymph node cells was reported to decrease with age, while spleen cells were observed in different studies to either decrease in activity with increasing age or show no change. In the mixed lymphocyte reaction, suppressor cells were increased with age in three out of four mouse strains (Gerbase-DeLima et al., 1974).

Both graft rejection and the graft-versus-host reaction were found to decrease in intensity with age in some cases, and to increase in others (Walters and Clayman, 1975). If animals showing decreased graft rejections with age were sensitized prior to grafting, there was no age difference in graft rejection (Menon, Jaroslow, and Koesterer, 1974). When bone marrow from animals of different ages was transplanted to irradiated hosts, secondary disease in the hosts was not observed to vary with age of the donor tissue (Chen, Price, and Makinodan, 1972).

There are some clear changes in immune responses with increasing animal age, but generalizations about mechanisms are not justified by current data. The most definitive change is the decrease in numbers of cells producing humoral antibody. Changes in some aspects of cell-mediated immunity also occur, but the data are quite variable in different studies. Functional decline is not only associated with aging of the animal, but also occurs during animal growth, as seen in altered cell-mediated immunity and in thymic atrophy. Functional decline does not appear to be at the level of individual cells. Many of the changes with age can be tentatively explained on the basis of an altered distribution of competent cells and smaller steady-state populations in the spleen. The cells that are present in older animals appear in most ways, including the capacity to proliferate, to be similar to cells in young animals. If smaller numbers of cells are present before stimulation, it would take longer to attain a given population size. The appearance of suppressor cells with age requires more study. It should be noted that many of the factors mentioned above that can influence the immune response, such as distribution and uptake of antigen, could change with age and could play roles in some age-altered responses that have been described.

Other studies of various functions and properties of reverting postmitotic cells have not provided evidence on the existence of intrinsic aging processes. Salivary gland cells synthesize DNA and divide in response to the drug isoproteronol. There is an age-related lag period in the induction of cell division, similar to the lag in enzyme induction discussed earlier. The age differences are abolished, however, with chronic administration of isoproteronol, suggesting the differences are secondary and reversible (Roth and Adelman, 1975). Mammary gland from 3-week-old and 12-month-old mice grows equally well in 3-week-old hosts but poorly in old hosts, indicating that aging of the environment is more important than cell aging with regard to growth (Young, Medina, and DeOme, 1971). Isolated liver cells from old rats have higher rates of endogenous respiration than cells from young animals (Van Bezooijen, Van Noord, and Knook, 1974).

Aging of short-lived fixed postmitotics

The distinction between cell growth and differentiation has long been appreciated by biologists. In general, cells that are dividing are unspecialized. In order for a cell to become differentiated, it apparently must stop dividing. It is as though a cell has limited resources and has the choice of either carrying out multiple syntheses associated with metabolism and cell division or synthesizing large amounts of a small number of substances.

All of the short-lived fixed postmitotics are highly specialized. Epithelial cells may produce keratin, mucus, sebum, or other secretions, or may have special organelles such as cilia or flagella. Erythrocytes are filled with hemoglobin and have an unusual dumbbell shape. Granulocytic leukocytes contain high concentrations of lysosomes. Spermatozoa, which represent a special type of fixed postmitotic, in being haploid, are adapted for rapid motion and penetration of the egg. They synthesize virtually no RNA or protein.

These cells all have very short life spans. Populations age in the sense that, in most cases, the probability of dying increases with increasing time. A population of red blood cells in the bone marrow has a life span of around 120 days in the human being. The percent survival, or rate of dying, curve is typical of an aging population (Eadie and Brown, 1953). In the dog, a similar curve showing red cell survival of around 110 days is obtained. In addition to the disappearance of cells from the circulation due to senescence, cells are also removed at random in some species such as the rabbit and cat. Resulting survival curves are between the curve for a random-hit process (first-order reaction) and the rectangular curve of an aging population.

Granulocytic leukocytes, on the other hand, appear to be removed from circulating blood and to be destroyed in a random fashion with a half-time of around 7 hours in the human being. This suggests that these cells are aged at the time they are released from bone marrow, in the sense that they are already unstable and that the rate of their destruction does not increase with increasing time.

Death in epithelial cells is clearly age-related, since cells at the surface are the ones that die, and it takes time for cells to reach this site. As an example of the short life span of such cells, the epithelium of the gastrointestinal tract in man is turned over every 6 days.

The question arises as to whether or not there is a difference in life span of these short-lived cells in animals of different ages. This question has received little attention. The study mentioned earlier, in which erythrocytes from young and old animals were cross-transfused, indicated that there was no difference in survival time (Mende, 1965). In the case of intestinal epithelium, also discussed earlier, the data suggested that postmitotic cells survive slightly longer in older animals because of slower replacement from the progenitor pool (Lesher, 1966).

What dying consists of, varies from one cell type to another. In some glands, products of the cells replace other components and distend the cells until they rupture. In a stratified squamous epithelium, the cells become filled with keratin, which replaces all other components. Finally, such cells are sloughed from the surface as scales. Red blood cells fragment, and the fragments are taken up by cells of the reticuloendothelial system and degraded. The fate of granulocytes is uncertain, but they are probably destroyed shortly after removal from the circulation.

Death of leukocytes and epithelial cells has been observed in vitro. There is no single characteristic change. The cell surface shows beading and pseudopod formation. Cells take up water. Some parts become more liquid, while other parts appear more gellike. Membranes rupture with the release of nuclear and cytoplasmic components. Vacuoles form in mitochondria, in nuclei, and in the cytoplasm. Leakage of enzymes and losses of lipids have been described. Functional deficiencies become apparent. For example, the fertilizing ability of aging spermatozoa decreases, while a variety of chromosomal abnormalities increase in the resulting blastocysts (Blandau, 1975). These changes can be characterized as a generalized morphological and functional degeneration.

Possible causes of death have not been systematically studied. In the previous chapter, reference was made to studies suggesting that calcium accumulation might shorten life spans of nerve cells. Cause of death is a particularly difficult problem since there is no simple way of distinguishing cause from effect when cell properties are found to be altered. It is often assumed that so many of the cell's resources are used in carrying out specialized functions that the cell is unable to renew enzymes necesary for life, or to generate high-energy compounds required for the maintenance of semipermeability of membranes and structural integrity of organelles. This would appear to be a reasonable hypothesis when one considers some extreme examples.

Cells in a keratinizing squamous epithelium become filled with keratin. Eventually all cellular components, including the nucleus, are replaced by this cell product. In the case of red cells, the cells are filled with hemoglobin and lose their nuclei. Lack of synthesis in spermatozoa was mentioned. Reasons for an inability to carry out normal metabolic reactions in these cells are obvious. The same factors, although less striking, very likely operate in the other short-lived fixed postmitotics. Since proliferating cells must synthesize all of the metabolic enzymes and organelles, this concept can explain in a general way why differentiating cells lose their ability to divide. The question then becomes one of determining the factors that cause a cell either to synthesize a special component or to synthesize the spectrum of basic enzymes and macromolecules.

Synthesis of special products may explain evolution of cell populations that turn over. If such synthesis leads to cell death, a mechanism must be available for the continuous replacement of dying cells.

Aging of long-lived fixed postmitotics

The full complement of long-lived fixed postmitotic cells is present at around the time of birth. These cells do not divide and, in terms of end points and altered function, should be convenient systems for the study of cell aging if in fact they do age. Neurones and skeletal muscle constitute a significant proportion of the body mass. In view of the functions of the nervous and muscular systems, any progressive alterations in large numbers of cells in these systems would be likely to have profound consequences. Oocytes serve as examples of this type of cell. The long-lived fixed postmitotics are also highly specialized, but not to the point at which they are unable to carry out basic metabolic and synthetic functions.

In the previous chapter we considered what is known about age-related changes in cell constituents. It is possible that progressive alterations in a cell might interfere with some cell functions, while still permitting the cell to survive. It is more likely, however, that if cell components are altered progressively in a population of cells, many of the cells will die. Rates of attaining the end point of death should then be of use in studying aging of these cells.

Oocytes are long-lived fixed postmitotic cells that are present in highest numbers before birth. Also, the total complement of these cells is apparently established before birth. Two different germ cell populations can be considered with regard to aging. One is the population of primary oocytes present before birth, which represents almost all oocytes. The second population consists of the very small fraction of cells that undergo ovulation. Cells in the latter population go through one cell division with the formation of a polar body.

The total number of germ cells in the human ovary as a function of age is shown in Figure 5.14. The peak is reached at around 6-months gestation, after which there is a rapid loss of cells. During the reproductive period, numbers are low, and the cells finally disappear at around 50 years of age. In some species, some oocytes persist beyond the end of the reproductive period. We should note that the curve for

Fig. 5.14   Total germ cell population in the human ovary as a function of age. (From Baker. Cited by Foote in Blandau, 1975.)

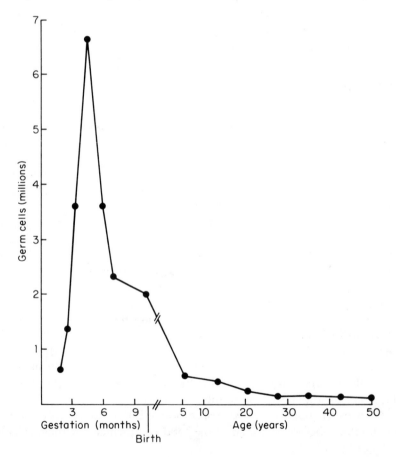

the numbers of cells surviving is not that of an aging population. Probability of dying is highest in very young cells. This would be expected if large numbers of cells were defective, or if they were killed at a certain time by environmental factors.

Practically nothing is known about the mechanism of this atresia of oocytes, or about what happens to surviving oocytes with the passage of time. In mice between 2 and 14 months of age, the chiasma frequency of oocytes decreases, and the percentage of oocytes with univalents at the first metaphase increases. Litter size drops off with age. Attempts have been made to discover if this is due to intrinsic aging of oocytes or to an aging environment of the reproductive system, by transplanting young and old ova to young and old recipients. The percentage of term fetuses was greater in young-to-young than young-to-old and old-to-young transplants in hamsters. In mice, however, the old-to-young transplants were as effective as young-to-young transplants, and young ova did not survive well in old mice. Thus, an old environment clearly has a damaging role in ova function. Results bearing on aging of ova are inconclusive.

Why some oocytes undergo ovulation while most die out is not known. The selection for ovulation appears random. After formation of the first polar body and ovulation, the ova age like short-lived fixed postmitotic cells. Aging in the oviduct is associated with decreasing fertilizability and with many structural abnormalities involving chromosomes, cortical granules, and the mitotic spindle. Atresia of oocytes and degeneration of ova have been extensively reviewed (Blandau, 1975).

Muscle cells are exceedingly responsive to functional demands. When a cell is not working, it rapidly loses structural proteins, and the patterns of protein synthesis and degradation and of metabolism become altered. Excessive or prolonged work has opposite effects. The consequences of inactivity or work can be recognized grossly in a muscle by atrophy or hypertrophy. These changes usually do not depend on the number of muscle cells, which do not divide, but rather on the number of myofibrils within a muscle cell. With lack of activity for prolonged periods, however, muscle cells disappear. The lability of muscle cells makes it difficult to evaluate changes with time, since any changes noted may be due to extracellular factors and to the generalized debility and progressive loss of activity that characterize aging of an animal, and may not be both progressive and irreversible.

Atrophy of striated muscle, representing both a decrease in size of muscle cells and a loss of cells, has been reported in aging animals. In the rat tibialis anterior muscle (Table 5.4), atrophy of white muscle

TABLE 5.4

Total Number of Muscle Fibers, and Fiber Diameter in Red and White Parts of the Tibialis Anterior Muscle of Adult and Old Rats. (From data of Tauchi, Yoskioka, and Kobayaski, 1971.)

| | 12 months old | | 24 months old | |
	Red	White	Red	White
Number of fibers				
Male	15020	10932	7616	13673
Female	15633	11147	6993	10350
Fiber diameter (μm)				
Male	28.7	38.5	24.8	24.0
Female	26.7	33.2	22.7	23.1

with age is due primarily to decreases in cell volume, while red muscle atrophy is caused mainly by cell loss.

It is not clear that such atrophy represents an intrinsic loss of ability of cells to carry out syntheses. Hypertrophy of rat plantaris muscle in response to exercise is not decreased with age (Tomanek and Woo, 1970), and heart muscle in 26-month-old mice undergoes hypertrophy in response to thyroxin to the same extent as the heart in 8-month-old animals, although there is a lag period in the response of older animals (Florini, Saito, and Manowitz, 1973). A role for the nervous system in age-related atrophy of some muscles is suggested by the observation that the number of motor units in human thenar muscle decreases with age (Brown, 1973).

Cells of the central nervous system have received considerable attention because, as fixed postmitotic cells, they would be expected to undergo changes with age. And because of their key role in regulation, any changes might be of importance in the aging of the whole animal. Most observations have dealt with the morphology of cell changes, as described in the previous chapter, and with loss of cells as a function of age. Very few studies of nerve cell function have been undertaken. It has been reported that the conduction velocity of a nerve decreases by about 15 percent between 30 and 90 years of age in man. Such a change could be due to progressive alterations in cell components, to diminished functional demand, or to selection of slower nerve fibers because of dropping out of faster cells. This question will be considered again in the next chapter.

It is often assumed that aging of the central nervous system is characterized by the loss of neurones, and this concept has found its way into popular journalism. Evidence bearing on this view, however, is not conclusive.

Numbers of nerve cells as a function of age have been counted in sections of different sites of the human cerebral cortex. There is some decrease at all locations, with the greatest change occurring in the external and internal granular layers. Most marked changes occur in the superior temporal gyrus. As shown in Figure 5.15, the most rapid decrease occurs between birth and maturity; loss after maturity is very slight. It has been suggested that the reported loss of neurones during growth may be only apparent because of the diluting out of neurones by the growth of nonneuronal elements. The loss occurring after maturity is roughly linear with time, suggesting a role for external factors in causing cell death. In terms of end points, human neurones do not represent an aging population; in fact, the probability of dying is greater, the younger the cell. Nevertheless, aging processes in terms of function may be found to occur in these cells when the appropriate studies are undertaken.

Studies of laboratory animals support the view that nerve cells do not die from aging processes; when these cells die in measurable num-

Fig. 5.15   Cell counts in the two areas of the human cerebral cortex which show the greatest change with age. (Drawn from data of Brody, 1955.)

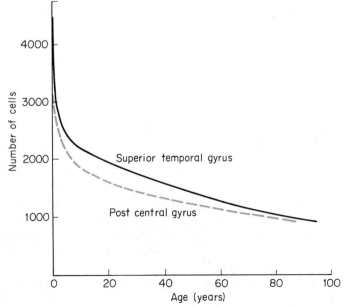

bers, death is due either to accidents or to external causes. If cell death is due to these nonprogrammed or extracellular causes, and the probability of dying is related neither to the age of the animal nor to the age of the cell, cell loss might not be detectable in a short-lived animal, since it may take 30 years for a measurable change to occur in such a cell population in human beings. Thus, no change in neurone density has been found with age in the rat cerebral cortex (Brizzee, Sherwood, and Timiras, 1968). Nor has an age-related change in numbers of rat sciatic nerve or ventral root fibers, or cat ventral root fibers been observed. An age-related decrease in number of myelinated fibers in mouse nerve has been described (Samorajski, 1974). Purkinje cells in the rat show a linear decline in number with age. In mice, nerve cells of the spinal cord are constant until 50 weeks of age, but show a 15 to 20 percent decrease by 110 weeks (Wright and Spink, 1959).

It is thus apparent that information dealing with what would appear to be a simple question is inconsistent. The world literature on neurone counts as a function of age has been reviewed by Hanley (1974) in an attempt to decide if loss of neurones is an intrinsic and universal property of nervous tissue. He concluded this was not the case, but that some species and tissues had a special vulnerability to factors that caused neurone death and disappearance.

None of the populations of long-lived fixed postmitotics that have been studied have been shown to give a survival curve characteristic of an aging population. This suggests that there is no progressive intracellular process occurring that increases the probability of dying with increasing time. Intracellular changes described in the previous chapter may thus be of no consequence, or may result in functional debilities that are unrelated to cell viability. Loss of cells with time, regardless of mechanism, could, of course, cause aging phenomena at higher levels of organization in an animal.

Aging of cells in development

Many of the cell populations we have been discussing, if they change at all with age, appear to change most rapidly during the period of growth in the animal. The lag period before regeneration of liver, the numbers of human cerebral neurones, and the generation time of intestinal epithelial cells all become altered to the greatest extent between birth and maturity. Lymphoid organs such as thymus and tonsils are prominent in infancy and become atrophic in the adults of many species, but function at the cell level appears to be maintained. In addition, several organs that are hormone-dependent undergo atrophic changes as hormone patterns change at various times in the life of an animal. In these instances, there is a decrease in cell number and in rate of cell division. These are all borderline aging processes in that some criteria of an aging process appear to be satisfied, while in no case are all criteria known to be fulfilled.

These examples illustrate the difficulty at times of disentangling developmental from aging processes. In addition, a number of cell populations die out as parts of early developmental processes (Biggers, 1964; Saunders, 1966). In general, rates of dying of these cells are characteristic of aging populations. Zones of dead and dying cells can be identified at many sites in developing embryos and in metamorphosing animals. The losses of tails and gills in anurans, of Mullerian and Wolffian ducts, and of pronephros and mesonephros occur largely by cell death and dissolution. Whenever lumens form in tissues, or separation, fusion, or invagination occurs, cell death is extensive. When it has been studied, cell death has been seen to consist of a generalized deterioration, associated with the presence of high concentrations of lysosomal enzymes.

It is not known to what extent death in these cells is due to intrinsic aging processes, and to what extent to external influences. A number of studies have shown that genetic factors, as well as environmental conditions, play key roles in programmed cell death. Several mutants are known in which cell death does not occur. Such animals develop a variety of abnormalities in morphogenesis.

Grafting experiments have been of use in evaluating factors required for cell death. For example, in sculpturing of the limb bud in the chick embryo, certain zones of cells die on schedule. If the presumptive necrotic zone is grafted onto somite tissue or placed in organ culture, the cells die at the usual time. If grafted to a site on the wing bud where necrosis does not occur, the cells survive and differentiate. It has been postulated that these cells will deteriorate and die when on their own, and that they require some substance for survival that can be provided by cells in areas where degeneration does not occur.

Cell death in some cases is under hormonal control. The thyroid hormone accelerates degeneration of cells of gills, tail, and musculature in the metamorphosis of tadpoles. In birds, involution of the Mullerian and Wolffian ducts is under the influence of testes and ovaries, respectively. Although treatment with androgens and estrogens can reproduce the gonadal effects, these hormones have not been shown to be present in significant concentrations in embryos. In mammals, the presence of testes is required for the degeneration of Mullerian ducts,

while involution of Wolffian ducts appears more genetically determined and intrinsic; unless a testis is present, Wolffian ducts degenerate.

Physical state of the immediate environment is important in at least
one instance. In the formation of bone from cartilage there is a definite
sequence in which cartilage cells mature, the extracellular matrix becomes mineralized, and the cells then die. If the matrix does not
mineralize, as in vitamin D deficiency, the cells do not die. It has been
suggested that mineralization of the matrix interferes with diffusion
processes, and that the cells starve or accumulate toxic waste products.

Finally, the opportunity of a cell to function may determine whether
or not it will survive. Spinal ganglia are all about the same size early
in the embryo. As limbs differentiate, they are innervated by certain
ganglia. In these ganglia large numbers of neurones survive, while in
other ganglia many of the cells die. With subsequent development,
ganglia supplying limbs remain large, and ganglia not innervating
limbs become small. Death of cells that have no function may explain
some loss of cells that occurs at a rapid rate in young animals.

Comments on temporary organs

It is clear that cell populations, tissues, and organs can have
life spans that do not coincide with life spans of the animals that contain them; their involution, deterioration, or death may in some cases
result from aging processes. Populations of oocytes, short-lived fixed
postmitotics, tissues in development, and the thymus gland have been
discussed.

In addition, there are organs that have distinct life spans and are
born, live, and die, at certain times or intervals over a mammal's life
span (Wolstenholme and Miller, 1956). Examples are the corpus
luteum, antlers, and the placenta. On examination of such organs, the
impression is gained that they undergo rapid aging; their death or loss
is clearly programmed, depending on how long the organs have been
in existence. The question arises as to what extent their deterioration
is due to intrinsic aging processes.

The corpus luteum is an endocrine organ that remains active for a
few days to two weeks in various species. It regresses rapidly unless
there is implantation of a blastocyst. The latter causes prolonged
survival. Degeneration is usually apparent about halfway through pregnancy, with regression then occurring rapidly and completely postpartum. Regression in normal cycles and following pregnancy is
associated with alterations in the blood supply, generally characterized

as closure of vessels or loss of vascularity, with consequent scarring of the organ.

The antlers of deer are annual organs composed of bone with a covering of soft skin, the velvet, during the period of growth. The antlers grow most rapidly in the spring, shed the velvet in September, and the antlers themselves are shed in midwinter. Growth and shedding are under the control of testosterone and a growth stimulating factor, presumably of pituitary origin. Castration during the first 8 months of life results in no antler growth. Castration in the presence of antlers causes retention of the velvet and failure of shedding. Administration of testosterone to castrated deer causes antler growth and shedding, but if it is administered after shedding of the velvet, shedding of the antlers is inhibited. Shedding is associated with obliteration of the blood supply at the antler-pedical junction, with resorption of bone and proliferation of connective tissue at this site, and finally with separation at the junction.

The placenta is a complex organ with varying structure and composition in different species. Different components appear, function, and regress at different times. The chorion laeve and decidua capsularis, for example, disappear by the fourth month of gestation in human beings. Many metabolic and chemical changes have been observed over the life span of the placenta. Some proceses do not change very significantly, and others become more active in older organs. Many processes show a slow progressive decline in function with placenta age, without any abrupt change as term is approached. In the latter part of a pregnancy, a number of degenerative changes occur. These are a thickening and fibrosis of arterial walls, thrombosis, infarcts and fibrosis of villi, and deposition of fibrin and calcium salts.

The term placenta remains a rather active organ metabolically, however, and is known to be capable of surviving beyond the gestational period. Pregnancy can be prolonged experimentally, in which case the placenta survives without any significantly increased degenerative changes. Many students of the placenta have gained the impression that its life ends because it is expelled, rather than because of intrinsic aging processes.

The major factors that regulate processes over the life spans of these transient organs, and that eventually cause their death or involution, appear to be extrinsic to the organs. The life of the organ ends because of something done to it, or withheld from it. On the basis of available information, there is no reason to believe that findings in these organs can be used to generalize about aging in systems where deterioration and death are due to intrinsic causes.

Some judgments

When very complicated systems exist over long periods of time, a number of changes would be anticipated. It is a continuing problem to decide which changes are important and which are trivial. From the data available, it is often impossible to know whether the changes represent aging changes in being universal, progressive, and irreversible. It is also usually impossible to tell whether the changes are intrinsic to the cell or are caused by environmental factors or control mechanisms.

An important change is one that causes an observable alteration in the function or properties of the system, or answers a question that a student of the system thinks is worth asking. In terms of cell dynamics —the number of cells present, rate of division, and generation time— changes over the life span of an animal appear trivial. In some populations, no changes in these parameters have been observed; in others, changes occur most rapidly during periods of maximum growth of the animal. It is possible that early in development there is a great excess of cells in various populations. As growth and development proceed there is a loss of some cells by decreased cell division and by death of cells, so that only cells that are called upon to function are maintained. There may be a re-sorting of cell populations so that a balance is achieved in the whole animal. Atrophy of nonfunctional tissue and the death of unused neurones support this notion. It is necessary to consider age changes in these cells because we shall have to evaluate their role in aging at higher levels of organization. Even negative data may be of use in this connection.

As noted earlier, the aging of cells cultured under optimal conditions does not appear to serve as a model for any process occurring in a cell population in an animal. Differences in potential cell doublings between cells derived from fetal, embryonic, and cancer tissue may be more relevant to questions about growth cessation and neoplasia than about aging per se. On the other hand, the culture of explants and of cells in sera of different ages may be of value in determining the effect of extracellular changes with age on cell proliferation and survival.

It has been more difficult to gain information on changes in cell function with age than on population dynamics. In the case of populations, many studies show no change, while some investigations indicate changes that occur most rapidly during rapid animal growth. A rare report describes significant enzyme variations between cells from adult and old animals. Such findings should be confirmed and extended, with particular reference to the criteria of universality, progression, and irreversibility.

It would be difficult to explain intrinsic age changes in intermitotics, although some possibilities were mentioned in the previous chapter. Long-lived fixed postmitotics would be likely candidates for change, however, certainly in components that are metabolically inert. Some morphological changes with age were described in the previous chapter. It is not known if there are any functional consequences of these alterations. Function of these cells with increasing age has received very little attention. Changes in an organ such as muscle tell us only that some alterations have occurred; alterations could be in the muscle cells, extracellular material, blood vessels, nutritional state, or recent history of the muscle in terms of training and exercise. Such cells as muscle and neurones could become altered in their specialized function, in membrane properties, for example, without any significant or detectable change in metabolic and synthetic processes necessary for life.

Deterioration and death of the short-lived fixed postmitotics are clearly the result of aging processes. Aging of populations of these cells does not appear to be related in any significant way to the life span of the animal. The postmitotics serve not only as examples of cell aging, but also as examples of systems in which differentiation occurs at the expense of cell growth and division. The interrelationship between specialization and aging in these cells is obvious.

Degeneration of cells in the developing animal demonstrates the type of programming that can occur in cell aging. Such programming may be intrinsic to the cells, or may reside in the environment or distant organs and probably has different bases in the case of different tissues. These cell populations, as well as temporary organs, also point out how various components of an organism can age independently of each other and of the aging of the entire animal. These cell populations age as the organism is growing and developing most rapidly.

Some useful studies

1. *Activities of intermitotics from animals of different ages.* Bone marrow cells or epithelial cells of various types could be studied with regard to enzyme content and rate of protein synthesis. It would be necessary to establish that cell samples from animals of different ages represented the same cell populations. Data from such cells after

several passages in tissue culture, so that environmental effects were abolished, would be useful additions to the small amount of information we have on this problem.

2. *Mechanism of death in short-lived fixed postmitotics.* Permeability of membranes, ion, and enzyme content could be determined in short-lived fixed postmitotic cells as they become specialized and die.

3. *Role of animal growth and activity in cell population dynamics.* By dietary means, animals could be made to grow slowly or rapidly. Animals could also be kept active by exercise, or be kept inactive. Cell populations in the animals could be studied in terms of numbers of cells present, numbers of stem cells, and generation time. It would be of particular interest to see if slow growth and inactivity reproduced any of the effects seen with age, and if these were reversible. Similar animals would be of use in studying the enzyme content of cells and rates of protein synthesis, in view of the changes that have been reported in cells from animals of different ages.

4. *Function of long-lived fixed postmitotics.* Studies of single isolated neurones and muscle cells from individuals of different ages, in terms of membrane permeability, depolarization, and conduction velocity would be feasible. Such activities as flow of axoplasm in nerve fibers and contraction of myofibrils might also be investigated. Such studies would indicate whether or not significant changes occur in these cells. They could be followed up by studies of cells from active and inactive or growing and nongrowing animals to determine the effects of extrinsic factors.

REFERENCES

Biggers, J. D. 1964. The death of cells in normal multicellular organisms. *In* A. V. S. de Reuk and J. Knight (eds.). Cellular Injury. Boston: Little, Brown and Company. Pp. 329–351.

Blandau, R. J. (ed.). 1975. Aging Gametes, Their Biology and Pathology. Basel: S. Karger.

Blau, J. N. 1972. DNA synthesis in the adult and ageing guinea pig thymus. Clin. Exptl. Immunol. 11:461–468.

Brizzee, K. R., N. Sherwood, and P. S. Timiras. 1968. A comparison of cell populations at various depth levels in cerebral cortex of young adult and aged Long-Evans rats. J. Gerontol. 23:289–297.

Brody, Harold. 1955. Organization of the cerebral cortex III. A study of aging in the human cerebral cortex. J. Comp. Neurology. 102:511–556.

Brown, W. F. 1973. Functional compensation of human motor units in health and disease. J. Neurol. Sci. (Amst.). 20:199–209.

Bucher, Nancy L., and André D. Glinos. 1950. The effect of age on regeneration of rat liver. Cancer Res. 10:324–333.

Bucher, Nancy L., Miriam N. Swaffield, and Joseph F. DiTroia. 1964. The influence of age upon the incorporation of thymidine-2-C14 into the DNA of regenerating rat liver. Cancer Res. 24:509–512.

Cameron, I. L. 1972. Cell proliferation and renewal in aging mice. J. Gerontol. 27:162–172.

Chen, M. G., G. B. Price, and T. Makinodan. 1972. Incidence of delayed mortality (secondary disease) in allogenic radiation chimeras receiving bone marrow from aged mice. J. Immunol. 108:1370–1378.

Cristofalo, V. J. 1972. Animal cell culture as a model system for the study of aging. Adv. in Gerontol. Res. 4:45–79.

Daniel, C. W. 1977. Cell longevity: In vivo. *In* C. E. Finch and L. Hayflick, (eds.). Handbook of the Biology of Aging. New York: Van Nostrand Reinhold. Pp. 122–158.

Eadie, G. S., and I. W. Brown, Jr. 1953. Red blood cell survival studies. Blood. 8:1110–1136.

Farrar, J. J., B. E. Loughman, and A. A. Nordin. 1974. Lymphopoietic potential of bone marrow cells from aged mice: Comparison of the cellular constituents of bone marrow from young and aged mice. J. Immunol. 112:1244–1249.

Florini, James R., Yoko Saito, and Ellen J. Manowitz. 1973. Effect of age on thyroxine-induced cardiac hypertrophy induced in mice. J. Gerontol. 28:293–297.

Franks, L. M. 1970. Cellular aspects of aging. Expt. Gerontol. 5:281–289.

Gerbase-DeLima, M., P. Meredith, and R. L. Walford. 1975. Age-related changes including synergy and suppression, in the mixed lymphocyte reaction in long-lived mice. Fed. Proc. 34:159–161.

Gerbase-DeLima, M., and R. L. Walford. 1975. Effect of cortisone in delineating thymus cell subsets in advanced age. Proc. Soc. Exptl. Biol. Med. 149:562–564.

Gerbase-DeLima, Maria, et al. 1974. Age-related decline in thymic-independent immune function in a long-lived mouse strain. J. Gerontol. 29:261–268.

Goodman, S. A., and T. Makinodan. 1975. Effect of age on cell-mediated immunity in long-lived mice. Clin. Exptl. Immunol. **19**:533–542.

Grant, Wilson C., and Mary C. LeGrande. 1964. The influence of age on erythropoiesis in the rat. J. Gerontol. **19**:505–509.

Hanley, T. 1974. "Neuronal fall-out" in the aging brain: A critical review of the quantitative data. Age Ageing. **3**:133–151.

Harrison, David E. 1975. Normal function of transplanted marrow cell lines from aged mice. J. Gerontol. **30**:279–285.

Harrison, David E., and John W. Doubleday. 1975. Normal function of immunologic stem cells from aged mice. J. Immunol. **114**:1314–1317.

Harrison, David E., C. M. Astle, and J. W. Doubleday. 1977. Stem cell lines from old immunodeficient donors give normal responses in young recipients. J. Immunol. **118**:1223–1227.

Hart, R. W., and R. B. Setlow. 1974. Correlation between deoxyribonucleic acid excision-repair and life span in a number of mammalian species. Proc. Nat'l. Acad. Sci. USA. **71**:2169–2173.

Hay, Robert J. 1967. Cell and tissue culture in aging research. *In* Bernard Strehler (ed.). Adv. in Gerontol. Res. **2**:121–158.

Hayflick, L. 1965. The limited *in vitro* lifetime of human diploid cell strains. Exptl. Cell Res. **37**:614–636.

Hirokawa, K., and T. Makinodan. 1975. Thymic involution: Effect on T cell differentiation. J. Immunol. **114**:1659–1664.

Krohn, P. L. 1962. Heterochronic transplantation in the study of ageing. Proc. Roy. Soc. London. **157**:128–147.

Lesher, S. 1966. Chronic irradiation and ageing in mice and rats. *In* Patricia J. Lindop and G. A. Sacher (eds.). Radiation and Ageing. London: Taylor & Francis Ltd. Pp. 183–206.

Makinodan, T., and W. H. Adler. 1975. Effects of aging on the differentiation and proliferation potentials of cells of the immune system. Fed. Proc. **34**:153–158.

Martin, G. M., C. A. Sprague, and C. J. Epstein. 1970. Replicative life-span of cultivated human cells. Lab. Invest. **23**:86–92.

Mathies, Margaret, et al. 1973. Age-related decline in response to phytohemagglutinin and pokeweed mitogen by spleen cells from hamsters and long-lived mouse strain. J. Gerontol. **28**:425–430.

Mende, T. J. 1965. Studies on Cr[51] labeled erythrocyte turnover in relation to age. Gerontologia. **11**:57–66.

Menon, Mira, Bernard N. Jaroslow, and Richard Koesterer. 1974. The decline of cell-mediated immunity in aging mice. J. Gerontol. **29**:499–505.

Meredith, Patricia, et al. 1975. Age-related changes in the cellular immune response of lymph node and thymus cells in long-lived mice. Cell Immunol. **18:**324–330.

Nordin, A. A., and T. Makinodan. 1974. Humoral immunity in aging. Fed. Proc. **33:**2033–2035.

Pisciotta, A. V., et al. 1967. Mitogenic effect of phytohaemagglutinin at different ages. Nature. **215:**193–194.

Rodey, G. E., R. A. Good, and E. J. Yunis. 1971. Progressive loss in vitro of cellular immunity with ageing in strains of mice susceptible to autoimmune disease. Clin. Exp. Immunol. **9:**305–311.

Roth, G. S., and R. C. Adelman. 1975. Age-related changes in hormone binding by target cells and tissues; possible role in altered adaptive responsiveness. Exptl. Gerontol. **10:**1–11.

Samorajski, T. 1974. Age differences in the morphology of posterior tibial nerves of mice. J. Comp. Neurol. **157:**439–452.

Saunders, J. W., Jr. 1966. Death in embryonic systems. Science. **154:**604–612.

Sharav, Y., and M. Massler. 1967. Age changes in oral epithelia. Progenitor population, synthesis index and tissue turnover. Exptl. Cell Res. **47:**132–138.

Stanley, J. F., D. Pye, and A. MacGregor. 1975. Comparison of doubling numbers attained by cultured animal cells with life span of species. Nature. **255:**158–159.

Stutman, O. 1974. Cell-mediated immunity and aging. Fed. Proc. **33:**2028–2032.

Tauchi, H., T. Yoshioka, and H. Kobayashi. 1971. Age change of skeletal muscles of rats. Gerontologia (Basel: S. Karger AG). **17:**219–227.

Tomanek, R. J., and Y. K. Woo. 1970. Compensatory hypertrophy of the plantaris muscle in relation to age. J. Gerontol. **25:**23–29.

Van Bezooijen, C. F. A., M. J. Van Noord, and D. L. Knook. 1974. The variability of parenchymal liver cells isolated from young and old rats. Mech. Ageing Dev. **3:**107–119.

Walters, C. S., and H. N. Claman. 1975. Age-related changes in cell-mediated immunity in BALB/C mice. J. Immunol. **115:**1438–1443.

Weksler, Marc E., and Thomas H. Hütteroth. 1974. Impaired lymphocyte function in aged humans. J. Clin. Invest. **53:**99–104.

Wolstenholme, G. E. W., and E. C. P. Millar (eds.). 1956. Aging in Transient Tissues. Vol. 2. Ciba Foundation Coll. on Ageing. Boston: Little, Brown and Company.

Wright, E. A., and J. M. Spink. 1959. A study of the loss of nerve cells in the central nervous system in relation to age. Gerontologia. 3:277–287.

Young, L. T. J., D. Medina, and K. B. DeOme. 1971. The influence of host and tissue age on life span and growth rate of serially transplanted mouse mammary gland. Exptl. Gerontol. 6:49–56.

Yuhas, J. H., and J. B. Storer. 1967. The effect of age on two modes of radiation death and on hematopoietic cell survival in the mouse. Radiat. Res. 32:596–605.

SIX

Aging of Animals:

Observations and

Questions

Aging usually denotes the phenomena or processes having to do with the deterioration and dying out of all members of a population of animals in a highly predictable and characteristic fashion with the passage of time. Deterioration and death occur in spite of the best possible nutrition, environment, life style, and combination of genes. The fact that these changes in populations occur in such a predictable fashion tells us that aging is as much a part of normal biology as growth and differentiation, and also indicates that changes with profound consequences must be occurring at the molecular and tissue levels.

Although we are now considering aging of animals, we know from previous discussions that aging processes occur at a variety of levels, from extracellular molecules to populations of cells. Some of these systems clearly age independently of aging of the animals that contain them, whereas changes in some systems are related to the life span of the animal. We have essentially surveyed changes with age at molecular and cell levels up to this point. A number of age-related alterations have been described, and where information is lacking, we have suggested possibilities and indulged in some speculations. Basic causes of animal aging most likely reside in some tissue changes that have already been discussed or postulated.

The single most important goal in the study of aging is to understand the inevitable aging of an intact animal in terms of molecular and tissue events. Before we return to a consideration of aging at these basic levels, it is necessary to consider what phenomena in aging animals must be explained by basic changes—in short, what is meant specifically by aging of an animal? When we know what must be explained—what types of questions to ask—we shall have some meaningful frames of reference for evaluation of the roles of tissue and molecular changes.

This chapter will deal with manifestations of aging—how aging is identified, described, and defined in an animal. Inferences are frequently made from life-table data—from rates and probabilities of dying in a population. It is necessary, however, to know what changes are progressing before the end point of death. For this reason, references will often be made to human populations. Man leaves much to be desired as an experimental animal. However, he is most useful for the study of aging, as much is known about rates of dying, causes of death, and metabolic and physiological changes over the life span of very large human populations. Heterogeneity of populations and environmental variations are frequently advantageous because the role of these factors can be evaluated; the experiments have been performed by nature. In recent years considerable information has accumulated on disease incidence and physiological changes in aging laboratory animals. Studies of these populations are becoming increasingly useful.

The dying out of populations

In Chapter One it was pointed out that populations dying out can be described by two extreme types of curve: the logarithmic die-away or first-order reaction rate curve for populations in which deaths are due to accidents or non-age-related causes, and the rectangular curve for populations in which deaths are due to aging. When percentage surviving is plotted as a function of age for animal populations, curves between these two extremes are obtained. We can then compare populations in terms of relative influences of accidental and age-related causes of death.

Figure 6.1 shows survival curves for a number of human populations and for a theoretical population dying out from non-age-related accidents. Shapes of the curves are dependent on standard of living and on technological attainments of the various societies. Population density, sanitation, and nutrition, rather than medical practices, play key roles in determining the shape of these curves. In underdeveloped societies there are large numbers of non-age-related deaths, or deaths

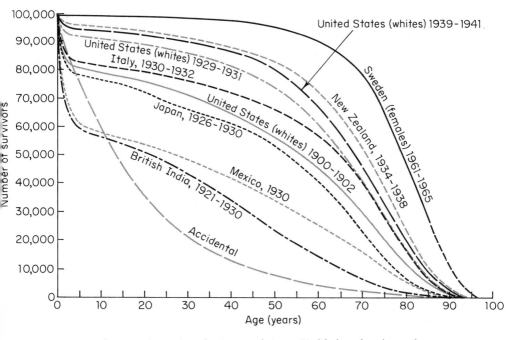

Fig. 6.1 Survival curves for various human populations. (Modified and redrawn from Ageing: The Biology of Senescence by Alex Comfort. Copyright © 1956, 1964 by Alex Comfort. Modified and reproduced by permission of Holt, Rinehart and Winston, Inc.)

that occur predominantly in young individuals. Most of these deaths are from infectious disease in malnourished individuals. As societies become more advanced, survival curves become more rectangular. In the most highly developed cultures, the curve becomes that of an aging population; most deaths are results of aging processes.

It can be seen from these curves that the maximum life span of 90 to 95 years is about the same in the different societies. This tells us that technological improvements and medical progress have had no effect on human life span as an intrinsic characteristic of populations. What has been changed is the probability of dying in younger age groups. More individuals can expect to live out the human life span in highly developed societies than in more primitive societies.

We also know from these curves that as research on specific diseases leads to effective means of prevention or treatment, the survival curve will become slightly more rectangular, with no change in maximum survival. In other words, the human life span will not be altered until underlying causes of aging are slowed or inhibited. This is because most of the non-age-related diseases involving large numbers of people have already been dealt with rather successfully in the most advanced societies.

The effects of progress can be illustrated in life expectancy at birth, which is a useful overall measure of the health status of a population. As shown in Figure 6.2, progress as manifested by life expectancy virtually ceased in the United States at around 1955. Although life expectancy at birth has shown marked improvement in this century, life expectancy at 65 years of age has only gone from 11.9 years in 1900–1902 to 14.8 years in 1969 (Siegel, 1975). Some subgroups of the population have not even done this well. White males, for example, had an expectancy of 11.5 years at 65 years of age in 1900–1902, and only 13.0 years in 1969. What this all means is that progress has not had much effect on the aging population, and that in the more highly developed societies, greater fractions of the population have survived to an age where they can die of aging processes. In advanced societies, about 10 percent of the population is over 65 years old. Almost all mem-

Fig. 6.2   Life expectancy at birth as a function of year for U.S. populations. (From U.S. Vital Statistics.)

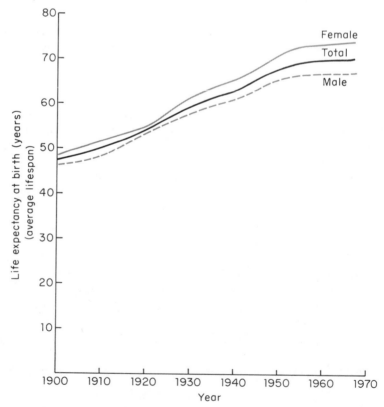

bers of this group are debilitated or sick in one way or another. The diseases and debilities of this population comprise the most important public health problem in all modern societies.

The question of the duration of the human life span has been confused by reports that certain populations have excessively long lives. An Andean village in Ecuador, the Hunza tribe in Kashmir, and the people of Soviet Georgia are often cited in this regard; individuals in Soviet Georgia have been reported to live for 168 or more years. Data on these populations have been critically reviewed by Medvedev (1974). Records on the Hunza and Ecuador populations are too scanty for any conclusions. Quite a bit more is known about the Georgian population. Medvedev's conclusion is that the apparent longevity of this population is due, for a variety of reasons, to people lying about their age; people in Soviet Georgia probably do not live longer than people in other healthy environments. The maximum life span that has been reasonably well documented is 113 years, according to the *Guiness Book of World Records*.

If different inbred strains of mice are looked after very well and, in particular, are protected from epidemics, a family of survival curves is obtained (Figure 6.3). All of these curves are somewhat rectangular, indicating that most deaths in all of the strains are age-related. It might

Fig. 6.3 Survival curves for mice of various inbred strains. (From Green (ed.), Biology of the Laboratory Mouse by the Staff of the Jackson Laboratory. Copyright © 1966 by McGraw-Hill, Inc. Used with permission of McGraw-Hill Book Company.)

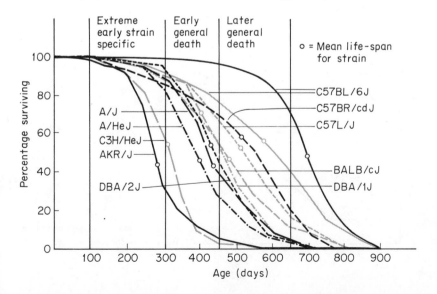

appear that some strains age sooner than others. It turns out, however, that the short-lived strains are highly susceptible to certain fatal diseases. Virtually all individuals of strain AKR/J, for example, develop leukemia and die at an early age. In such a population the onset and progression of leukemia could be considered aging processes. This disease would represent an aging process only in those members of the population that were destined to die from it. The mouse strains susceptible to certain diseases were selectively bred for the development of these diseases. However, the characteristic survival curve for the mouse as a species would probably be that for strain C57BL/6J. These animals die from a variety of age-related causes.

An important way of characterizing an aging population in terms of end points was discovered by Gompertz, an English actuary, in 1825. He found that after maturity, the rate and probability of dying are exponetial with increasing age. If the life span is divided into short intervals, and the percentage of those alive at the beginning of each interval that die during the interval is plotted as a function of age, an exponential curve is obtained. If the logarithm of the mortality rate, or age-specific death rate, is plotted, a straight line is obtained (Figure 6.4). This tells us that rate and probability of dying double at regular intervals.

In the first chapter it was pointed out that if a homogeneous population dies out because of aging, and if the life span has an approximately normal distribution, then the age-specific death rate becomes exponential after the mean life span. In real populations the mortality curve becomes exponetial much earlier in life. This is because the life span has a skewed rather than a normal distribution; more individuals

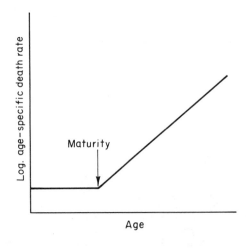

Fig. 6.4 Rate and probability of dying as a function of age. (Gompertz plot.)

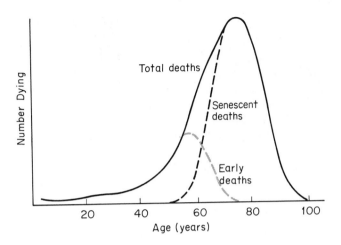

Fig. 6.5 Distribution of deaths in a human population. (Redrawn from Benjamin, 1959.)

die at earlier ages than would be the case if all died from the same age-related causes. Figure 6.5 shows the distributions of life spans for a human population. The curve for total deaths can be resolved into two curves: a normal distribution curve for that segment of the population that is rather homogeneous in dying off because of a small number of age-related processes, and a second curve for a heterogeneous population in which members die from nonrelated, or partially age-related causes, and as consequences of agelike changes occurring only in certain subgroups.

Life-span and survival data of these types have a number of uses. They indicate the extent to which end points of aging are characteristics of populations, and demonstrate that these end points are programmed and predictable. They can frequently tell us whether a given population is aging or not. Most importantly, they give an indication of what types of phenomena must be explained by changes at tissue and molecular levels. Progressive alterations must be occurring in the tissues to cause end points of death. A consideration of mechanisms of death will enable us to be more specific in trying to relate tissue changes to mortality data.

Diseases and aging

It is not always easy to determine cause of death, even after a very careful post-mortem examination. Frequently, the lesions noted do not appear severe enough to cause death, or no significant lesions are found, or there are so many different kinds of disease processes present in an individual that it is difficult to decide which was the primary cause and which were contributing causes of death. The latter difficulty, in particular, holds for individuals in old populations. When a number of severe diseases are present, it appears fortuitous that one kills rather than another. When very large populations are considered, however, it is likely that errors in judgment and observation would cancel each other out, and that an approximation of the truth would be achieved.

In Figure 6.6 the age-specific death rates for the most important diseases and accepted causes of death have been plotted as a function of age for the population of the United States. In this semilog plot, the curve for all deaths is a straight line in accord with the Gompertz function; the probability of dying doubles about every 8 years after maturity.

The majority of deaths are due to a rather small number of pathologic processes: arteriosclerosis, hypertension, and malignant neoplasms. The role of age in determining these end points can be evaluated by noting if the curve for a given cause of death is parallel to or rises faster than the all-causes curve, or if it falls away from the all-causes curve with increasing age. Deaths due to arteriosclerosis, which includes arteriosclerotic heart disease, most vascular diseases of the central nervous system, and the majority of chronic renal diseases, are clearly age-dependent. The curve for hypertension similarly parallels the all-causes curve, although very late in the life span it drops away slightly. Respiratory infections, such as influenza and pneumonia, and accidents become more age-dependent with increasing age, so that curves for these end points rise faster than the all-causes curve in the later decades of life. This indicates that basic aging processes increase the susceptibility to death from respiratory infections and accidents very markedly in the later decades of life. On the other hand, the curve for malignant neoplasms drops away from the all-causes curve in later decades. This tells us that the probability of dying from a neoplasm does not increase as fast as the probability of dying, and that neoplasms affect only a certain segment of the population. As this segment dies off, the probability in the remaining population of becoming afflicted rises at a lower rate or actually declines. The divergence of such a curve from the Gompertz function is characteristic of those diseases that are either present or absent, rather than present to some degree in all, and are either cured or rapidly prove fatal. Many diseases in this category, syphilis for example, are only very peripherally related to aging processes.

These mortality curves can be used for calculating what would hap-

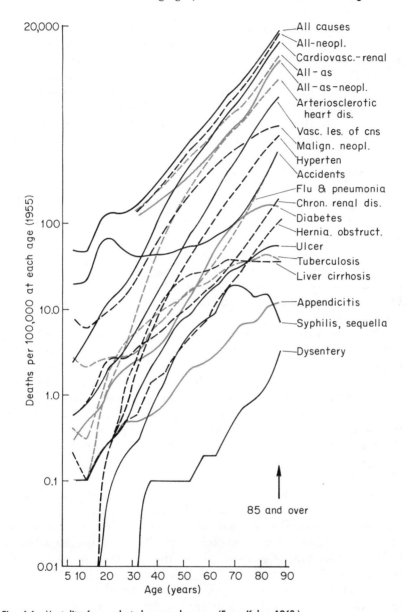

Fig. 6.6 Mortality from selected causes by age. (From Kohn, 1963.)

pen if some present efforts in biomedical research were wholly success-
ful. (See Figure 6.6.) For example, if no one died from cancer, the
all-causes curve would be replaced by the "All-neopl." curve, and life
expectancy at birth would be increased by about 2 years. If arterio-

sclerosis were conquered, the all-causes curve would become "All-as," and about 7 more years of life would be expected. A population free of these two major diseases would gain 9 to 10 years of life (curve "All-as-neopl."). What diseases would then kill the population? Deaths would be due to the miscellaneous group of other diseases—particularly respiratory infections and accidents, which increase so rapidly as causes of death in the older populations. In fact, from extrapolating the curves for influenza and pneumonia and accidents, it would appear that a population free of cancer and arteriosclerosis would be cut down very quickly, and that the estimated increase of 9 and 10 years is probably overly optimistic. This bears out the earlier assertion that progress in research on specific diseases might make the survival curve more rectangular but would not lengthen the total life span by very much.

The diseases with which large numbers of aging individuals die can be classified in three ways in regard to aging: (1) Diseases that are aging processes themselves, (2) diseases that show increasing incidence with increasing age, and (3) diseases that have more serious consequences with increasing age.

The diseases that are aging processes themselves occur in all members of the population and are progressive and irreversible under usual conditions. Arteriosclerosis, or atherosclerosis, is the best example of such a disease. The terms *arteriosclerosis* and *atherosclerosis* are often used interchangeably. This can be confusing because "arteriosclerosis" literally means hardening of the arteries; whereas "atherosclerosis" is the formation of lesions—of plaques involving the inner lining of arteries, and deaths are due to these plaques. The phrase "arteriosclerotic heart disease" really means disease due to atherosclerotic plaques of the coronary arteries.

A variety of factors—nutritional, metabolic, and genetic—and the presence of other diseases influence the rate of progression of atherosclerosis. However, the essential fact of this disease is that it consists of a chronic inflammatory reaction in the walls of arteries, characterized by the proliferation of small vessels, by the accumulation of minerals, lipids, and glycoproteins, and by scarring associated with the formation of large amounts of collagen. Many of these changes occur diffusely through the vessels, but at certain sites they are severe enough to cause the formation of plaques. This disease progresses in everyone, and increasing age is the most important risk factor. Figure 6.7 compares aortas from a young adult and an old individual. The older artery is dilated, the wall is thickened and stiff, and the inner surface shows many atherosclerotic plaques, several with ulcerations and with adherent blood clots. Those who die from atherosclerosis do so from

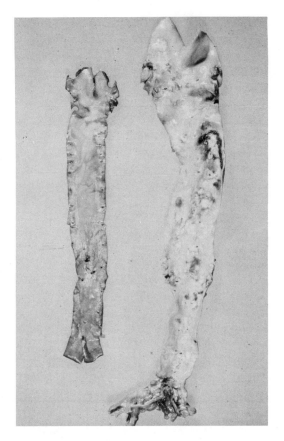

Fig. 6.7   Opened aortas from adult (left) and old (right) human beings.

complications involving smaller arteries: growth of a plaque, or hemmorrhage within a plaque or from a blood clot forming on the plaque, so that the lumen is occluded and the distal tissue dies.

Hypertension results from several different processes. Although some forms are secondary to kidney and adrenal disease, the great majority of cases are of the so-called essential type and are not related to any specific known disease. The mechanism of death in hypertension is heart failure, kidney failure, or stroke, which all depend on a certain severity and duration of high blood pressure. Hypertensive deaths are a very indirect measure of high blood pressure in a population. We would like to know if increasing blood pressure is an aging process, in occurring in all members of an aging population.

If blood pressure is measured in a large population in a modern so-

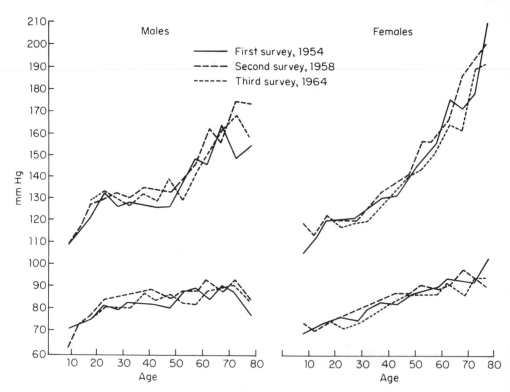

Fig. 6.8 Relationship between age and blood pressure in a Welsh population. (From Miall and Lovell, 1967.)

ciety, the impression is gained that increasing systolic blood pressure is an aging process, in occurring in the entire population, whereas diastolic pressure seems to increase in all females, but not in males, as shown in Figure 6.8. However, if blood pressure is determined in a large number of individuals over a 25-year interval, and individual changes over this period are calculated, it is seen that most individuals show increases in both systolic and diastolic blood pressure, a very small number shows no change, and a few individuals even show lower blood pressure at the greater age (Figure 6.9). Also, some primitive societies show little or no increase in blood pressure with increasing age. Thus change in blood pressure lacks the universality of a true aging process.

Systolic blood pressure is determined to a great extent by stiffness of the large arteries, and increased diastolic blood pressure is largely dependent on increased peripheral vascular resistance. Blood pressure is decreased by decreased cardiac output, by an increased volume of

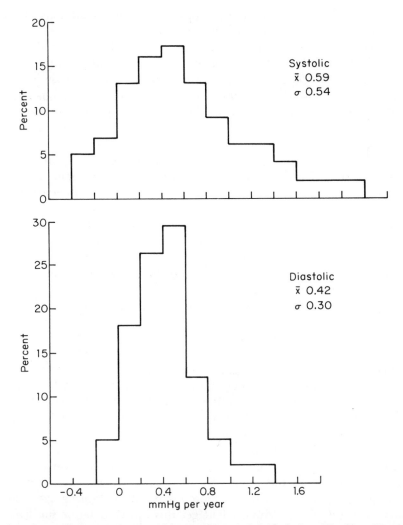

Fig. 6.9 Distribution of changes in blood pressures in individuals from 25-to-30 to 50-to-54 years of age. (From Harris and Forsythe, 1973; by permission.)

large arteries, and by dilatation of small peripheral vessels. Some observations suggest that increasing arterial stiffness and increasing peripheral vascular resistance are aging processes; the inference would be that blood pressure should go up with age. It would appear, however, that some individuals and populations compensate for the tendency to increase blood pressure, perhaps by making use of mechanisms that lower pressure. Whatever the mechanism, hypertension develops with increasing age only in subgroups of human populations. This brings us to the second way of classifying diseases.

The second category of diseases, consisting of diseases that do not occur in all members of the population but that show an increasing incidence as the population ages, do not, in the strictest sense, represent aging processes because the criterion of universality is not satisfied. If, however, only the population destined to develop such a disease or to die from it is considered, the disease becomes an aging process for that population. Many, if not most diseases, can be considered in these terms. Progressive muscular dystrophy of childhood, for example, is fatal for essentially the entire afflicted population by the age of 20 years. If only this population were being observed, the mortality data would be those for an aging population with a maximum life span of around 20 years. Most diseases affecting a segment of the population, however, are not relevant to a consideration of aging of the entire population, or of aging as a normal biological process. Nevertheless, certain diseases must be considered because their incidence does increase exponentially, or at least very rapidly in the later decades of life, and because they play some role in determining the shape of the survival curve.

The increasing incidence of certain types of hypertension is another example of the second category of diseases. Perhaps the best example is malignant neoplasms. Malignancies as a whole, as a cause of death, parallel the all-causes curve, or rise faster over part of the life span, but then drop away in the last decades (Figure 6.6). Reasons for the varying shape of this curve can be appreciated when mortality data for different types of tumors are examined.

Figure 6.10 shows the age-specific death rates for certain selected tumors. Cancer of the colon is quite common and appears to represent an aging process to the extent that the incidence increases with increasing age, and the increase is more rapid with increasing age. The curve suggests that everyone might get this cancer if he or she lived long enough. On the other hand, deaths due to cancer of lung and kidney drop off late in life. If an individual has not developed cancer of the lung by around 70 years of age, or of kidney by 82 years, the probability of getting these cancers drops off significantly in succeeding years. In addition, it is seen that there is a risk of kidney cancer in childhood that disappears by about 12 years. This is due to a specific kind of embryonal kidney tumor. Similarly, there is a maximum risk of death due to bone tumors at around 13 years. This is due to two special types of bone neoplasms. The remaining curve for bone tumors is irregular because of specific types of tumors that have characteristic age incidences. Leukemia also exists in a childhood form and in forms that show a strong age-dependent incidence. A similar pattern of dif-

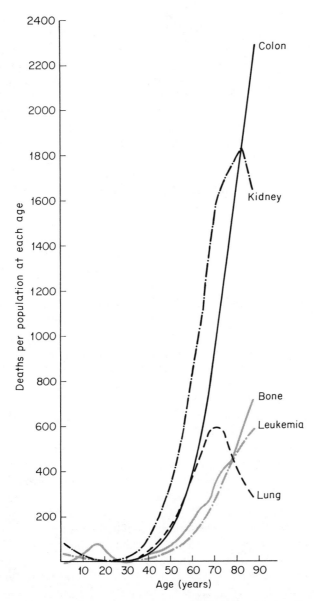

Fig. 6.10 Age-specific death rates for several neoplasms: colon, lung, and leukemia per 10^8 people; bone and kidney per 10^7 people. (From U.S. Vital Statistics, 1965.)

ferent age incidences for different kinds of neoplasms is seen in small laboratory mammals (Peters et al., 1972).

Some tumors clearly occur in only a segment of the population.

Others might eventually occur in all, but this cannot be ascertained because the entire population dies off while the incidence is still rising. Although all criteria of an aging process are not satisfied by malignant neoplasms, the obviously important role of age in determining incidences justifies an attempt to understand the types of age-related molecular and tissue events that might be responsible.

A neoplastic disease occurs in several stages: neoplastic transformation of cells is followed by growth and tissue invasion, spread and metastasis to distant sites, and growth and invasion at those sites. The course of a neoplastic disease depends on properties of the malignant cells and on a number of poorly defined host factors that influence the viability, spread, and invasive capacity of tumors.

The role of age in the various phases of neoplasia has been studied in experimental animals by the induction and transplantation of tumors. Many of the most conspicuous age differences occur between birth and maturity. Thus, weanling or very young animals are more susceptible than mature animals to viral-induced leukemia, the mammary tumor agent, and to the induction of liver tumors by urethane. The growth of a transplanted rat sarcoma is greatest in newborn animals, and drops to a low level at about the time of weaning. On the other hand, the effectiveness of estrogen treatment in causing development of leukemia in mice appears greatest at around the time of sexual maturity, and the induction of skin cancer by a carcinogen has been reported to be more effective in skin grafts from old than from young mice (Ebbesen, 1974).

Several reports indicate that changes after maturity favor the spread and growth of tumors. Older animals develop more metastases than young after the injection of ascites tumor cells. Certain human tumors have been successfully transplanted to old, but not to mature, mice. It has been reported that transplanted lymphosarcomas grow better in old animals, whereas liver tumors and the Walker 256 carcinosarcoma do better in younger animals (Kerkvliet and Kimeldorf, 1973). The growth of skeletal muscle tumors is unrelated to age.

Many of the results quoted in experimental neoplasia studies may be due to changes over the life span in endocrine status and in immunological competence (Teller et al., 1964; Hanna, Nettesheim, and Snodgrass, 1971). Immaturity of immune mechanisms in very young animals may be of particular importance in tumor induction. The role of immune reactions in "spontaneous" tumors is controversial at present, and the problem is further complicated by observations on transplanted tumors. The relevance of animal experiments, particularly those employing induced tumors, to relationships between age and neoplasia in natural populations is uncertain. Perhaps the appropriate generality is that age-related factors appear to be of importance in the various stages of experimentally induced and transplanted neoplastic diseases, and that studies of possible underlying aging processes are now required.

A third category of diseases, as noted earlier, consists of those diseases that also do not occur in all individuals; they also do not show very consistent age-related incidences, but when they do occur, they have more serious consequences, the older the individual. It is this miscellaneous group of diseases and insults, particularly accidents and respiratory infections, that perhaps best characterizes the relationship between age and disease. It has been noted above to what extent these diseases would cause a Gompertz-type mortality curve in the absence of certain diseases that now cause the majority of deaths in a human population.

Bronchopneumonia occurs at all ages. As individuals become older, however, and particularly if they have some debilitating illness or have experienced some trauma such as an accident or surgery, they frequently develop pneumonia and die. What is of interest in regard to aging processes is that the tissue damage from the pneumonia may be very slight. Young individuals with the same degree of lung involvement as the older person who died would quickly recover. In other words, basic aging processes are occurring that decrease the probability of the individual surviving rather trivial insults. This age-related decrease in resistance holds for a variety of infections and for internal accidents such as hernias, intestinal obstructions, and ulcers.

The diseases that are responsible for the doubling of rate of dying every 8 years, and that enable us to characterize a human population as an aging one, have little relationship to one another in terms of development and progression of specific lesions. Thus, an atherosclerotic plaque, cancer of the colon, rigid arteriole, lung infection, and hernia appear to have little to do with each other. Yet, as causes of death in the later decades of the human life span, they all increase more or less exponentially. It should also be noted that many individuals have these diseases concurrently, and that it is often fortuitous that one is a cause of death rather than another. This information gives rise to the concept that there may be one or a small number of basic aging processes in tissues that cause or predispose to all of these diseases. Aging processes would then constitute a 100 percent fatal disease that everyone has, and the age-related diseases could then be viewed as complications.

This view is supported by plotting deaths due to various major causes in a cohort of human beings. Modal values for age of death from such apparently unrelated causes as arteriosclerotic heart disease, hy-

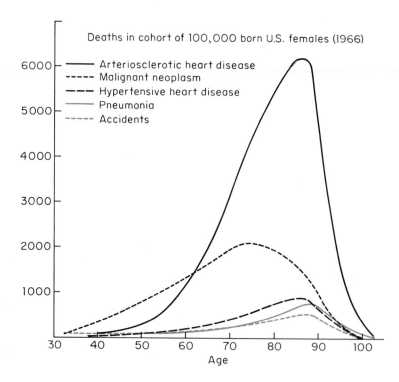

Fig. 6.11 Deaths in U.S. female cohort from specific major diseases. (From U.S. Vital Statistics.)

pertension, pneumonia, and accidents in females, who are healthier than males, are 86 to 89 years (Figure 6.11). The life span for human beings as a species thus appears to be around 87 to 88 years. Cancer deaths occur at earlier ages, as shown in Figure 6.11, representing those diseases in which incidence increases as a function of age. Populations with these diseases do not live out the full life span.

Less is known about causes of death in aging animals other than man. However, the same generalities applied to human diseases will also hold for laboratory animals undergoing natural aging; in simple terms, the probability of dying doubles at regular intervals, and if an individual does not die from one disease, it will die from another. Diseases of animals may also be categorized in the same three ways in relationship to age. In Figure 6.12 the incidences of the most common diseases in a strain of laboratory rat are plotted as a function of age; infections and certain neoplasms that also occur in this strain are excluded. The presence of these diseases is determined by examination

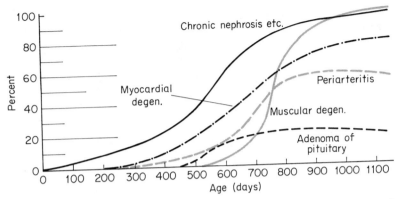

Fig. 6.12 Percent incidence of major lesions in rats as a function of age. (From Simms, 1965. Aging and Levels of Biological Organization, Univ. of Chicago Press, Chicago. © 1965 by the University of Chicago.)

of tissues, and although the data of Figure 6.12 might give the impression that the lesions are all-or-none phenomena in individuals, some of these lesions represent aging processes since they occur in all members of the population. The lesions are recognized, however, only when a certain level of severity is attained. Thus, chronic nephrosis and muscular degeneration are aging processes because they eventually affect the entire population. The other diseases afflict only a fraction of the population, but are clearly age-dependent. In animals, more often than in man, cause of death cannot be determined. Many older animals that die show minimal tissue changes. This indicates the increasing probability of dying from trivial insults, or the decreasing efficiency of resistance factors with age.

The lesions commonly identified in aging rats and mice, in addition to infections and tumors, are inflammations of small vessels, hypertension, chronic inflammatory reactions of kidneys, and scarring of the heart muscle.

When attempting to evaluate various basic processes in regard to their possible importance in the actual aging of an animal, it would be difficult to take any process seriously that could not explain the development and progression of diseases that are responsible for the increasing probability of dying of a population.

Some additional aging diseases

We have been considering diseases as cause of death. There are additional diseases, however, that satisfy the criteria of universality, progression, and irreversibility, and that are generally not fatal.

There is often a wide variability in severity of these diseases. Some may cause severe debility and even death; others cause only slight functional decline. In some cases it is difficult to decide if some debility should be considered a disease rather than a part of the generalized decline that is so characteristic of aging, and which will be described in later sections.

Degenerative joint disease or osteoarthritis is a disease that occurs in the joint cartilage, particularly of weight-bearing joints, of all aging human beings. The cartilage becomes split and fragmented and eventually disappears at many sites. There is an excessive production of underlying bone and of bony and cartilaginous growths from bone ends. This debility is most likely caused in part by a combination of mechanical trauma and the age-related stiffening of collagen in articular cartilage.

Some changes associated with the disease emphysema appear to satisfy the criteria of an aging process. There is an increase in the size of air spaces and increasing lung stiffness. There is also a marked variability in the degree of these changes in an aging population.

Osteoporosis or loss of bone is another disease or process that occurs to some extent in all members of an aging human population. It also shows marked variability, and is particularly severe in some postmenopausal females. Many factors are known to affect the amount of bone present. Bone formation and degradation are labile processes and are dependent on functional demand. It is very likely that disuse of the musculoskeletal system plays some role in the osteoporosis associated with aging.

Amyloid, as mentioned in an earlier chapter, is found in the tissues of increasing numbers of an aging human population. When more sensitive analytical methods are available, it may be found that amyloid accumulates in everyone.

Basic processes at molecular and tissue levels must underly these aging diseases, in addition to promoting atherosclerosis and deaths secondary to the inability to withstand various insults and injuries.

Disease and the acceleration of aging

There are several diseases of human beings in which it appears that some aspects of aging are accelerated. The most common of these is diabetes mellitus. Individuals with diabetes have an earlier onset and very rapid progression of atherosclerosis. Their arteries, lungs, and joints become stiff at an earlier age than normal, and they show early thickening of basement membranes (Schuyler et al., 1976). The basic causes of diabetes are not known, and it is not known of course how these might be related to aging. Fibroblasts from diabetics do not survive well in culture. And it is of particular interest that collagen from individuals with diabetes appears to have undergone accelerated aging by the criterion of resistance to collagenase digestion (Hamlin, Kohn, and Luschin, 1975).

There are two disease states characterized by an apparent acceleration of aging. The victims, while chronologically in childhood or young adulthood, look like little old people. They also show various debilities and lesions that are characteristic of aging. These diseases are progeria, or the Hutchinson-Gilford syndrome, and Werner's syndrome.

Less than 100 cases of progeria have been reported (DeBusk, 1972). Severe growth retardation is apparent in the first year of life. There is loss of hair and of subcutaneous fat. The clavicle and mandible are poorly-developed. Eyes are prominent and the nose is beaked. Atherosclerosis is marked; death is caused by cerebral or coronary artery disease at an average of $13\frac{1}{2}$ years. These individuals do not show other age changes such as degenerative joint disease, far sightedness, and intracellular lipofuscin accumulation. Pedigree analyses show a high degree of consanguinity. Both autosomal recessive and dominant mutation forms of inheritance have been suggested. Fibroblasts from these individuals appear defective in culture (Goldstein and Moerman, 1975).

Werner's syndrome has been reported in some 125 individuals (Epstein et al., 1966). It is recognized later than progeria—generally in the third and fourth decades. The afflicted individuals have short stature, greying and loss of hair, cataracts, and severe osteoporosis, and show atrophy of skin, lymphoid tissue, muscle, and fat. Mild diabetes is present in about one-half of the cases. Very severe arteriosclerosis and atherosclerosis are present, and there is calcification of blood vessels and heart valves. Lipofuscin accumulation is not accelerated. Genetic analyses are consistent with an autosomal recessive mode of inheritance. Cells from these individuals also grow poorly in culture and may show defective DNA repair.

None of these diseases mimic the aging syndrome with complete accuracy. Each has enough in common with natural aging, however, to suggest that an understanding of mechanisms will give some insight into aging processes. Abnormalities can be detected in cultured cells in each of these diseases, suggesting a genetic basis, and that studies of functions of these cells might provide useful information on mechanisms of disease.

Age and responses to stress

Declining resistance to stress, in the form of disease, is one of the most characteristic features of an aging population. Such declining resistance, with reference to cause of death such as respiratory infections, was mentioned previously. This phenomenon has been studied more directly by subjecting animals of various ages to controlled stresses, and observing their capacity to react or compensate in terms of some end point, usually death.

When mice were cold-stressed by being placed at temperatures of 6 to 7°C for 14 days, the percentage surviving decreased linearly with age (Figure 6.13). What is really being measured here is the ability of animals to keep warm. The production and conservation of body heat depend on a large number of metabolic and physiologic processes. It is of interest that the survival curve is linear with age, rather than showing an increasing rate of dying, or an increasingly negative slope, as would be seen in the case of a natural stress such as pneumonia. This suggests that either the severity or incidence of such a natural stress increases with age. On the other hand, the linear decline is quite characteristic for loss of function, as will be dealt with in a later section.

It has been possible to gain estimates of the actual ability to react

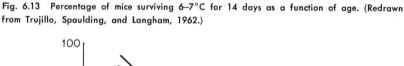

Fig. 6.13 Percentage of mice surviving 6–7°C for 14 days as a function of age. (Redrawn from Trujillo, Spaulding, and Langham, 1962.)

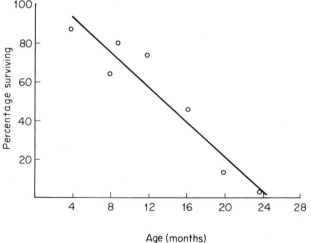

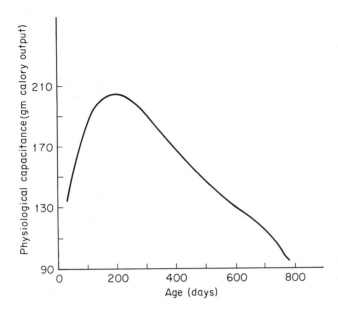

Fig. 6.14 Physiological capacitance as a function of age in mice. (Redrawn from Hensley, McWilliams, and Oakley, 1964.)

to stress as a function of age. Mice of various ages were forced to do continuous work at elevated temperature to the limit of their endurance. The end point was the onset of convulsions. Physiological capacitance in terms of gram calorie expenditure could be determined for each mouse. As shown in Figure 6.14, physiological capacitance increases during maturation and then undergoes a linear decline with age.

It can be seen that if a certain output of energy or level of performance is required in order to maintain life in the face of stresses that are relatively constant over the life span, then the percentage unable to survive will increase with increasing age. Or the amount of stress required to kill an animal will decrease with increasing age. Results of many different types of experiments support this concept. Thus, if animals are bled and the amount of blood that must be lost in order for death to occur is determined as a function of age, it is found that the blood loss required drops off linearly with age after maturity (Figure 6.15)—the older the animal, the less the blood loss that can be tolerated.

The curve of Figure 6.15 represents a quantity, and is linear with age. Such data, including standard deviations at each age, can be used

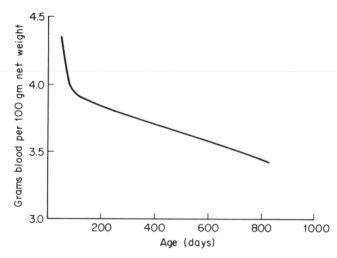

Fig. 6.15 Blood loss required to cause death of rats as a function of age. (Redrawn from Simms, 1942.)

to calculate probability of dying from a given blood loss as a function of age. These calculations have yielded a log, or Gompertzian mortality curve.

As a final example, we can consider the survival time of mice exposed to a standard daily dose of X rays. Ionizing radiation is not an ideal injurious agent for a study of the role of aging in reaction to stress because dividing cells are more sensitive to irradiation than resting ones, and young, growing animals contain more dividing cells than old animals. Mean survival time of mice did not change very conspicuously with age, as would be expected, since any generalized decreased resistance secondary to age might be balanced off by an increased cellular resistance. However, a very striking age-related increase in variance in survival time was observed (Figure 6.16). This means that as a population ages, the individuals become increasingly different from one another.

This increase in variance has been noted in several different types of measurements, such as barbiturate toxicity, body weight, and cardiac lipofuscin concentration (Storer, 1965). It is as though young animals are uniformly programmed, but that with age there is a progressive randomization within the population. This suggests that rates of aging are influenced to some extent by individual life histories, although it would be difficult to explain how a highly inbred mouse strain caged under very uniform conditions could contain individuals with different histories. Some variance might be explained on the basis of an in-

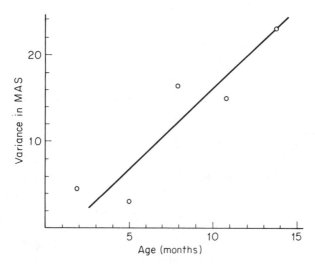

Fig. 6.16 Variance in survival time, under 100 r per day, in mice as a function of age. (Redrawn from Storer, 1965. Aging and Levels of Biological Organization, Univ. of Chicago Press, Chicago. ⓒ 1965 by the University of Chicago.)

crease with age in the amplitude of fluctuations of a component or property. Sampling or measuring at a given time might then give greater variation in an aging population.

There are certain types of stresses to which animals might develop resistance as they become older. Cell resistance to radiation could be an example of this. Another might be certain infectious agents to which immunity is lacking in very young animals, but to which the adult population may be resistant. However, if we restrict our consideration to changes occurring after maturity, it is probably safe to predict that any stress or insult capable of killing an animal will kill an increasing percentage of the population as the population becomes older. Or as animals become older, stresses of decreasing magnitude will be sufficient to cause death.

In summary, one category of causes of death, and one that is most characteristic of an aging population, is comprised of the miscellaneous diseases that kill off the population at a logarithmic rate as a function of age because of a decline in resistance factors. These experiments done by nature have been reproduced in the laboratory using controlled stresses of various kinds. To be able to explain the progressive decline in resistance factors in terms of cell and tissue changes is a major goal in aging research. We know enough already to go beyond the general concept of declining resistance factors, and can now consider those reactions and mechanisms that are responsible for maintaining resistance and steady states.

Physiologic processes and homeostatic mechanisms

The internal conditions under which life can exist are very restricted. Living processes within an animal are possible only within very narrow temperature and pH ranges, and only in the presence of a very delicate balance of ions, both intracellular and extracellular. Levels of nutrients, hormones, gases, and metabolites must not vary beyond rather close limits. A healthy animal maintains homeostasis, or relatively constant internal environment, under a variety of circumstances—at rest, or in a rapidly changing external environment, or during severe alterations in activity and feeding cycles.

If we were to observe any isolated component or property of the internal environment, we would find that it does not remain constant but is continually undergoing fluctuations or perturbations around some mean value. Each factor is under the control of several governors, as it were. Whenever deviation in one direction occurs, a control mechanism acts to make the factor return, so that there is a resulting overshoot in the other direction, at which time another control mechanism begins to act, and so on. These governors or control mechanism are the body's physiological processes.

Studies of the efficiency of physiological process as a function of age have been very informative. The pattern that has emerged is one of an increasing sluggishness and inefficiency of all processes. The overall change with age was seen in Figure 6.14. Figure 6.17 contains data for function of the heart, kidney, and lungs. Although there is considerable individual variation at each age in measurement of function of these organ systems, which is not shown in the figure, it can be seen that function of these vital organs drops off linearly with age after maturity.

The decline in physiological efficiency with age applies to all systems. The decline in muscle strength is shown in Figure 6.18. Declines in hearing ability and in accommodation of the eye have frequently been documented. In the eye, also, transparency of the lens declines, and its refractive properties become altered with age. The ability of the stomach to secrete acid in response to food intake diminishes linearly with age (Figure 6.19).

Any number of examples could be given. It is probably safe to state that the ability of *every* organ or organ system to function declines progressively with age. This declining efficiency may be observed in some cases only when the system is stressed (Shock, 1960). Resting body

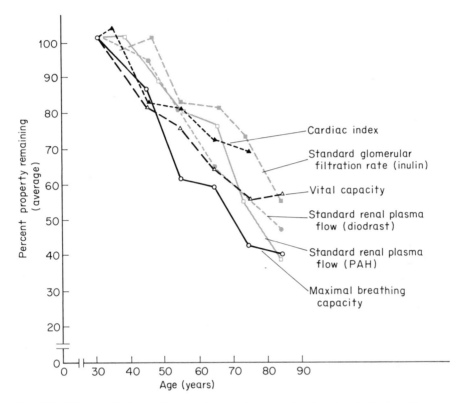

Fig. 6.17 Efficiency of human physiological mechanisms as a function of age. Level at 30 years is assigned a value of 100%. (Modified from Shock, 1960.)

temperature, for example, is the same in old and young animals. However, it was pointed out earlier that with age, animals are less able to produce and conserve heat when cold-stressed. Or when animals are maintained at elevated temperature, old animals show a greater rise in body temperature. Similarly, blood sugar levels are comparable in healthy young and old animals, but when sugar is administered, the rise in the blood concentration is greater in older animals, and more time is required for the drop to resting levels. The same applies to blood pH, which is the same in young and old, but which shows a greater rise in old animals in response to an alkali stress, and takes longer to return to the optimal level.

We can now appreciate the meaning of the decline in resistance factors, and can understand how older animals might die from insults that they would have resisted at an earlier age. The important con-

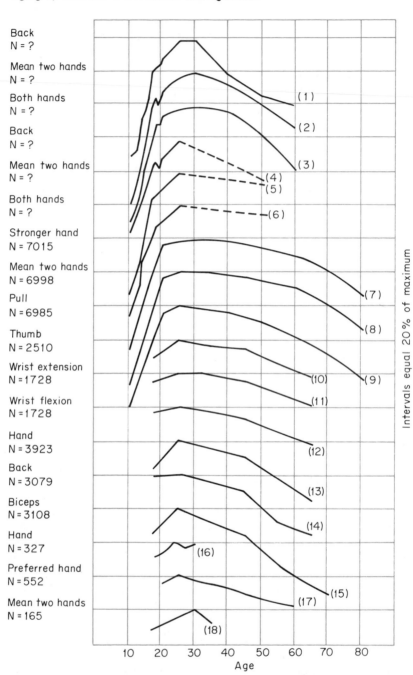

Back
N = ?

Mean two hands
N = ?

Both hands
N = ?

Back
N = ?

Mean two hands
N = ?

Both hands
N = ?

Stronger hand
N = 7015

Mean two hands
N = 6998

Pull
N = 6985

Thumb
N = 2510

Wrist extension
N = 1728

Wrist flexion
N = 1728

Hand
N = 3923

Back
N = 3079

Biceps
N = 3108

Hand
N = 327

Preferred hand
N = 552

Mean two hands
N = 165

Intervals equal 20% of maximum

Age

Fig. 6.18 Effect of age on strength of various human muscles. (From Rodahl and Issekutz, 1962.)

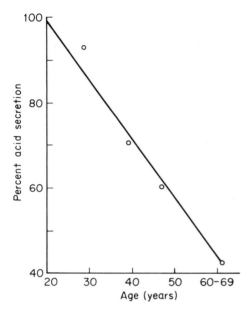

Fig. 6.19 Acid secretion in response to a test meal as a function of age of human males. (Redrawn from Ivy and Grossman. Problems of Aging. © 1952, The Williams and Wilkins Co., Baltimore.)

cept here is that this progressive sluggishness of physiological processes occurs throughout the body; changes cannot be ascribed to a single organ or organ system. This means that we will eventually want to consider tissues common to all organs.

Measurements of physiological processes in an animal are rather gross assessments of the consequences of processes occurring at molecular and tissue levels. Although there is an enormous number of physiological processes that can be measured, these depend on a small number of different types of reactions at the microscopic level. One type of reaction is cell and membrane movement. All physiological processes depend to some extent on the ability of such tissue as lung or blood vessel walls to dilate and to contract, and on the contraction and relaxation of heart and of smooth muscle cells in walls of arterioles. A second type of reaction that plays a role in most physiological processes is the passage or transport of substances across membranes, from vessel to cell, or from cell to cell through the extracellular compartment. The elastic or contractile properties of tissues and the transport of substances within the body are determined largely by reactions of the vascular system, and the passage of materials is frequently affected by local states of dilatation or contraction, as in the case of gas diffusion in the lung, where transfer can occur efficiently only when the alveoli are open.

The heart, of course, is the major contractile structure, and its func-

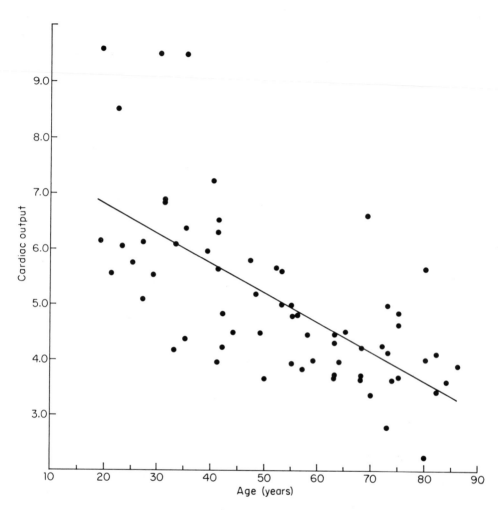

Fig. 6.20 Cardiac output as a function of age in human beings. (From Brandfonbrenner, Landowne, and Shock, 1955, Changes in cardiac output with age, Circul. 12:557–566. Reproduced by permission of the American Heart Association, Inc.)

tion as a pump, regardless of the method of measurement used, declines in efficiency with age (Lakatta et al., 1975). Cardiac output declines about 0.7 percent per year, with marked variability at each age (Figure 6.20). The amount of work performed per heart beat similarly drops off at a rate of about 1.0 percent per year. Studies of mechanical properties of samples of myocardium have demonstrated increased stiffness with age. An example of these observations is in Figure 6.21.

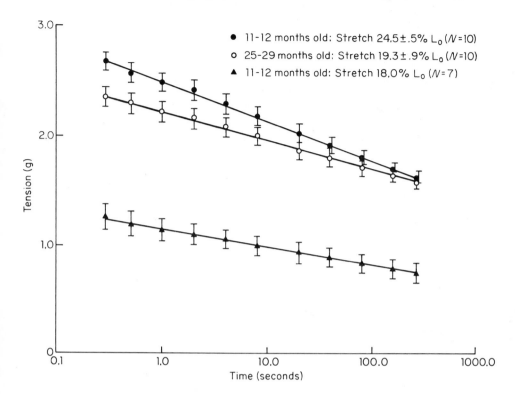

Fig. 6.21 Stress relaxation in trabeculae carnae. Upper plots are from trabeculae of 11 to 12- and 25 to 29-month-old rats stretched to length achieved after 1 hour at 1.75 g tension. Lowest plot is for muscles from 11 to 12-month-old rats stretched to 18% of L_o. (From Weisfeldt, Loeven, and Shock, 1971.)

When the heart contracts, the blood surges into the aorta, causing it to dilate. Energy of the stroke volume is then stored temporarily in the aorta. As the heart relaxes, the aorta contracts, driving the blood into the distal circulation. As the pressure wave travels down the aorta, it undergoes an amplification. The amount of this amplification between the aortic arch and iliac artery has been studied as a function of age in living human subjects. As shown in Figure 6.22, the amplification drops off very markedly in a linear fashion with age. This has been attributed to a progressive loss in distensibility of peripheral vessels. In an independent study it was calculated that total peripheral resistance to blood flow increased 1.7 percent per year.

The distensibility of human thoracic aortas was studied directly by measuring the volume increase due to a constant inside pressure of 100 mm Hg, which is a pressure within the normal or physiological

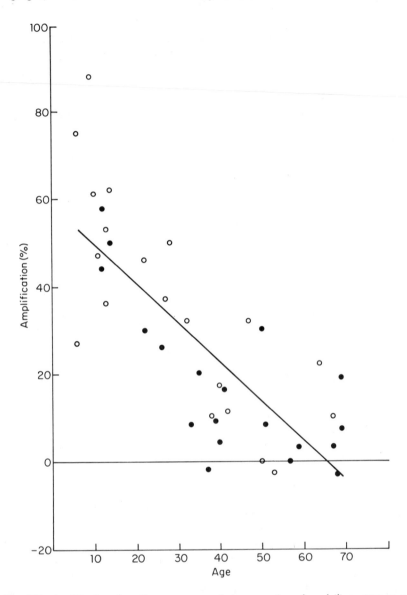

Fig. 6.22 Amplification of aortic pressure wave between aortic arch and iliac artery as a function of age in human beings. (Redrawn from O'Rourke et al., 1968.)

range. The distensibility fell off very markedly with increasing age (Figure 6.23). By 85 years of age the aorta took on the elastic properties of a rigid tube. Such increasing stiffness of vessels has been observed in several peripheral arterial beds as well.

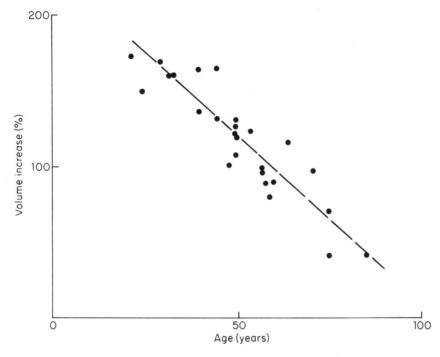

Fig. 6.23 Volume increase of human thoracic aorta under standard pressure as a function of age. (Redrawn from Bader, 1967.)

The combination of decreasing cardiac efficiency, increasing rigidity of the arterial system, and increasing peripheral resistance results in a sluggish tissue perfusion (Bender, 1965). The decreased renal plasma flow shown in Figure 6.17 is a good example of this. It is not known to what extent other factors, such as a decreased capillary density, might influence this age-related decrease in organ blood flow. A large number of studies yield the conclusion that blood flow through organs decreases with age (Hollenberg et al., 1974). Such decreases, however, are not uniform throughout the body. It has been reported, for example, that blood flow in the forearm increases with age (Bender, 1965). This could be due to an arteriovenous shunting of blood or to loss of muscle tone with age. Further studies on blood flow at various sites are required.

Other tissues undergo changes in elastic properties with age. An increasing flaccidity of the skin has been frequently observed. The lung has a normal tendency to contract because of its elasticity. It is kept expanded by the chest, so that there is a negative pressure in the potential space between lung and chest wall. With age this negative

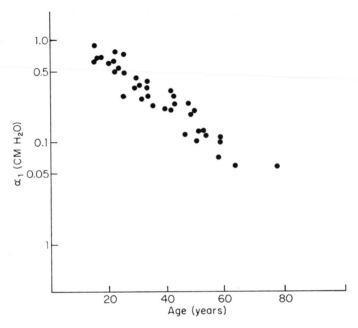

Fig. 6.24 Lung elasticity (α_1) as a function of age in human beings. (From Niewoehner, Kleinerman, and Liotta, 1975.)

pressure decreases; and the contractile force of the lung, due to its intrinsic elasticity, progressively diminishes. When pressure-volume relationships of human lungs of different ages are determined, a very marked loss of elastic behavior with increasing age is apparent (Figure 6.24).

Studies of alterations in tissue permeability and in diffusion processes have scarcely begun. Pulmonary diffusing capacity of gases in the lung has perhaps been studied most extensively in this regard. There is a progressive loss in diffusing capacity amounting to about 8 percent per decade in human beings (Cohn, 1964). It has been assumed that this is due to increasing membrane resistance, since total lung volume and number of alveoli have not been shown to change with age. A possibility that has not been excluded is a decreasing density of lung capillaries.

The age-related decrease in glomerular filtration rate shown in Figure 6.17 represents a decline in diffusion, but because of the complex capillary-membrane-cell relationships, the site of the alteration cannot be ascertained.

A number of other isolated studies have been undertaken (Sobel,

1967; Bender, 1965). When labeled albumin was injected into dogs, it was found that with increasing age, less and less of the albumin had diffused from the circulation into the extravascular compartment of the heart. A saline solution injected into the skin has been reported to take longer to be absorbed in the case of old human beings than in young. When histamine is injected into the skin, vascular permeability is altered so that serum proteins can more readily diffuse out of the vessels. When adult and old rats, previously injected intravenously with a dye that binds to serum proteins, were injected intradermally with histamine, it was found that less bound dye diffused into the skin in the old animals (Kohn, 1969). In an in vitro study, it was found that a silver proteinate diffuses into joint cartilage more slowly with increasing age. On the other hand, there is one report that when a solution of Na^{22} is injected intradermally, it disappears faster from skin of the forearm of older people than of younger people, and that there is no age-related difference in disappearance from skin of the hand and face. Injected tracers of various kinds, as well as antigens (Hanna, Nettesheim, and Snodgrass, 1971), disappear more slowly from the circulation of older animals. Such clearance, however, may be a measure of combinations of transport, diffusion, and blood flow.

For any organ in which blood circulation or perfusion rate becomes sluggish with age, and in which permeability is altered, it would be possible to explain a decline in its functional efficiency with age. Such alterations would also be of use to us in that they would indicate that we must search for molecular and tissue changes with age that could explain them. It is obvious that many more systematic studies are required to demonstrate, organ by organ and tissue by tissue, changes with age in vascular dynamics and permeability.

In summary, the pattern that emerges is one of progressive decline in all physiological functions after maturity. The declines are associated with increasing stiffness of mobile organs such as heart, arteries, and lungs, and with decreased gas exchange and blood flow. If we consider health as the optimal physiological state, we can view all individuals as becoming progressively sicker after maturity.

It is apparent from inspection of the foregoing physiological data that there is a marked variability at each age. Some of this variability is undoubtedly due to true biological differences, and some must result from the procedures used for measurements. It is also likely that an individual's location within a range depends in part on previous nutrition and activity patterns. For example, an individual could be in poor nutritional and physical condition, and at the lower end of the range of some measurement. Perhaps by a training program he could improve his relative position within the range for his age and actually show improved performance over a limited period of time. Because of aging processes, however, it would appear that even the best performers must inevitably deteriorate.

Aging in the abstract: models

Aging populations die out according to the Gompertz function; the age-specific death rate is exponential, whereas losses of physiological function appear to take place linearly. There have been several attempts to gain insight into how a linear decline in function could result in an exponential rate of dying, and how these phenomena might be altered in different populations and environments. These attempts have resulted in the construction of theoretical models of aging populations. It was pointed out earlier in this chapter that by calculations employing the standard deviation at each age in the measure of a quantity that falls off linearly—in that case, the amount of blood loss required to cause death—the probability of dying from a standard blood loss is found to increase according to the Gompertz function. Another way of looking at this question is shown in Figure 6.25.

For a rather homogeneous population a linear decline in total physiological function is shown. An increasing variability, characteristic of changes in reactivity in an aging population, is indicated. At any age, such as *A,* for example, there will be a mean value and a distribution of values as shown in the small graph. A threshold level is indicated, below which life cannot be maintained in the face of stresses and injuries that occur throughout life. As members of the aging population reach this level, they will die off, yielding the distribution of deaths shown in the bottom graph of the figure. These deaths have a distribution identical to the senescent deaths in Figure 6.5. If one or more additional populations dying of age-related diseases with earlier modal values are added, the age distribution of deaths for the whole population is obtained, as shown in Figure 6.5. If these deaths are plotted as an age-specific death rate, the exponential or Gompertzian increase with age is obtained.

We shall now examine a second model—one based on the Strehler-Mildvan theory (Strehler, 1962). This theory is based on the concept that an organism is composed of systems whose functions are continually being displaced by randomly occurring internal and environmental stresses. The systems must do work in order to reestablish a steady state. The maximum rates at which these systems can expend energy constitute the viability of the organism. Death occurs when the de-

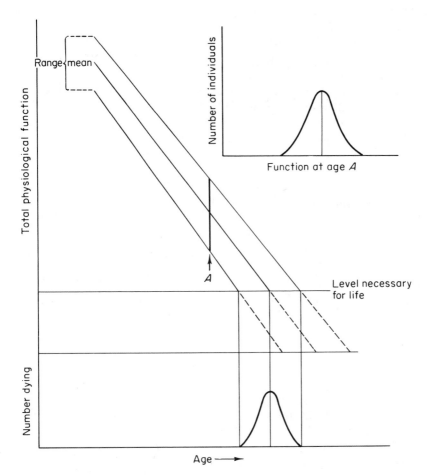

Fig. 6.25 Theoretical relationship between physiological decline and distribution of deaths in an aging population.

mands on one or more systems surpass the ability of these systems to expend energy.

The theory assumes that the demands for energy are due to random fluctuations in the internal or external environment, and that the magnitudes of these stresses have a distribution similar to the distribution of kinetic energy of gas molecules according to the Maxwell-Boltzmann equation.

The Gompertz function can be expressed as:

$$R_m = R_0 e^{at}$$

where R_m is the mortality rate at time t, R_0 is the rate at birth, and a is a constant. R_0 is obtained by extrapolating the exponential curve back to zero time and does not truly represent the mortality rate at birth because Gompertzian kinetics do not hold for the period of growth and development.

If X, the frequency of stresses capable of killing, is substituted for N', the number of molecules having energies greater than that required for activation in the Maxwell-Boltzmann equation, and ΔH, the size of energy fluctuations just sufficient to kill (vitality), is substituted for E, the energy required for activation, then,

$$X = K'e^{\Delta H/RT}$$

where RT represents the average size of energy fluctuations, and K' is a constant. Since the death rate (R_m) is proportional to the frequency of stresses capable of killing (X), then

$$R_m = R_0 e^{at} = CX = CK'e^{-\Delta H/RT} = Ke^{-\Delta H/RT}$$

ΔH, the vitality, can be considered physiological efficiencey. If we solve for this as a function of time, letting ΔH_0 represent vitality at time zero, then

$$\Delta H = \Delta H_0 \left(1 - \frac{at}{\ln \dfrac{K}{R_0}} \right)$$

Since a, K, and R_0 are constants,

$$\frac{a}{\ln \dfrac{K}{R_0}} = B$$

where B is the linear decay constant of vitality, and

$$\Delta H = \Delta H_0 (1 - Bt)$$

If the rate of loss of function, B, is calculated for an aging population, a close agreement is found between the curve obtained and that obtained by measurements of physiological function. In other words, this model predicts a linear decline in function.

Furthermore, the model predicts an inverse relationship between the log of the zero time mortality rate, R_0, and the slope of the Gompertz function, a. By calculating these variables for different societies with different environments and different stresses, an inverse relationship was found.

Exercises of this type do not lead to experiments that will provide information on mechanisms of aging at the cell or tissue level. Some of these exercises also require assumptions that might be exceedingly difficult or impossible to justify. They do serve, however, to point out that the relationship between a linear decline in function and an exponential death rate need not be a mysterious one.

Functional changes in some selected systems

A decline with age in function of the major organ systems responsible for maintaining homeostasis—the heart, blood vessels, kidney, and lung—is unequivocal. Every organ system in the body and every physiological process could be discussed in terms of aging. However, we shall restrict further discussion to certain systems that should be considered because of various arguments and hypotheses concerning basic mechanisms of aging that will be presented in the next chapter. The systems to be considered are the central nervous system, the endocrine glands, and the system responsible for immune reactions.

In the previous two chapters we considered evidence that aging processes occurred in the cells that function in these systems. Here we are not concerned so much with whether it is possible to demonstrate any changes with age, but whether or not any changes with age in the function of these systems cause any real problems at the level of the intact animal.

One way of assessing function of the central nervous system is by psychological and behavioral testing, in accordance with the notion that behavior is a product of neurones analogous to the production of bile by the liver. There is an enormous and very interesting literature on the psychology of aging (Ordy and Brizzee, 1975). Most of this material would not be appropriate for inclusion here since our primary concerns are with structural, chemical, and physiological alterations. However, some concepts from these studies can be summarized by noting that psychological reactions undergo the same types of changes with age that occur in the function of other organs; that is, the psychological reactions become increasingly sluggish and inefficient. Psychomotor speed, learning ability, perception, and manipulative ability decline; speed of reaction also declines. Such declining function is also observed in the organs of special sense. There are, for example, increases with age in auditory reaction time and pupil latency period.

The role of age in the complex interrelationships between the central and autonomic nervous systems has been studied in terms of autonomic conditioning. A representative investigation was carried out

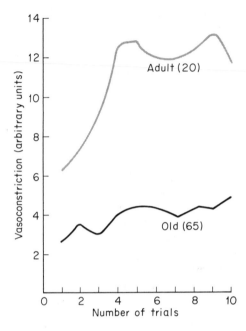

Fig. 6.26 Vasomotor conditioned responses for human males. Mean ages in years are indicated. (Modified from Shmavonian, Yarmat, and Cohen, 1965.)

with a group of young adults with a mean age of 20 years, and an older group averaging 65 years of age. The subjects were exposed to a musical tone and at the end of the tone were given electric shocks. The conditioned response measured over a series of trials was the extent of constriction of small blood vessels, an autonomic nervous system function. As shown in Figure 6.26, the young subjects became very quickly conditioned, whereas the old group was almost entirely nonreactive.

Behavioral and conditioned reactions depend on a sequence of events beginning with a sensory perception and ending with a physiological response. For any alteration, a variety of interpretations regarding causal mechanisms would be tenable, since neuronal, neurohumoral, permeability, vascular, and muscular factors are usually involved.

Changes with age in neurones, particularly in functional aspects, have not been studied in much detail. As mentioned in the previous chapter, there is some loss of human cortical neurones with age, but this is not generalized, there being no loss from the hypoglossal nucleus, for example. In short-lived laboratory mammals, cortical neurone loss has not been demonstrated. Lipofuscin pigment accumulation with age has been observed in neurones, but no attempts have been made to correlate the presence of this material with any functional property. Limited chemical analyses of brain lipids have not revealed any age difference. In comparing protein synthesis in immature and old rat neurones, it was found that incorporation of a labeled amino acid occurred to a lesser degree in the old animals, but that turnover rates were similar in the two groups.

Regarding neuronal function, the conduction velocity of nerves in animals of different ages has received some attention. A preliminary study indicated that the fastest fibers of the sciatic nerve in 30-month-old rats conducted at a significantly slower velocity than those of 16-month-old animals (Retzlaff and Fontaine, 1965). That this age difference may be due in part to extraneuronal factors is indicated by the finding that prior exercise of the animals caused a marked increase in the conduction velocity of the fastest fibers. In the 16-month-old rats, exercise increased conduction velocity from an average of 51 to 70 meters per second. In the 30-month-old animals, conduction velocity increased from 20 to 45 meters per second because of exercise. Since neuromuscular activity appears capable of strongly influencing neuronal function, it is conceivable that part, at least, of the decline with age in reactivity of the nervous system is secondary to the general physiological decline associated with aging.

Neuromotor functional decline may be in part due to muscular weakness, as discussed in an earlier chapter. In addition, degenerative changes with increasing age have been described in preterminal nerve fibers and motor end plates. The number of nerve fibers innervating a muscle appear to remain constant.

Among the extraneuronal factors that would be expected to influence nervous system function is blood supply. Decreases in cerebral blood flow and in oxygen consumption and a rise in cerebral vascular resistance with age have been observed (Bender, 1965). There is considerable scatter of values at each age, and carefully selected, healthy old individuals give values for cerebral blood flow comparable to those in young adults. This relates to the problem alluded to earlier concerning the difficulty in dissociating arteriosclerosis, a disease that occurs in everyone and progresses at different rates in different individuals, from basic aging processes at the tissue level in all individuals. It would also be useful to know what the relationship of age to cerebral blood flow would be if the system were stressed in such a way that flow would increase to the maximum rate. Age differences in other physiological processes often cannot be demonstrated unless the system is stressed for maximum performance.

The declining function of the nervous system, which is undoubtedly of importance in the generalized aging syndrome, cannot be ascribed to intrinsic neuronal aging on the basis of current evidence. Although neuronal alterations could be responsible, many more systematic studies are required in order to determine the roles of activity of other systems, of vascular reactivity, and of tissue permeability, and to determine whether primary cell changes precede or are correlated with age-related declines in neurone function.

Since the syndrome of aging is generalized throughout the mammalian body, attention has frequently been directed toward control or integrative systems; any age-related alteration might be expected to have widespread consequences. The endocrine glands, in particular, have a long history as a focal point in considerations of aging. These organs play key roles in growth, metabolism, homeostasis, and reaction to stress. They are of prime importance in bringing about sexual maturity. The endocrines would be likely suspects for a role in aging, and at various times it was believed that aging must be due to endocrine failure and could be prevented by some type of endocrine therapy or gland replacement.

We would like to know if there are age changes in the capacity of the endocrine glands to synthesize and secrete hormones, in the ability to deliver biologically active hormones to target cells in appropriate concentrations, and in the ability of target cells to respond. Data of these types would be difficult to obtain, and in most cases inferences must be made from hormone concentrations in the blood, or from the urinary excretion of hormones or their degradation products. Such levels may vary with rates of degradation, excretion, and utilization, as well as with rates of synthesis and secretion. Hormone utilization and target organ reactivity might be influenced by vascular and permeability factors, or by the immediate past history of the animals in terms of generalized physiological activity.

Profound changes in the secretion of hormones have been observed early in development, and are associated with growth and the attainment of sexual maturity. These changes are not relevant to our discussion. After maturity there are declines in the production of sex hormones synthesized by the gonads (Bellamy, 1967). In females, the drop-off of estrogen production is associated with the disappearance of ovarian follicles, follicular cells being responsible for estrogen synthesis. There is similarly a decline in the secretion of 17 ketosteroids by the testes. When testes of rabbits of different ages are perfused with gonadotropic hormones, testosterone secretion declines with age. The administration of gonadotropins to human beings shows age-related declines in 17β-estradiol and testosterone responses, but percentage increase over baseline values is quite constant with age; absolute and relative estrone responses are constant with age (Longcope, 1973). There is apparently no age-related loss in interstitial cells of the testes, and it has been proposed that the endocrine dysfunction may be associated with a progressive peritubular fibrosis occurring with age. The decrease in gonadal steroid secretion is accompanied by increases in pituitary gonadotropin production. These are examples of organ aging. However, they are not of significance in the aging of animals since the gonads are not necessary for life; removal of the gonads does not result in shortened life spans.

Sex hormones are also produced by the adrenal glands, and the amount of circulating hormones would be a function of the activity of gonads and adrenals, plus possibly rates of degradation, utilization, and excretion. From determinations of urinary excretion it has been concluded that total estrogen levels in human males do not change significantly with age, but they decline somewhere between 40 and 60 years of age in the female and then remain quite constant. Androgens and 17 ketosteroids drop off logarithmically in both males and females. Studies of the role of age in the adrenal androgen response to ACTH are inconclusive.

The adrenal corticosteroids that are necessary for life appear less affected by age than the sex steroids. The level of circulating and excreted corticosteroids does not vary significantly with increasing age in human beings or rats. Old individuals appear capable of an adequate steroid secretion in response to stress. The blood corticosterone level in response to the stress of fasting was found to decrease with age in rats (Adelman and Britton, 1975). There is no assurance, however, that the stress of fasting is as severe in old animals as it is in younger ones. The blood level of thyroid hormone, measured as protein-bound iodine, does not change with age.

There is an age-related decrease in the insulin response to a standard glucose dose; the amount of glucose required to cause a standard rise in insulin increases with age (O'Sullivan et al., 1971). The decrease in blood glucose in response to insulin becomes sluggish with increasing age, and the resulting high levels in older individuals, after glucose administration, may actually cause hyperinsulinemia. The pancreas and isolated islets of old animals apparently give an adequate insulin response to glucose.

Analyses of hormone concentrations in human pituitary glands have revealed no significant changes with increasing age in adrenal- and thyroid-stimulating hormones or in growth hormone, and have shown age-related increases in follicle-stimulating and luteinizing hormones. Control of LH reaction has been reported to become sluggish with age in the rat (Reigle and Meites, 1976). The concentration of insulin in the human pancreas has not been found to change with age.

Regarding reactivity of target tissues, the administration of insulin is less effective in reducing blood glucose with increasing age (Muggeo et al., 1975). Diabetes is one of the diseases that shows an increasing incidence with age in a subgroup of the general population. A relationship between this disease and response to insulin has not been established. Administered insulin results in an age-related decrease in growth hormone response, and no age difference in cortisol response (Muggeo et al., 1975). As noted in the chapter on intracellular aging, there is no consistent pattern with age in the stimulation of enzymes by hormones, or in binding of hormones to membrane receptors.

There have been many experiments in which old animals and human beings were treated with hormones in attempts to rejuvenate them. Some of these treatments have been beneficial in increasing performance—muscle strength, for example—or in stimulating a sense of well-being. However, such responses probably have little to do with aging, since many pharmacologic agents would be expected to have beneficial effects independent of the age of the subjects. Reports that aging has been inhibited or reversed in terms of life span, turn out on careful examination to indicate that maximum life span has not been altered, but that the percentage survival curves become slightly more rectangular. This is most consistent with the view that old debilitated animals with diseases are kept alive a short while longer, in the same way that human beings dying of congestive heart failure may survive longer when treated with pressor agents; their heart failure is not caused by a deficiency in such agents.

We can conclude that there is no characteristic endocrine gland failure, with respect to the hormones necessary for life, that is associated with aging. Such observations as a loss of tissue response to insulin treatment and a variability in response to vasopressin raise some interesting possibilities. If the reactivity of small blood vessels and control of passage of metabolites into cells become altered, many of the debilities of age could be explained. At the level of target organs, the amount of an agent delivered to cells would depend on small blood vessel density and reactivity and on permeability factors. It has already been shown that peripheral resistance in small vessels increases with age. It would obviously be useful to know whether altered response to hormone action depends on intrinsic cellular changes, or on changes in the extracellular environment.

The complex series of reactions leading to antibody formation and function constitutes a unique type of system. In contrast to physiological processes, which work continuously to maintain a constant internal environment, immune mechanisms are called upon at irregular intervals to react to new or repetitive stimuli. The reactivity depends on the past history of the system in terms of antigenic stimulation, and on genetic factors. Aging processes may further influence reactivity.

In view of the different types of antigens, measurements, and species that have been employed in studying the relationship between age and immunity, it is not surprising that many findings are not consistent with each other.

As in so many of the systems we have considered, profound changes occur early in life in immune mechanisms. These deal with maturation of the immune mechanism and with immune tolerance. We shall be concerned here primarily with changes occurring after maturity and in overall responsiveness of the immune system. Age-related changes at the cell level were discussed in the previous chapter.

Much older data on immunological phenomena as a function of age have been reviewed by Ram (1967). The levels of naturally occurring antibodies decline with age. This holds for the isoagglutinins anti-A and B, and for antibodies against red cells of foreign species. If animals are immunized against a specific antigen early in life, there are progressive decreases over the life span in the percentage of animals with measurable antibody, and in the mean antibody titers of the responders.

When animals of different ages are injected with antigens, responses are variable. The antibody response to bovine serum albumin in rats and to horse serum in humans declines with age. In the case of *Salmonella* immunization, there is a decrease in the percentage of individuals who respond to the somatic antigen, but in those of the older groups who respond, the level of response is comparable to that of young individuals. No age-related decline in response to the flagellar antigen is observed. In mice, the primary antibody response to flagellin does not change, but on secondary challenge, there is marked decline in response as a function of age. In humans, no decline in the ability to respond to typhoid or Rh factor immunization has been demonstrated, and an enhanced response has been noted with age in response to an influenza vaccine. Antibody response to a single injection of coliphage decreases with age in dogs, but on multiple injections, the old animals make as much antibody as the young (Jaroslow, Suhrbier, and Fritz, 1974).

Older animals give a diminished anaphylactic reaction. This has been shown with both guinea pigs and rabbits sensitized with horse serum. The number of animals dying of anaphylactic shock declines with increasing age. The same phenomenon is noted when antibodies are passively transferred to animals of different ages, indicating that the difference in reactivity is not due to the ability to produce antibodies. The decreasing sensitivity to anaphylactic shock appears to be an exception to the previous generality that there is an increasing sensitivity to insults with age. This might be explained on the basis of a decreased ability of blood vessels and bronchioles to constrict, these reactions being required for anaphylaxis.

Cell-mediated immunity appears, by sensitive tests, to be depressed in old animals and man (Toh et al., 1973). However, the skin response to tuberculin appears adequate in old human beings (Joris and Girard, 1975). The possible significance of an age-related decline in cellular immunity is cast in doubt by the observation that there are no differences between 3- and 18-month-old mice in the ability to reject skin homografts (Ram, 1967).

The delayed type of hypersensitivity, manifested by skin reactions, drops off with age. This has been observed in the guinea pig reaction to poison ivy antigen, in human sensitivity to dinitrochlorobenzene, and in human food allergies. It has been reported that the blood level of thymosin, a hormone postulated to convert stem cells to T cells, decreases after maturity in human beings (Goldstein et al., 1974).

In addition to the above changes in normal function of immune mechanisms, increasing age is associated with certain immunologic abnormalities in increasing percentages of the population. Autoantibodies and autoimmune diseases show increasing incidences with age in mice and man. Abnormal antibodies of the types found in rheumatoid arthritis and systemic lupus erythematosis are seen in increasing fractions of aging populations. Such age changes reflect special susceptibilities in subgroups of the population. They lack the universality of true aging processes.

Altered immunological function may not be due to aging of immunocompetent cells, but could result from changes in the microcirculation or in the cell environment. Clearance of a protein antigen from the blood, for example, shows a decline with age (Figure 6.27). There is virtually no clearance in $2\frac{1}{2}$-year-old mice. The decreased clearance with age probably has the same basis in part, as decreased organ perfusion described earlier.

Although many age differences in immune function have been observed, it is probably incorrect to view aging animals as undergoing progressive immunological failure, or to conclude that debilities characteristic of aging have an immunological cause—at least on the basis of current evidence. Furthermore, it is not known if the changes that have been observed are due to progressive and irreversible changes in cells of the immune system.

Growth and aging

Changes with age at molecular, cell, and tissue levels that are used to explain aging of an animal in terms of debilities and death rates must also be capable of explaining, or at least be not incom-

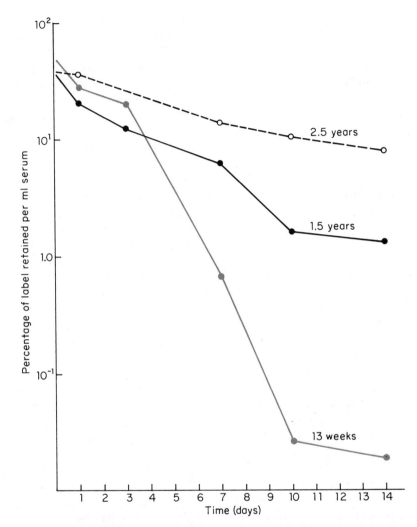

Fig. 6.27 Clearance of an antigen, human gamma globulin, from the blood of mice of different ages. (From Hanna, Nettesheim, and Snodgrass, 1971.)

patible with, certain observations and correlations that characterize aging populations. One of the most significant observations in this category is a relationship between growth rate and rate of aging.

Animals that have a clearly defined life span are those that have a species-specific size. These animals go through a period of growth, attain a size that is characteristic of the species, and grow no more. Furthermore, the debilities that we have been considering appear to begin, or at least to accelerate, at around the time at which this size is attained. This is particularly clear in the cases of death rates and physiological processes.

Animals that do not have characteristic sizes, or that continue to grow indefinitely, have poorly defined life spans, or we are not able to say what their life spans are. A number of reptiles and fish grow in proportion to their food supply and continue to grow as long as they live. It would appear that they do age, and that the rate of aging is probably inversely proportional to their rate of growth, in that with increasing time they grow more slowly and perhaps age more rapidly, but we are unable to assign them characteristic life spans.

The relationship between growth and aging in mammals was brought out by experiments undertaken by McCay, a nutrionist, in the 1930s. McCay allowed his control rats to eat a well-balanced diet, rich in calories, at will. These animals grew rapidly until around 6 months of age and then gained weight more slowly until around 18 months, when their size and weights became stabilized. Experimental groups were then given all essential nutrients but were starved for calories. They grew at very slow rates, so that at around 18 months of age they weighed approximately one-fourth as much as the controls. At various times, up to 1000 days of age, groups from among those starved for calories were put on the control diets. They rapidly gained weight, approaching that of the control group at the same age. The animals that grew slowly for a period beyond that over which rats normally grow, and which had periods of accelerated growth late in life, had greatly lengthened life spans (McCay, 1952).

Subsequent studies by McCay and others suggested that aging was truly inhibited by prolonging the growth period because the onset of diseases characterisic of aging was delayed in underfed animals (Simms, 1965). Lengthening of life span would also appear to be the result of continuing growth rather than small size of the animals, since keeping animals stunted at a constant size by dietary manipulation does not increase life span very markedly.

For any postulated mechanism of aging, an explanation of how the mechanism might be inhibited by growth processes would appear to be required.

Nutrition and aging

The point has just been made that growth inhibits aging processes. Growth depends on nutrition, so there would appear to be a relationship between nutrition and aging. Another association between these two factors would result from a high level of nutrition enabling an animal to grow to maturity faster than an undernourished animal and thereby start aging earlier. Variations in nutrition might affect basic molecular and tissue aging processes, either directly or indirectly through effects on other systems such as the nervous system or endocrine glands. Variations in nutrition could also cause differences in incidence and progression of certain age-related diseases, and while not affecting aging directly, could alter life expectancy and death rates in an aging population.

Longevity can be readily modified by differences in nutrition. In the rat, life-long restriction of carbohydrate and calory intake results in longer lives. Dietary restriction instituted after maturity also results in greater life expectancy. The life expectancy is inversely related to growth rate, as noted in the previous section, and to body weight. In effect, animals that are fat do not live as long as thinner animals.

It turns out that such nutritional effects on life span are almost entirely due to variations in certain disease. The kidney disease glomerulonephritis is clearly related to nutrition; groups of rats with the longer life spans have lower incidences of the disease (Ross and Bras, 1965). The tumor risk, in terms of incidence and age at onset, is directly and exponentially related to caloric intake; heavier rats have greater tumor risks. The correlation between body weight and tumor incidence is striking (Ross and Bras, 1965).

The nutrition effect on disease raises some important and challenging questions, but it would appear that aspects of nutrition that have been studied do not have a direct effect on basic aging processes. The effects on such processes would be by altering growth rates, and the effect on life span would be by the role of nutrition in incidence and progression of certain diseases.

Correlations among life span, body weight, brain weight, and metabolic rate

It is likely that different species of mammals age by similar mechanisms. Since there are great differences in life span among various kinds of animals, there must be factors characteristic of each kind of animal that determine rates at which aging processes proceed.

We can attempt to gain information on what these factors might be by considering what properties of different animal species are correlated with life span. Maximum life span is the most useful measure of aging end points, since there are not enough data available for many families and genera of mammals for estimations of life expectancies and modal life span values.

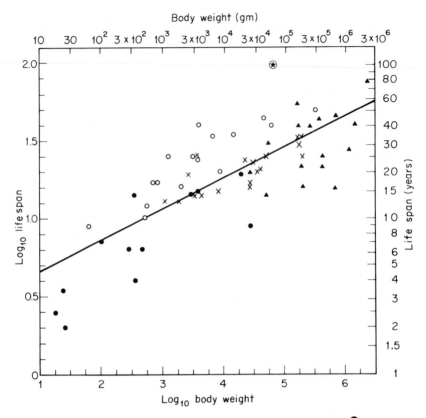

Fig. 6.28   Relation of life span to body weight for 63 species of mammals. **O** —primates and lemurs, **●** —rodents and insectivores, **X** —carnivores, **▲** —ungulates and ele-phants, **⊛** —man. (From Sacher, 1959.)

There is a clear relationship between body size and life span (Figure 6.28). The regression of log life span in years, x, on log body weight in grams, y, is

$$x = 0.198y + 0.471$$

and accounts for 60 percent of life span variance.

Brain weight is a better predictor of life span than body weight (Figure 6.29), the regression of log life span on log brain weight accounting for 70 percent of the life span variance. The significance of this is not clear, since brain weight follows body weight to a large extent, and other organs might be equal or better predictors of life span. Brain weight and body weight together can be associated, by calculation, with most of the variance in maximum longevity. Furthermore, it is possible to calculate a brain quantity, the index of cephali-

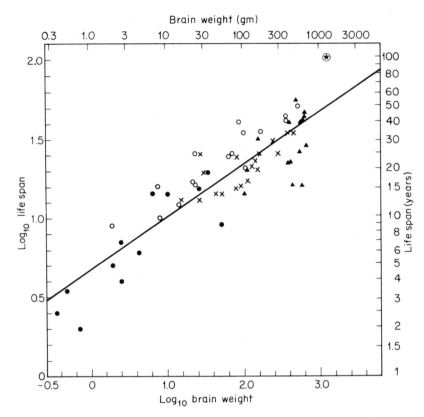

Fig. 6.29   Relation of life span to brain weight for species of animals. Symbols and source as in Figure 6.28.

zation, which is a measure of brain development independent of body size. This quantity also correlates with life span, suggesting that some aspect of brain development per se influences rates of aging or probability of dying (Sacher, 1959). It may be that smarter animals are better able to interact with their environment to avoid certain debilitating factors. We should note, however, that there is no evidence, or reason to believe, that large brains result in more effective regulation of the internal environment of animals.

Metabolic rates of animals of different species are also functions of body size. As animals become smaller, their metabolic rates increase. The smaller the animal, the larger the ratio of body surface to volume; heat loss would surpass heat production if metabolic reactions that produce energy did not increase with decreasing body size. The regression of log metabolic rate, m, on log body weight, y, is

$$m = -0.266y + 1.047$$

and the correlation coefficient is over 0.99. This means that we can substitute metabolic rate for body weight and obtain a relationship with life span as in Figure 6.28, except that the plot would be a mirror image of the Figure 6.28 data; the faster animals live, the shorter their life spans.

Sacher (1977) has extended these studies of constitutional factors and comparative aging with detailed considerations of rodents and other orders, in attempts to identify the most important differences between animals with different life spans, and to understand why species with roughly the same size or metabolic rate can have quite different apparent rates of aging. Man and anthropoid apes, for example, live longer than they should by such criteria as body size, as is apparent in Figure 6.28. Sacher's calculations indicate: (1) If brain weight is held constant, larger species have shorter life spans, (2) if body temperature is constant, increased metabolic rate is associated with shorter life spans, (3) if metabolic rate is held constant, increasing body temperature is associated with longer life span, and (4) if body weight is constant, life span is inversely related to rate of entropy production and is independent of index of cephalization.

Such conclusions have not explained why different species of mammals age at different rates, and we should be aware of other possible explanations of some of the variance in life span at given metabolic rate or body size. It is assumed that cause of death and processes leading to death are the same in the different species in these studies, and that only the rates vary. It is also accepted that maximum life spans from zoo records are true maximum life spans. It is likely that many of these species die from different causes and have not lived out their full life spans. The fraction of the life span taken up by growth is also not taken into consideration in many calculations, and aging does not proceed at a significant rate until growth slows or stops. Human beings, for example, grow for an excessively long period for an animal of their species specific size. On the other hand, the rodent *Peromyscus* lives much longer than *Mus,* even though the two are similar in size, and *Peromyscus* grows for a shorter period than *Mus.*

The above correlations do not tell us anything about cause and effect. We have the choice of speculating that something about body or organ size, or about metabolic rate, body temperature, or entropy production, influences rates of basic aging processes; or that additional unknown factors influence these dimensions and that the latter are independent of each other. Speculation about factors responsible for different rates of aging in different species becomes of limited usefulness in the absence of agreement on key basic aging processes at the tissue and molecular levels that would be affected by such factors. The constitutional factors that correlate with rates of aging do, however, indicate that rates of basic aging processes must be capable of regulation by one or a small number of factors. Some of these aspects of comparative aging will be mentioned again when discussing mechanisms of aging and genetics and evolution of aging in the next two chapters.

Radiation-induced life-shortening

There is a zone of interaction between radiation biology and the study of aging that has given rise to a number of questions for both of these disciplines. When laboratory mammals were given doses of whole-body radiation early in life, it was observed that those that did not die of acute injury appeared to recover, but with the passage of time they lost hair, looked debilitated, demonstrated decreased activity, and died off at increasing rates, all of these changes occurring earlier than similar changes associated with natural aging. It thus appeared that irradiation accelerated the rate of aging or hastened the onset of aging processes.

Treatment of mice at 4 weeks of age with a single dose of whole-body radiation results in the types of percent survival curves shown in Figure 6.30. The major effect of radiation is a displacement of curves to earlier ages. The amount of displacement is dose-related. This phenomenon has been studied in detail in the mouse. The amount of life-shortening varies linearly with dose in certain strains, but the

Fig. 6.30 Survival curves of mice irradiated with 457 r and 198 r at 4 weeks of age. (Redrawn from Lindop, 1965. Aging and Levels of Biological Organization, Univ. of Chicago Press, Chicago. © 1965 by the University of Chicago.)

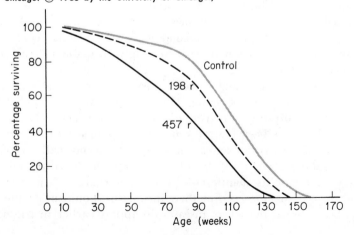

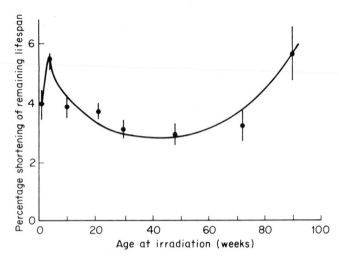

Fig. 6.31 Amount of life-shortening caused by 100 r given at different ages in mice. (Redrawn from Lindop, 1965. Aging and Levels of Biological Organization, Univ. of Chicago Press, Chicago. © 1965 by the University of Chicago.)

relationship is curvilinear in C57BL/6J, and the curve plateaus at high doses in A/J mice (Yuhas, 1969).

Age at irradiation also influences life-shortening. When the percentage shortening of remaining life span is calculated for mouse populations irradiated at different ages, data of Figure 6.31 are obtained. Young and old animals are most sensitive; greatest resistance is at maturity. This curve follows rather closely that for the role of age in sensitivity to acute radiation injury, determined by the amount of radiation required to kill 50 percent of a population. The data suggest that radiation life-shortening may occur by two mechanisms: one is associated with the growth of animals, possibly depending on the number of dividing cells, and the second represents a nonspecific injury in aging animals, as they become increasingly incapable of reacting to injuries of all types.

Survival curves for animals irradiated early in life suggest that radiation hastens the onset of aging. However, any number of harmful treatments could cause animals to die off at earlier ages. A large number of studies have been undertaken to discover to what extent irradiated animals demonstrate an earlier appearance of normally occurring age changes (Casarett, 1964). If radiation simply hastened the onset of aging with all of its manifestations, diseases characteristic of aging should have earlier onsets, but their incidences should be unaffected. It has been shown that these diseases do appear earlier in irradiated animals, but that the incidences vary somewhat from those in control populations. Neoplasms of certain types, particularly leukemia, have increased incidences. However, incidences of these lesions depend on the age at which animals are irradiated; this may simply mean that the well-known carcinogenic effect of ionizing radiation is manifested in these animals, in addition to the life-shortening or age-simulating effect. Most importantly, life-shortening in irradiated animals is not due to a specific disease, or to diseases not seen in control animals; irradiated animals die from a variety of diseases associated with normal aging. This would indicate that radiation accelerates basic aging processes, or that aging processes and the consequences of radiation may act through some final common pathways.

Mammals contain an intrinsic, or physiological, clock that is of use in considering factors that alter life spans. This is collagen, which, as described in a previous chapter, becomes increasingly cross-linked with age. The degree of cross-linking can be used as a measure of biological age. Collagen is extremely resistant to radiation, and collagen present at the time of irradiation does not undergo accelerated cross-linking. Thus, the effect of radiation is not a straightforward acceleration of biological aging.

In the case of radiation-induced life-shortening, as in natural aging, attention must be directed to the tissues in order to gain an appreciation of possible mechanisms. Because of the mutagenic effect of radiation, genetic damage would be a likely suspect. Very shortly after receiving a life-shortening dose of radiation, the liver cells of mice show large numbers of gross chromosomal aberrations—about two times as many aberrations as are found at the end of the normal life span. However, at the time of the greatest number of altered cells, the animals do not appear aged; apparent aging comes later. Also, the percentage of altered cells drops off with the passage of time, either by intracellular repair mechanisms or by replacement of damaged cells. In other words, the number of liver cells with aberrations is not related to the apparent age of the animals. It is not known if this lack of correlation between altered chromosomes and life span holds for other organs. Offspring of irradiated animals age and die off at the same rates as control mice, suggesting that genetic alterations affecting gametes are not responsible for life-shortening.

Histological examination of tissues of irradiated mice reveals the lesions and degenerative diseases of age. In addition, characteristic and widespread changes have been observed in the small blood vessels (Casarett, 1964; Cottier, 1965). Walls of arterioles and small arteries are thickened by the deposition of connective tissue elements, and fibrous connective tissue is laid down in and around the walls of capillaries. These changes have been referred to as arteriolocapillary fibrosis, or hyalinosis. Arteriolocapillary fibrosis may represent a low-grade inflammatory response to the injury of endothelial cells by the radiation. These changes may be of help in attempting to relate aging and late radiation effects at the tissue level.

The questions

We have now characterized aging mammals as animals that all have certain progressive diseases, that show increasing incidences of other diseases, and that show increasing mortality from yet a third group of injuries and insults of many types. Reactions to stress in these animals are diminished because of declining efficiency of all physiological processes and homeostatic mechanisms. We have examined the role of age in some factors influencing physiological reactivity and homeostasis, and in tissue motility, contraction, and transport processes. Any aging processes at the tissue or molecular level postulated to be causes of animal aging must be capable of explaining these characteristic manifestations.

Furthermore, we have noted that growth inhibits aging, that different kinds of mammals age at different rates, and that low doses of ionizing radiation and age have similar consequences. Basic causes of aging must be related to, or capable of being influenced by, these phenomena. In other words, any postulated basic mechanism whose function is inconsistent with these observations is probably not an important cause of aging.

Some needed studies

1. *Microphysiology.* Information is required on changes with age in microvascular perfusion at various sites, permeability of tissue, diffusion of substances between vessels and cells, and elastic properties of small vessels and tissues. Since the most prominent change with age might be in dynamic processes, in vivo studies, in which systems are stressed for maximum performance, would probably be most informative.

2. *Neuromuscular function.* As noted in the previous chapter, studies are required on functions of the long-lived fixed postmitotic neurones and muscle cells, and on their interrelationships. Data on age changes in nerve conduction, motor end-plate function in terms of acetylcholine

production and degradation, and myofiber reactivity and contractabil-ity would be of great value. Ideally, experiments would be performed on neuromotor units isolated from their blood supply and environ-ment, and obtained from animals that had exercised to the same extent.

3. *Reactivity of target cells.* Information on reactivity might be obtained by in vitro studies of the effects of such hormones as insulin and vasopressin on cells and tissues removed from animals of different ages. Again, the immediate past history of animals would have to be taken into account, and comparisons between animals that had had the same amount of activity would be most useful.

4. The role of possible age changes in immunoreactive cells in aging could be tested by transplanting young immunocompetent cells into older animals and observing the recipients for life span and for the development of age-related disease and debility.

REFERENCES

Adelman, R. C., and G. W. Britton. 1975. The impaired capability of bio-chemical adaptation during age. Bioscience. 25:639–643.

Bader, Hermann. 1967. Dependence of wall stress in the human thoracic aorta on age and pressure. Circ. Res. 20:354–361.

Bellamy, D. 1967. Hormonal effects in relation to ageing in mammals. *In* H. W. Woolhouse (ed.). Aspects of the Biology of Aging. Symposium of the Soc. for Expt. Biol. XXI. Cambridge, England: Cambridge University Press.

Bender, Douglas A. 1965. The effect of increasing age on the distribution of peripheral blood flow in man. J. Amer. Geriatric Soc. 13:192–198.

Benjamin, B. 1959. Actuarial aspects of human lifespan. *In* G. E. W. Wolsten-holme and Maeve O'Connor (eds.). The Life Span of Animals. Ciba Foundation Colloquia on Ageing, Vol. 5. London: J. & A. Churchill. Boston: Little, Brown and Company. Pp. 2–15.

Brandfonbrener, Martin, Milton Landowne, and Nathan W. Shock. 1955. Changes in cardiac output with age. Circul. 12:557–566.

Casarett, G. W. 1964. Similarities and contrasts between radiation and time pathology. *In* B. L. Strehler (ed.). Advances in Gerontological Re-search, Vol. 1. New York: Academic Press. Pp. 109–163.

Cohn, J. E. 1964. Age and the pulmonary diffusing capacity. *In* L. Cander and J. H. Moyer (eds.). Aging of the Lung. New York: Grune & Stratton. Pp. 163–172.

Comfort, Alex. 1956. The Biology of Senescence. New York: Rinehard & Co.

Cottier, Hans. 1965. Histopathological differences between natural and radiation-induced aging. *In* Austin M. Brues and George A. Sacher (eds.). Aging and Levels of Biological Organization. Chicago: Univ. of Chicago Press. Pp. 255–262.

DeBusk, F. L. 1972. The Hutchinson-Gilford progeria syndrome. J. Pediatrics. **80**:697–724.

Duffy, P. H., and G. A. Sacher. 1976. Age-dependence of body weight and linear dimensions in adult *Mus* and *Peromyscus*. Growth. **40**:19–31.

Ebbesen, P. 1974. Aging increases susceptibility of mouse skin to DMBA carcinogenesis independent of general immune status. Science (Wash., D.C.). **183**:217–218.

Epstein, C. J., et al. 1966. Werner's syndrome. Medicine. **45**:177–221.

Finch, C. E. 1976. The regulation of physiological changes during mammalian aging. Quart. Rev. Biol. **51**:49–83.

Goldstein, A. L., et al. 1974. Thymosin and the immunopathology of aging. Fed. Proc. **33**:2053–2056.

Goldstein, S., and E. Moerman. 1975. Heat-labile enzymes in skin fibroblasts from subjects with progeria. N. Engl. J. Med. **292**:1305–1309.

Green, E. L. (ed.). 1966. Biology of the Laboratory Mouse, 2nd ed. New York: McGraw-Hill Book Co. Pp. 511–519.

Hollenberg, Norman K., et al. 1974. Senescence and the renal vasculature in normal man. Circul. Res. **34**:309–316.

Hamlin, C. R., R. R. Kohn, and J. L. Luschin. 1975. Apparent accelerated aging of collagen in diabetes mellitus. Diabetes. **24**:902–904.

Hanna, M. G., Jr., P. Nettesheim, and M. J. Snodgrass. 1971. Decreasing immune competence and development of reticulum cell sarcoma in lymphatic tissue of aged mice. J. Natl. Cancer Inst. **46**:809–824.

Hensley, John C., Paul C. McWilliams, and Glenda E. Oakley. 1964. Physiological capacitance: A study in physiological age determination. J. Gerontol. **19**:317–321.

Harris, R. E., and R. P. Forsythe. 1973. Personality and emotional stress in essential hypertension in man. *In* G. Onesti, K. E. Kim, and J. H. Moyer (eds.). Hypertension: Mechanisms and Management. New York: Grune & Stratton. Pp. 125–132.

Ivy, A. C., and M. I. Grossman. 1952. Digestive system. *In* A. I. Lansing (ed.).

Problems of Ageing. Baltimore: The Williams & Wilkins Co. Pp. 481–526.

Jaroslow, Bernard N., Katherine M. Suhrbier, and Thomas E. Fritz. 1974. Decline and restoration of antibody-forming capacity in aging Beagle dogs. J. Immunol. 112:1467–1476.

Joris, F., and J. P. Girard. 1975. Immune response in aged and young subjects, following administration of large doses of tuberculin. Int. Arch. Allergy Appl. Immunol. 48:584–596.

Kerkvliet, Nancy L., and Donald J. Kimeldorf. 1973. The effect of host age on the transplantability of the Walker 256 carcinosarcoma. J. Gerontol. 28:276–280.

Kohn, R. R. 1963. Human aging and disease. J. Chron. Dis. 16:5–21.

Kohn, R. R. 1969. Age variation in rat skin permeability. Proc. Soc. Expt. Biol. Med. 131:521–522.

Lakatta, Edward G., et al. 1975. Prolonged contraction duration in aged myocardium. J. Clin. Invest. 55:61–68.

Lindop, Patricia J. 1965. "Life shortening in an irradiated population of mice." *In* Austin M. Brues and George A. Sacher (eds.). Aging and Levels of Biological Organization. Chicago: Univ. of Chicago Press. Pp. 218–255.

Longcope, Christopher. 1973. The effect of human chorionic gonadotropin on plasma steroid levels in young and old men. Steroids. 21:583–588.

McCay, C. M. 1952. Chemical aspects of ageing and the effect of diet upon ageing. *In* A. I. Lansing (ed.). Problems of Ageing. Baltimore: The Williams & Wilkins Co. Pp. 139–202.

Medvedev, Zhores A. 1974. Caucasus and Altay longevity: A biological or social problem? The Gerontologist. 14:381–387.

Miall, W. E., and H. G. Lovell. 1967. Relation between change of blood pressure and age. Brit. Med. J. 2:660–664.

Muggeo, Michele, et al. 1975. Human growth hormone and cortisol response to insulin stimulation in aging. J. Gerontol. 30:546–551.

Niewoehner, D. E., J. Kleinerman, and L. Liotta. 1975. Elastic behavior of postmortem human lungs: Effects of aging and mild emphysema. J. Appl. Physiol. 39:943–949.

Ordy, J. M., and K. R. Brizzee (eds.). 1975. Neurobiology of aging. New York: Plenum Press.

O'Rourke, Michael F., et al. 1968. Pressure wave transmission along the human aorta. Circ. Res. 23:567–579.

O'Sullivan, John B., et al. 1971. Effect of age on carbohydrate metabolism. J. Clin. Endocrinol. Metab. **33**:619–623.

Peters, Robert L., et al. 1972. Incidence of spontaneous neoplasms in breeding and retired breeder BALB/cCr mice throughout the natural life span. Int. J. Cancer. **10**:273–282.

Ram, J. S. 1967. Aging and immunological phenomena—A review. J. Gerontol. **22**:92–107.

Retzlaff, E., and J. Fontaine. 1965. Functional and structural changes in motor neurones with age. *In* A. T. Welford, and J. E. Birren (eds.). Behavior, Aging and the Nervous System. Springfield, Ill.: Charles C. Thomas. Pp. 340–352.

Riegle, G. D., and J. Meites. 1976. Effects of aging on LH and Prolactin after LHRH L-dopa, methyl dopa and stress in male rat. Proc. Soc. Exptl. Biol. Med. **151**:507–511.

Rodahl, Kaare, and Bela Issekutz. 1962. Physical performance capacity of the older individual. *In* Kaare Rodahl and Steven M. Horvath (eds.). Muscle As a Tissue. New York: McGraw-Hill Book Co. Pp. 272–301.

Ross, M. H., and G. Bras. 1965. Tumor incidence patterns and nutrition in the rat. J. Nutrition. **87**:245–260.

Sacher, G. A. 1959. Relation of lifespan to brain weight and body weight in mammals. *In* G. E. W. Wolstenholme and Maeve O'Connor (eds.). The Lifespan of Animals. Ciba Found. Colloq. on Aging, Vol. 5. Boston: Little, Brown and Company. Pp. 115–133.

———. 1977. Evaluation of entropy and information terms governing mammalian longevity. *In* R. G. Cutler (ed.). Molecular Gerontology. Basel: S. Karger.

Schuyler, M. R., et al. 1976. Abnormal lung elasticity in juvenile diabetes mellitus. Am. Rev. Resp. Dis. **113**:37–41.

Shmavonian, B. M., A. J. Yarmat, and S. I. Cohen. 1965. Relationships between the autonomic nervous system and central nervous system in age differences in behavior. *In* A. T. Welford and James E. Birren (eds.). Behavior, Aging and the Nervous System. Springfield, Ill.: Charles C. Thomas, Publisher. Pp. 235–258.

Shock, N. W. 1960. Age changes in physiological functions in the total animal: The role of tissue loss. *In* Bernard L. Strehler (ed.). The Biology of Aging. AIBS, Washington, D.C. Pp. 258–264.

Siegel, J. S. 1975. Some demographic aspects of aging in the United States. *In* A. M. Ostfeld and D. C. Gibson (eds.). Epidemiology of Aging. DHEW Publ. No. (NIH) 75-711. Washington, D.C.: U.S. Gov. Printing Office. Pp. 17–82.

Simms, Henry S. 1942. The use of a measurable cause of death (hemorrhage) for the evaluation of aging. J. Gen. Physiol. **26**:169–178.

———. 1965. Nutrition, pathologic change, and longevity. *In* Austin M. Brues and George A. Sacher (eds.). Aging and Levels of Biological Organization. Chicago: Univ. of Chicago Press. Pp. 87–121.

Sobel, H. 1967. Aging of ground substance in connective tissue. Adv. Gerontol. Res. **2**:205–283.

Storer, John B. 1965. Mean homeostatic levels as a function of age and genotype. *In* Austin M. Brues and George A. Sacher (eds.). Aging and Levels of Biological Organization. Chicago: Univ. of Chicago Press. Pp. 192–204.

Strehler, B. L. 1962. Time, Cells and Aging. New York: Academic Press.

Teller, M. N., et al. 1964. Aging and cancerogenesis, I. immunity to tumor and skin grafts. J. Nat. Canc. Inst. **33**:649–656.

Toh, B. H., et al. 1973. Depression of cell-mediated immunity in old age and the immunopathic diseases, lupus erythematosis, chronic hepatitis and rheumatoid arthritis. Clin. Expt. Immunol. **14**:193–202.

Trujillo, T. T., J. F. Spaulding, and W. H. Langham. 1962. A study of radiation-induced aging: Response of irradiated and nonirradiated mice to cold stress. Radiat. Res. **16**:144–150.

Weisfeldt, M. L., W. A. Loeven, and N. W. Shock. 1971. Resting and active mechanical properties of trabeculae carnae from aged male rats. Am. J. Physiol. **220**:1921–1927.

Yuhas, J. M. 1969. The dose response curve for radiation-induced life shortening. J. Gerontol. **24**:451–456.

SEVEN

Aging of Animals:
Possible Mechanisms

The manifestations of age that we have considered are not very subtle. Aged animals are very different from mature ones. Therefore one might expect early agreement among students of aging on the tissue changes that are most likely responsible for the aging syndrome and on the types of studies and experiments required for an understanding of cause-and-effect relationships. However, such an agreement has not been the case; rather, notions about causes of aging have generally followed the fashions of the times, and virtually every conceivable phenomenon has been proposed at some time in the past, or is currently under consideration as a primary cause.

Although basic mechanisms of aging are currently at the level of hypotheses or theories, any mechanism that is capable of explaining observations discussed in the previous chapter and is consistent with all established data should be worthy of serious consideration. Conversely, any tissue change or hypothesis that cannot be related to the manifestations of age or is inconsistent with established information should be rejected as an explanation of aging.

The consequences of age are clear. Of the various causes that have been postulated, some are known to exist, while others have been argued on the basis that if they do occur, they would be reasonable explanations of aging. For example, latent viruses have been postulated as a cause of aging. It would first have to be shown that viruses become more widespread in tissues or become more active with age, and second, a reasonable explanation of how viral activity might cause the debilities of age would have to be advanced. On the other hand, it is known that lipofuscin pigment accumulates in muscle cells and in neurones with age. If one could explain debilities on the basis of this accumulation, lipofuscin would be a more reasonable cause than viruses.

A useful rule in scientific reasoning has been that if there are several ways in which a phenomenon might be explained, one should favor the mechanism that requires the fewest assumptions. In considering causes of aging, therefore, we should perhaps first attempt to rule out mechanisms that are known to exist rather than those that we assume or guess are operative. Also, we have observed that aging debilities occur throughout the mammalian body. We cannot ascribe consequences of age to a single organ. We might assume that the major manifestations of age result from one change or a small number of changes in a system that is common to all organs. Otherwise, we would have to make multiple assumptions about different types of alterations in the various systems and tissues, all proceeding at similar rates to cause debilities at different sites at about the same time.

Theories of aging deal with various levels of abstraction. It has been proposed that aging is due to tissue wear and tear, to random "hits" or mutations, or to the formation of free radicals, without specifying how any of these might cause debilities. Other theories are based on autoimmunity, on the accumulation of inert or harmful substances, and on cross-linking of macromolecules.

Since the cause of aging must reside in chemical changes in cells or tissues, it would be profitable to direct our attention to what is known or what can be reasonably assumed about aging processes at these sites and their effects at higher levels of organization. It should be emphasized that although there are large gaps in our knowledge of basic processes, an enormous number of studies have been carried out, and we have a great deal of information, as indicated in earlier chapters. This information should at least permit the rejection of some hypotheses while favoring one or more of the others, and should indicate the types of studies required to support or negate likely possibilities.

Role of cells in animal aging

Most attempts to explain animal aging have, for obvious reasons, been based on cell alterations. It has been assumed that there must be widespread cell death or injury underlying the aging syndrome. Recent discoveries and concepts in biology have been applied to this assumption. It has been frequently postulated that aging is caused by alterations in the DNA code, or in transcription or translation.

A theory that aging is due to autoimmunity is based on abnormal serum globulins and autoantibodies found in increasing percentages of an aging population, and on some similarities between aged animals and animals with runt disease, a disease caused by antitissue immune reactions. The view that aging is due to injury caused by free radicals arises from knowledge of how free radicals could alter cellular components, and from suggestive evidence that free radicals increase in the blood with increasing age.

There are several a priori considerations that weaken the view that cell loss is a cause of animal aging. If there were a random loss of cells throughout the body, even a very large number (one-third of the total cells, for example), individuals would simply be smaller by that amount. There is no obvious reason why this should lead to debilities. If cells at some sites remained relatively constant in number, while those in other organs decreased with age, the imbalance might then result in functional impairments. This would require a number of assumptions to explain selective cell loss and its consequences, which would not be justified on the basis of current information.

If aging were due to selective cell loss, the loss would have to be very great indeed, and some mechanism would have to appear that would interfere with cell replacement. The reserve of cells in organs is enormous; animals survive quite well with only 40 percent of a liver, part of one kidney, one lung, and with large areas of the brain destroyed. In order to cause decreased organ function, cell loss would have to reduce organ size to below these limits. We also know that regeneration would restore cell numbers in those organs where cell division can occur, and that no significant decrease in regenerative capacity with age has been demonstrated. Similarly, the short-lived fixed postmitotic cells appear to be replaced adequately in animals of all ages.

Most importantly, studies of aging tissues have not revealed cell losses after maturity that would begin to depreciate the known reserve. Some losses of cells occur, particularly in the nervous system of man, as discussed in Chapter Five, but these can only be described as trivial in terms of losses required for functional impairment and the widespread debilities of age.

In summary, the view that the mammalian organism is a collection of cells analogous to a complex tissue culture and that aging is caused by the dying out of these cells is untenable.

If aging is not caused by the death and disappearance of cells, perhaps it is due to cell injuries or alterations. However, some of the same problems in attempting to explain aging in terms of cell death are encountered in considering cell alterations, except that cells that remain viable but deficient in function may be more likely to result in debilities than cells that simply disappear.

Aging of cells and their components was discussed in Chapters Four and Five. The short-lived fixed postmitotic cells, which clearly age, appear to do so independently of the animals that contain them; there is no evidence that these cells in an old individual are significantly different from those in younger animals. In other types of cell populations, no pattern of generalized loss of enzymatic activities or of ability to synthesize cell components is apparent. Occasional observations of decreases in these factors might depend on changes in cell environment or on the physiological state of the animals.

It is of interest that while these life-maintaining factors in cells are unchanged, or show equivocal changes with age, organ function declines markedly and progressively. This would suggest that only components required for specialized function become altered, or that the declining function of organs does not depend on cellular changes.

There are not many ways in which cells could be permanently altered without killing them. Mutations, in particular, would be more likely to result in dead than altered cells. And effects of mutations, such as defects in the synthesis of specific proteins, have not been observed in cells of aging animals.

Observations underlying the somatic mutation theory of aging are, as described in Chapter Four, an increasing frequency of chromosomal aberrations in liver cells with age and a larger number of aberrations in short-lived, as compared to long-lived, mice. The mutagenic effect of radiation also serves to relate radiation life-shortening to an explanation of aging based on mutations.

There is no reason to believe, however, that the short-lived strain of mice undergoes accelerated aging; such strains are known to have an increased susceptibility to certain diseases. Primary lung tumors, for example, develop in one-third to one-half of the animals in the short-lived strain used. Furthermore, there is no relationship between the actual number of aberrations and life span in the two groups, and aberrations do not increase significantly after growth cessation. More significantly, following radiation, the percentage of aberrations is about twice as high as that attained at the end of the life span; but rather than being dead, the irradiated animals survive, and the percentage of aberrations decreases. It is rather difficult to demonstrate an age-related decline in liver function, and liver failure per se is not a cause of death in old mammalian populations. This indicates that chromosomal aberrations in liver cells, which have been described in 80 percent of the cells under certain experimental conditions, do not cause functional impairment.

If such aberrations do not impair liver function at the instant they are present, there is no reason why similar changes should be damaging at other sites, regardless of differences in rate of cell replacement. In accord with this view, when the mutagen, nitrogen mustard, was administered in very high doses to mice for two-thirds of their life span, no life-shortening occurred. It must be concluded on the bases of these data that somatic mutations of the type that have been described cannot be a cause of aging.

Cell function may be impaired by the accumulation of substances. Lipofuscin accumulation occurs in neurones, and in cardiac and skeletal muscle. Other substances such as minerals may also accumulate, and may not have ben discovered as yet because they are invisible by light microscopy. If the accumulation of substances such as lipofuscin interfered with nerve transmission, cardiac contractility, or reactivity of smooth muscle cells in blood vessels, many of the debilities of age could be explained. In a limited study, no correlation was found between the concentration of lipofuscin and cardiac function, but it could be argued that the heart may be able to compensate to a degree, and that there is considerable individual variation in this ability. An important role for the accumulated lipofuscin and other substances has not been excluded.

Other possibilities for cell alteration are in the cell membranes and structural components such as myofilaments and myelin. These structures contain macromolecules, some of which are polymerized and rather inert metabolically. On the basis of what is known about chemical aging, we would suspect changes in the nature of cross-linking or the binding of small molecules. The aging of these structures has not been studied in any detail. Alterations in membranes might influence permeability of cells, while changes in structural proteins of muscle could hinder contractility. Decreases in nerve myelin with age have been reported. This requires more study. If any of these changes were widespread in the body, many of the declines in physiological function with age could be explained.

As noted earlier, the debilities of age cannot be accounted for on the basis of cell alteration or failure known to occur in any specific organ or system. Endocrine failure, long suspected to be a cause of aging, may be ruled out as playing a key role in the major manifestations of age. Although there is suggestive evidence that neurone function decreases with age, more studies are required to show that this is an intrinsic and irreversible cellular phenomenon, unrelated to cell environment and physiological state of the animal. The declines that have been demonstrated in the function of the immune system may mean that older animals have impaired reactivity to certain antigens, and may be more susceptible to some infectious diseases. It is also likely that increasing (though small) percentages of an aging population undergo tissue damages because of autoantibodies. However, in view of the characteristics of an aging population, described in the previous chapter, and the lack of tissue evidence of immune reactions, except in certain subgroups and certain inbred mouse strains, the notion that autoimmunity is a major cause of aging in natural populations is tenuous.

Some possibilities remain for a major role for cellular alterations in causing aging. It is also likely that certain types of cell changes will be found to result in some debilities in aging populations. We have been unable to build a strong case, however, for the major characteristics of aging animals being caused by the aging of their cells as it is presently understood.

Role of connective tissue in animal aging

Components of connective tissue and their changes with age have been described in Chapter Three. The most characteristic age change appears to represent a progressive intermolecular cross-linking of collagen. This is associated with decreases in concentrations of mucopolysaccharides at some sites. The discussion to follow will deal with collagen, although, in addition to the probable significance of changes in this molecule, collagen may serve as a model for similar alterations and consequences likely to be associated with reticulin, elastin, and structural proteins of basement membranes.

It was pointed out that collagen constitutes 25 to 30 percent of the total body protein, and is distributed in and around walls of all blood vessels, and around cells. Contraction and relaxation of muscle cells occur in a collagen-containing matrix, and the passage of materials between blood vessel and cell takes place through this type of tissue. Studies combining physical measurements and morphological observations indicate that collagen functions to maintain form and to limit deformations of tissues.

Progressive cross-linking of collagen, which appears to occur throughout the body, would tend to interfere with the flexibility of fibrils, and thereby make tissues less mobile. Tissues become more rocklike, a state incompatible with life.

Physiological impairment might occur at several levels. Cardiac muscle would be unable to contract efficiently, as it has already been shown that the capacity of the heart to work drops off with age, and the heart muscle becomes more rigid. Large arteries would be less able to transmit contractile force, since with increasing age these arteries become more like rigid tubes. At the level of capillaries and tissues, mobility would be damped. In the extracellular space, actual movement of substances might be hindered by excessively cross-linked structural proteins. Decreases with age in perfusion of organs and in tissue permeability, and increased peripheral vascular resistance were described in the previous chapter.

Inadequate perfusion of tissues, impaired passage of materials between vessels and cells, and increasing stiffness of tissue per se form the bases of arguments relating debilities of age to cross-linking of collagen. Since all physiological processes depend on tissue movement and diffusion of substances, the generalized physiological decline with age could be explained on these bases. An impaired passage of gases, nutrients, metabolites, hormones, antibodies, and accumulated toxins would, furthermore, explain why aging animals become increasingly susceptible to being killed by miscellaneous diseases, injuries, and insults. Some cell death and altered function secondary to altered passage of materials would be expected.

If physiological decline with age is due to connective tissue alterations, this would explain why organ function *in situ,* kidney function, for example, declines markedly with age, while studies based on preparations in which vessel-connective tissue-cell relationships are destroyed show only equivocal changes, or none.

A stiffer connective tissue with increasing age could also play major roles in the brittleness and fragmentation of articular cartilage that characterize degenerative joint disease, and in the lung stiffness that accompanies emphysema of the aged. The general physiological decline could, by disuse, cause some of the osteoporosis and muscle atrophy associated with aging.

We cannot discuss here all of the specific diseases characteristic of aging in various mammalian populations. We can consider human populations, however, in terms of some diseases that are aging processes themselves. The complications of atherosclerosis constitute by far the most common cause of death. The blood supply to inner layers of large blood vessels is limited even in young individuals because small vessels from the outer layer do not penetrate very deeply. Decreased permeability and diminished perfusion with age could result in tissue ischemia, and in the trapping of lipids, glycoproteins, and minerals. Resultant inflammatory reactions would constitute the lesions of atherosclerosis.

Hypertension would result from the increasing rigidity of large vessels and the increasing peripheral resistance.

Diseases such as atherosclerosis and hypertension are complex; there are obviously predisposing and exacerbating factors. The above deals only with the specific role of macromolecular aging in pathogenesis.

The diseases that show increasing incidences with age are not aging processes themselves, and populations would age and die off even in their absence. One of these, malignant neoplasms, however, bears an interesting relationship to age, and kills off a sufficiently large segment of older populations to justify special consideration. One might speculate on roles of connective tissues changes in carcinogenesis, in terms of tissue hypoxia causing cells to become neoplastic, or aged connective tissue being more readily invaded by tumors, such invasion being necessary for the spread of a tumor. However, these notions require a large number of assumptions that go far beyond established information. Some other ways in viewing the role of age in neoplasia will be mentioned in a later section.

With regard to growth and aging, it will be recalled that newly synthesized collagen is soluble, and that it matures into insoluble collagen by the formation of intermolecular cross-links. As long as an animal is growing, it will synthesize young, or soluble, collagen. Therefore, its collagen will continually be diluted by young collagen. The amount of young collagen will be proportional to growth rate rather than chronological age. Collagen as a whole will not be able to age until growth has stopped. Reduction of food intake and decreased growth of rats have been shown to inhibit aging of collagen fibers (Everitt, 1971).

The inhibition of aging by growth would hold for any system in which aging is caused by reactions involving nonrenewable molecules. Growth processes would dilute any such population of molecules. One theory of aging that is inconsistent with the known inhibitory effect of growth on aging is that aging results from an accumulation of somatic mutations, resulting in altered but viable cells; growing animals should have more dividing cells, which would be more, rather than less, susceptible to mutations.

In the previous chapter it was pointed out that rate of aging correlates with metabolic rate and, negatively, with body and organ size.

It is possible that metabolic rate is governed in part by body size, and that rate of aging is influenced by metabolic rate. There are at least two ways in which cross-linking of collagen could be accelerated by an increased metabolic rate. If an enzyme such as amine oxidase plays a role in the oxidative deamination of lysine leading to cross-linking, a generalized increase in metabolism might cause increased concentrations of such enzymes. Alternatively, it has been shown that stresses exerted on collagen fibers in vitro cause the fibers to take on the physical properties of more densely cross-linked structures. Animals with higher metabolic rates would have higher frequencies of tissue stresses, which could result in more rapid cross-linking of collagen.

The effects of irradiation late in life have been tentatively explained on the basis of widespread arteriolocapillary fibrosis, which has been shown to occur. Fibrosis at the capillary level would be expected to have effects on tissue mobility, perfusion, and permeability similar to those caused by increasing cross-linking of collagen due to natural aging. Any new collagen forming secondary to irradiation would also become aged by cross-linking. The fact that irradiation has more of an agelike effect, the younger the animals irradiated, may depend on more time being available for the collagen that is laid down in response to radiation injury to age itself by natural cross-linking.

Other theories of aging are compatible with the correlation between metabolic rate and rate of aging, and with the radiation effect. Roles for free radicals (Harman, 1965), somatic mutations, and autoimmunity due to altered tissue antigens (Walford, 1967), could be argued in terms of radiation and metabolic rate. As indicated earlier, however, either these theories are contradicted by other data, or not enough is known about their existence and possible consequences to construct a very plausible cause-and-effect sequence ending with the debilities of old age.

A variety of chemical agents that interfere with the maturation of collagen and elastin have been discovered. The most thoroughly studied of these are certain nitriles, known as lathyrogens, and penicillamine. These agents have been given to rats and mice in an attempt to inhibit aging—without success. Since the fibrous proteins of connective tissue are synthesized in response to stress and in amounts appropriate to the degree and type of stress, tissues probably compensate for a partial defect in maturation by the synthesis of greater amounts of collagen and elastin. Any agent given in sufficient concentration to cause a permanent decrease in absolute amounts of insoluble protein would be too toxic. Since the cross-linking of collagen which is an aging phenomenon occurs in mature insoluble collagen, it might be possible eventually to find an agent that will maintain the collagen in its optimal mature state by inhibiting the formation of additional cross-links. An undertaking of this type would provide important evidence for or against the view that cross-linking of collagen causes animal aging, as well as possibly demonstrating the feasibility of inhibiting mammalian aging.

The speculative nature of the foregoing discussion is obvious. The value of the theory of aging based on cross-linking of extracellular macromolecules lies in its starting with established information on aging of collagen, proceeding to impaired function of all organs by making use of additional known facts, and its being capable of explaining major debilities. It also satisfies the criterion of being compatible with relationships between radiation, growth, and metabolic rates, and aging. Since it is this theory that is best able to explain aging in terms of current information, perhaps it should receive the highest priority for future investigations.

The view that macromolecular cross-linking causes aging is a variation of one of the oldest theories of aging—that aging is caused by syneresis of body colloids. This view also supports the cliché that a man is as old as his arteries, and suggests that when Leonardo da Vinci claimed that aging was due to thickening of tunics of veins that restricted the passage of blood, he may not have been very far from the truth.

Age and neoplasia

There is a clear relationship between age and the incidence of tumors in mammalian populations, in that different types of tumors appear on schedule, and that ages of maximum incidence are different for different kinds of malignancies. The possible role of host factors in controlling viability, growth, invasion, and spread of tumors has been mentioned previously. Future studies may show that physiological decline with age, as manifested in altered tissue permeability, vascular reactivity, or immunological reactions, permits the growth and spread of tumors. Since incidence of tumors appears to be the major age-related phenomenon, however, some theoretical aspects of time and the malignant transformation of cells will be considered.

In order for a cell to be malignant it must have a certain small number of properties. One would be some alteration in the rate of cell division or destruction so that the number of cells increases. The cells also have to be able to invade, to separate from one another in order to metastasize. And they must in some way avoid controls on growth and function exerted by other tissues. The number of properties we select is arbitrary, but the number required is probably small—four would be convenient for consideration. Some of these properties are shared with certain normal cells; for example, many cell populations can increase in number. Leukocytes normally spread throughout the body, and both leukocytes and trophoblast tissue have invasive ability. Also, benign tumors would have some of these properties that are not present in the cell of origin. Each cancer cell, however, would require all of these abilities.

In order for a cell to have all of these properties, it must be subjected to events or "hits" that bring about the alterations. Hits could be mutations, viral infections, or any other events whose consequences would be transmitted to subsequent generations.

Of course, a specific number of hits could be required for the alteration of a single biological property. Or a sequence of events might be necessary for the accumulation or depletion of some component, for the expression of viral activity, or for the loss of immune surveillance.

Age becomes an important factor because time would be required for a given number of hits to occur in a cell. By using probability theory, the time required for a certain number of hits per cell, or the probability of a certain number of hits as a function of time, can be calculated. However, such calculations assume that the frequency of mutation or similar change is constant with time, that the probability of hits or successes remains constant, and that the probability of a hit is independent of the number of previous hits. Since some of these assumptions may not be true, it will be just as useful for our purposes to assume only that more time is required for more hits per cell.

Starting with a large population at birth, we know from human and laboratory animal data that with the passage of time certain segments of the population will die off with characteristic types of malignancies. An idealized view of this pattern is shown in Figure 7.1, where *A* represents tumors of early development; *B*, malignancies characteristic of growth and maturation; and *C, D,* and *E,* tumors of the aging population.

Two questions arise: (1) Why do some tumors appear earlier than

Fig. 7.1 Deaths of subgroups of a population from different kinds of neoplasms as a function of age.

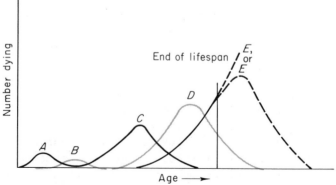

others? (2) Why does the incidence of all tumors not increase with age regardless of age at onset? Age of maximum incidence could depend on the number of additional hits required by certain cell types in order to have the required four hits. For example, tumors of young animals could be of a cell type in which only two hits are required because the cell normally has properties equivalent to the other two hits. Or the susceptible subgroup could be born with a genetic pre-disposition—that is, could be born with one or more hits. In order for the incidence not to rise indefinitely with age, the probability of getting new hits of the inborn type would have to be very low when compared to the probability of getting postnatal hits.

The appearance of different malignancies as the population ages could be due to the number of postnatal hits required for different tumors. For example, the cells of cancer C may have had two hits to start with, and require two more; cancer D may originate from cells that already had one hit and require three more; E may require all four hits, and show an increasing incidence at the time the whole population dies off.

The frequency of hits for certain types of tumors could also increase with age in subgroups because of special types of risks. Cigarette smoking might provide a hit in the population of heavy smokers, for example.

In addition to a priori considerations, evidence for the accumulation of hits is found in carcinogenic effects of mutagens and viruses, and in the development of malignancies in benign tumors and premalignant lesions. Cancers are more likely to develop in these lesions than in tissues of origin, possibly because such lesions already have some of the required hits.

Decending limbs of the curves in Figure 7.1 are most readily explained in terms of the susceptible group for each type of tumor dying out, while the resistant segment of the population survives. This would be the case if the susceptible population had a genetic predisposition or inborn hits, and if the probability of hits of this type for affecting the general population was very low. A susceptible group might also be one exposed to certain hazards; cigarette smokers, radiologists, and uranium mine workers would be candidates for more hits than would the general population. Members of a group may be more susceptible to sustaining a permanent hit than the general population. The entire population may be exposed to a virus, for example, but while one group becomes infected—that is, sustains a hit—the remaining population may halt the infection, become immune, and not have a future risk of that type of hit.

These concepts indicate the need for a search for evidence of hits before final malignant transformation. This would be most feasible in certain mouse strains. Over 90 percent of the animals in strain AKR develop lymphatic leukemia on schedule, between 6 to 10 months of age. These mice are born with one hit in the form of a vertically transmitted C-type RNA leukemia virus. A second hit involves the thymus gland; thymectomized mice do not develop the typical leukemia. Comparative studies of lymphocytes over the life span in animals of this strain and of a strain that does not develop leukemia might demonstrate additional hits in the AKR cells.

REFERENCES

Everitt, A. V. 1971. Food intake, growth and the ageing of collagen in rat tail tendon. Gerontologia. **17**:98–104.

Harman, D. 1965. The free radical theory of aging: Effect of age on serum copper levels. J. Gerontol. **20**:151–153.

Kohn, R. R. 1966. A possible final common pathway for natural ageing and radiation induced life-shortening. *In* P. J. Lindop and G. A. Sacher (eds.). Radiation & Ageing. London: Taylor & Francis, Ltd. Pp. 373–392.

Walford, R. L. 1967. The general immunology of aging. Adv. in Gerontol. Res. **2**:159–204.

EIGHT

Evolution, Control,

and Programming

of Aging

In a previous chapter it was stated that the most important questions about aging dealt with the inevitable deterioration and death of all members of a population in spite of the optimization of everything, including the best possible combination of genes. Although the connotation of this question is that aging occurs in the absence of deleterious genes, and it can be stated at the outset that there is no evidence that aging in mammals is caused by any specific and direct gene action, we are left with the challenging question of how aging evolved within a species.

The progression of various aging processes in animals is obviously under some kind of control. Rates of these processes may vary between individuals and between strains within a species as consequences of genetic or environmental factors, and as a result of direct control or of secondary effects of other processes. The very marked differences in rates of aging processes between different orders and families of mammals must result, directly or indirectly, from gene action.

The most useful approach to understanding control of aging would be to study rates and factors regulating rates of molecular aging processes. Not many studies of this type have been undertaken. More often, life span has been used as a measure of aging rate. As noted earlier, the latter approach would appear to be legitimate if true maximum life spans are known, and if it is known that animals with

217

different life spans die from the same aging processes. These criteria are usually not satisfied.

Origin of aging within a species

In the systems in which aging can be most readily observed—macromolecules, short-lived fixed postmitotic cells, and animals—changes are clearly programmed in that they can be predicted with considerable precision. One might assume that the program resides in genes. However, this view is insufficient because it does not provide insight into mechanisms at higher levels, and molecules and structures are likely to participate in reactions not intended by genes.

Evolution may be related to aging in several different ways. For example, age changes could be the necessary consequences of some useful property or function that was selected for; that is, in order for a molecule or cell to carry out a necessary function, it must be constructed in such a way that age changes are unavoidable. Or aging processes could be selected for on the basis of some benefit to the organisms or species. Or age changes could be essentially accidental—unrelated to any function, and occurring because no mechanism has evolved to prevent them.

At the level of macromolecules, there is every reason to believe that the program follows from the molecular structure, and that, at least in some cases, aging is the unavoidable consequence of development required for specific function. The function of collagen requires the formation of strong fibers and fibrils. Therefore, collagen molecules are programmed to aggregate and undergo cross-linking. This cross-linking does not stop at maturity of the fibrils, however, but continues and is responsible for collagen aging. Apparently no mechanism has evolved to prevent this excessive cross-linking or to cause significant turnover of mature collagen. Aging of collagen might be viewed as both an unavoidable consequence of a necessary trait and as a continuation of developmental processes.

Other macromolecular reactions such as the accumulation of lipofuscin might, again, depend on programs built into the molecular structure, but be accidental in terms of any function. Accumulation could then occur if no mechanism were available for removal of aggregates.

Organelles and enzyme molecules that have regular turnover rates may deteriorate by denaturation or by reactions of other types as mentioned in Chapters Two and Four. Since function depends on structural integrity, mechanisms for destruction and replacement of altered molecules and organelles would have to have evolved concomitantly.

Reasonable explanations for the deterioration of short-lived fixed postmitotic cells are that their specialized functions utilize so many of the cell's resources that vegetative processes cannot be maintained, or that cells are killed as a result of some specialized reactions. In such cases, aging would be an unavoidable byproduct of properties that were selected for. Again, this would necessitate the concomitant evolution of mechanisms for the removal and replacement of altered and dead cells.

Degeneration and death of cells in development appear necessary in most cases for organogenesis. Such aging processes must have been selected for in some way. Either specific lethal reactions might be selected for, or mechanisms for protecting or replacing these cells could have been selected against.

The role of evolution in aging of animals has been the subject of considerable speculation. Selection for a trait can be most readily explained if the trait gives a reproductive advantage and has survival value during the reproductive period. It is more difficult to explain how some trait that is manifested in the postreproductive period could be selected for. Animals with such a trait would not tend to leave any more descendents than animals without the trait. It has been suggested that in some social animals, old, nonreproducing animals compete with younger animals for food, and thereby hinder reproduction of the young. Therefore, if some genetic trait appeared that caused animals to die as their reproductive capacity declined or ceased, this would be selected for. On this basis it has been suggested that early in the evolution of a species, animals were essentially immortal or had indefinite life spans, and that aging was brought about by selection for shorter life spans.

Although selection for aging processes may occur in some species, there are more plausible explanations for mammalian aging based on the relationship between growth and aging, and on selection for longer life spans operating during the reproductive period. It was pointed out in the previous chapter that animals that show the most clearly programmed aging are those that have a species-specific size. Having a specific size is probably of great adaptive value for various animals in different ecological niches. This would lead to the selection of factors that cause growth cessation. Molecules and structures that are metabolically inert would then not be diluted or turned over by growth, but would persist and age.

Few animals in the wild have the opportunity to age and die of degenerative processes. Early in the evolution of a species it is likely that animals were killed off by many different types of diseases, both intrinsic and environmental, very early in life. There would be great selection pressure for the development of defenses against these diseases during the reproductive period. This would result in a progressively longer life span until reproductive capacity declined markedly or was exhausted. Selection would also occur over the period in which young offspring must be cared for. After this period there would be no mechanism by which defenses or life-lengthening processes could be selected for. Nonreproducing animals or those with very diminished reproductive capacity would then be left with some uninhibited lethal processes or susceptibilities.

In terms of one theory of aging—that based on the cross-linking of collagen—in the nongrowing, nonreproducing animal, there would be no pressure for the evolution of mechanisms that would cause collagen to turn over, or inhibit cross-linking. Aging of animals would be the unavoidable consequences of molecular aging.

According to the above view, the evolutionary origins of aging are in the processes that restrict growth and in the duration of the reproductive period. The latter depends primarily on gonadal function (Foote, 1975). Aging processes in gonads, particularly depletion of ova, as seen in human beings, or failure in oocyte maturation or ovulation, as seen in prosimians, are probably of major importance in determining when more generalized aging begins or accelerates.

To return to the question of genes and the inheritance of aging processes, aging is, of course, inherited in the sense that genes determine whether an animal will be a rat or a man, and a rat ages faster than a man. It is more useful to ask if studies of gene action will provide insight into mechanisms causing aging of a species. On the basis of current information it would appear that such studies might tell us why or how aging processes are initiated, but would not indicate which processes occur subsequently, nor provide important details of their progression.

Variability between individuals and strains

When considering variability in aging rates, it is of course essential that the same processes in different animals and strains be examined. There are great differences in life spans in different strains of animals, and it might appear that the different strains age at different rates. It is clear, however, that the differences are due almost entirely to differences in genetic susceptibility to specific diseases. C57BL mice live to around 3 years of age and die off from a variety of diseases. AKR mice die between 6 and 10 months of age from leukemia. It would certainly be erroneous to conclude that AKR mice age faster than the C57BL. If, by definition, aging processes are those processes responsible for debility and death when all genetic and environmental factors are optimized, a very large number of factors could cause early deaths without representing accelerated aging.

Hybrids often live longer than inbred strains of animals. This increased fitness is known as heterosis or hybrid vigor, and is associated with heterozygosity. Extensive homozygosity is unhealthy. Certain diseases are expressed in the homozygous recessive state. Also, if alleles are pleiotropic with different alleles being more adaptive with different traits, a heterozygote will be more adaptive than either homozygote. There is no evidence that the greater vigor of hybrids is due to a slowing of aging processes rather than to a decreased susceptibility to certain diseases and debilities that may be only peripherally related to aging.

If we adhere to previous definitions of aging processes and look for genetic variability in rates of these processes, we do not find clear evidence that there is any greater variability between strains or between heterozygotes and homozygotes than there is between individuals within a species.

Variations in aging rates between individuals may be in regulatory processes at high levels of biological organization, and may be on a genetic basis, but are also capable of being influenced by environmental factors. Individuals who stop growing early would be expected to show earlier expression of aging processes and shorter life spans. Genetic, hormonal, and nutritional factors could determine when growth ceases. Variations in metabolic rate could similarly be on genetic, hormonal, or environmental bases, and it would be expected that all processes including aging processes would be accelerated in individuals with higher metabolic rates. The apparent slower aging in human females, as compared to males, could be due in part to the lower metabolic rate in females.

The role of brain size has been emphasized by Sacher (1975) in the evolution of longevity, and the correlation between brain size and life span in animals is impressive. We should note, however, that there is no known mechanism by which brain size per se affects any aging process.

Information on control and genetic variability of aging processes at the molecular and tissue level would be very useful, but this subject has not been dealt with systematically, and only isolated bits of information are available. The stability of collagen, presumably due to increased cross-linking, is perhaps the best characterized basic aging process and has been invoked previously in theorizing about mechanisms of aging. Any variation in overall aging rate in an animal should be manifested in, or associated with, variation in age changes in collagen. Variability in rate of molecular age changes could result from systemic causes or could be caused by factors operating specifically at the molecular level. At the molecular level, true variations in rates of aging processes could occur, or reactions could take place that simulate acceleration or retardation of aging processes, but by mechanisms not involved in natural aging.

The possible effects of growth and metabolic rate on aging of collagen have been discussed. Collagen aging is also subject to some direct and indirect endocrine control. Hypophysectomy causes an early apparent acceleration of collagen aging because of growth inhibition, but later there is an inhibition of aging (Delbridge and Everitt, 1972). The inhibition appears to be due to lower activity of an amine oxidase, an enzyme that plays a role in the cross-linking of collagen (Howarth and Everitt, 1974). In the genetic disease, alkaptonuria, homogentisic acid accumulates and causes cross-linking of connective tissue structures and acceleration of an agelike brittleness of these structures. It was mentioned in an earlier chapter that collagen from individuals with diabetes mellitus appears to undergo accelerated aging. It is not known if true age changes are accelerated in diabetic collagen or if some additional reaction occurs, as is the case in alkaptonuria.

There are thus many ways in which apparent rates of molecular aging might vary or be controlled in different individuals. In most cases, the molecular differences appear secondary to an overall control process or an additional factor. It has not been shown in any case that variation is due to a simple acceleration or slowing of a basic process.

Variability between different kinds of animals

The marked variability in life span between different orders and families of mammals was cited in a previous chapter. It is assumed this variability represents differences in rates of aging. The correlations between life span, body weight, metabolic rate, and brain size were noted. Since metabolic rate, which correlates inversely with body size, is involved in the acceleration or slowing of virtually every process in the body, it may be invoked in a general explanation of at least some aspects of very marked differences in aging rates. Differences in metabolic rate cannot explain cases where some smaller animals live longer than larger ones, or where animals of very different sizes have similar life spans.

The inhibition of aging by growth was described previously, and it was argued that longer life spans could be selected for during the reproductive period. Human females have reproductive failure at around 45 years of age, and growth ceases in human beings at around 18 years of age. Although cattle are much larger, they grow until perhaps 4 to 5 years of age, and experience reproductive failure when around 20 years old. The excessively long growth and reproductive periods in man may explain, at least in part, why man lives longer and apparently ages more slowly than larger animals such as horses and cattle. Rats are around 10 times as big as mice, but they have similar life spans. Both grow for 6 to 9 months and experience reproductive failure at around $1\frac{1}{3}$ years. Thus, genetic variability in aging may not be by direct effect on aging processes as much as on processes such as growth and reproduction that determine when aging processes start or accelerate. Variability in size and growth, however, cannot explain differences in aging rate between some species, such as *Peromyscus* and *Mus* described in Chapter Six.

We would assume that if animals age at different rates, basic aging processes at the molecular and tissue levels would occur at different rates. Very few comparative studies of basic aging processes in different species have been carried out, and the data that are available may be misleading. It is essential that changes occurring during growth be separated from those occurring during aging, and that the phenomenon under study be known to be a true aging process. Properties of solubilized collagen from 2-year-old calf, dog, rat, and cat have been studied (Deyl et al., 1971). However, the calf would still be growing and synthesizing large amounts of collagen, while the other species would have matured at different ages and would have been aging for different periods. Furthermore, solubilization of collagen results in loss of the most characteristic age changes. Factors affecting aldimine bonds in collagen from different species of different ages have been studied (Vančikova and Deyl, 1973), but it is not known whether changes in these bonds are important in the aging of collagen.

An overview of the appearance and regulation of aging

A plausible explanation for the evolutionary origins of aging is available. This is based on progressive and irreversible processes occurring in animals that experience growth cessation or slowing and failure of reproduction. Other possible explanations have been advanced, but this problem does not appear amenable to solution by new observations or experimental means.

Much variability in aging between individuals and species can tentatively be explained on the basis of variability in metabolic rate and in duration of the periods of growth and reproduction. Growth differences would appear to be central to variability of aging in that both metabolic rate and duration of reproduction are related to amount and duration of growth.

Much more information is required about basic aging processes in animals that appear to be aging at different rates. If there are true differences in rates of aging in animals, there should be differences in rates of most, if not all, of their basic aging processes. In particular, if a basic process is proposed as a cause of aging, its rate of change should be related to the rate of aging in different animals, assuming these different animals age by the same basic mechanism. It should not be assumed, however, that there is necessarily a linear relationship between rate of animal aging and rate of some basic process. That is, if one kind of animal has a life span one-half that of another, a key aging process would not have to take place twice as fast in the first animal. Even after allowing for differences in duration of growth, it is possible that a given degree of basic change in tissues may cause different degrees of debility in different animals because of other factors in the animals such as functional demand in the tissues.

In the case of a basic process such as the stabilization of collagen it would be useful to know the degree of stabilization at the end of the life span of animals with very different rates of aging, as manifested in properties of insoluble collagen that are known to change characteristically with age. Additional information is also required on the stabilization of collagen in certain genetically influenced diseases such as diabetes mellitus, progeria, and alkaptonuria, in which agelike changes in tissues appear accelerated.

In view of the above considerations, the contributions of either classical or molecular genetics to the understanding of aging would appear to be limited. It is important not to confuse the genetics of aging with the genetics of the susceptibility to certain diseases. If a disease represents an aging process, the genetics of that disease would, of course, bear on aging. There are many genetically influenced diseases that afflict aging populations but do not, however, play a role in aging as defined here. The role for gene action in agelike processes observed in diseases such as diabetes mellitus and progeria remains to be demonstrated.

REFERENCES

Cutler, R. G. 1976. Evolution of longevity in primates. J. Human Evol. 5:169–202.

Delbridge, L., and A. V. Everitt. 1972. The effect of hypophysectomy and age on the stabilization of labile cross-links in collagen. Exptl. Gerontol. 7:413–415.

Deyl, Z., et al. 1971. Aging of the connective tissue: Collagen cross linking in animals of different species and equal age. Exptl. Gerontol. 6:227–233.

Foote, R. H. 1975. The gametogenic function of the aging ovary in the mammal. *In* R. J. Blandau (ed.). Aging Gametes, Their Biology and Pathology. Basel: S. Karger. Pp. 179–200.

Howarth, D., and A. V. Everitt. 1974. Effect of age, hypophysectomy, cortisone and growth hormone on amine (lysyl) oxidative activity in rat aorta. Gerontologia. 20:27–32.

Sacher, G. A. 1975. Maturation and longevity in relation to cranial capacity in hominid evolution. *In* R. Tuttle (ed.). Primate Functional Morphology and Evolution. The Hague: Mouton Publ. Pp. 417–441.

———. 1977. Life table modification and life prolongation. *In* C. E. Finch and L. Hayflick (eds.). Handbook of the Biology of Aging. New York: Van Nostrand Reinhold. Pp. 582–638.

Strehler, B. L. 1962. Time, Cells, and Aging. New York: Academic Press, Inc. Pp. 219–225.

Vančiková, O., and Z. Deyl. 1973. Aging of connective tissue: solubilisation of collagen from animals varying in age and species by reagents capable of splitting aldimine bonds. Exptl. Gerontol. 8:297–306.

NINE

Some Judgments
About the Study
of Aging

We have seen from the various levels at which aging processes occur that these processes constitute a major area of biology. In fact, these processes deal with the added parameter of time for most living systems. Furthermore, they underlie the most important public health problems in modern societies. It is inevitable that aging will receive increasing attention in biomedical research. In the case of intact animals, there are no reasons why aging processes will not be completely understood eventually, and methods devised for their inhibition.

Progress in the formulation and acceptance of concepts has been slow. This is not due to lack of data, but is the result of difficulties inherent in the field. It is frequently difficult to know what basic system to study or what types of studies to undertake to answer questions about alterations occurring at higher levels of organization. Aging processes are easily defined in the abstract, but it may be difficult to identify a process under observation as an aging one, and to distinguish it from a disease in a certain subgroup. An aging population is changing in many ways, and conclusions may be based on statistical artifacts. Distinguishing causes from effects is a common problem, and when several different causes might have a certain effect, there is often disagreement on the cause most likely to be the true one. In addition, a great deal of confusion has arisen because of the tempta-

226

tion to generalize from an observation about one type of animal or system.

The view that aging is aging and that one can study any system and generalize to all systems is clearly not tenable. If a question is asked about the aging of the entire animal, there would be little justification for studying intermitotic cells in detail unless preliminary studies showed that changes in these cells were associated with significant changes in function of the animal. Similarly, the liver would probably be a poor choice for an organ to study in regard to animal aging because it does not appear to be a major contributor to the debilities of age, presumably because of its enormous cell reserve and regenerative capacity. On the other hand, if the question were about cell aging, it would be more reasonable to study fixed postmitotic cells than turning-over cells, or organ function where extracellular factors may be important.

The type of animal chosen for the study of animal aging should, again, depend on the specific question being asked. Coelenterates consist largely of turning-over cells, and members of at least some species may be immortal. Insects and rotifers are composed of fixed postmitotic cells, while mammals contain all types of cells, large amounts of extracellular substances, and a complex cardiovascular system. There is little reason to believe that such animals with very distant phylogenetic relationships and very different types of architecture age by similar mechanisms.

Most successes in science result from following a certain procedure. An observation is made in nature. A hypothesis is then constructed to explain the observation, and an experiment is designed to test the hypothesis. The experiment can be on the phenomenon itself or on a model in which some aspect of the phenomenon is isolated and reproduced in the laboratory. A great deal of aging research has started with a model, with the hope or faith that what is discovered will be found to also occur naturally and be of importance in man. Thus, many aging studies are carried out on tissue cultures, invertebrates, and plants, even though there is little reason to believe that what is discovered in these systems will necessarily apply to mammals. Again, the question being asked is the key to significance; if one is asking why insects or tissue cultures age, then clearly insects or tissue cultures are the systems to study.

If life span is used as a measure of aging, it is essential that something be known about mechanisms of death. Mayflies might seem to be convenient for the study of aging since adults live only a day or so. Death, however, is due to starvation because mouth parts are atrophied.

The mouse as a species has a mean life expectancy of around 24 months. Therefore, if a mouse population under observation has a mean life span of only 16 months, deaths are almost certainly due to a specific disease and not to aging processes, as usually defined. Any changes in life span of such a population due to experimental manipulations would be of uncertain significance. Similarly, since life-shortening can be caused by any number of treatments, it should not be accepted as accelerated aging unless it can be shown that physiological decline and mechanisms of death follow the same patterns as those in the naturally aging population. On the other hand, experimental lengthening of life span beyond that recognized as maximum for the species would be likely to represent inhibition of aging.

A major problem inherent in the study of aging animals is that there can be no really satisfactory controls—that is, animals existing in time without aging. Longitudinal studies in which the same animals are studied over their life spans would be more meaningful than studies based on sampling of animals of different ages. Also, as a population ages, a continual selection occurs as members are removed by death. This can give very misleading data. For example, if some harmful substance or a byproduct of some harmful reaction accumulates with age, and if animals die when this reaches a high level, studies of populations of different ages may indicate that the concentration of this substance remains constant with age, or actually appears to decrease in old animals.

Other misleading data could result from not taking into account differences between development and aging. A system may change in a rat between birth and 10 months of age, and remain rather constant thereafter, representing an aspect of maturation. If 3- and 18-month-old animals are studied, conspicuous differences would be observed, and might be assumed to represent an aging process. However, the same differences would be observed in 3- and 10-month-old animals, and little change might be detected between 12 and 30 months.

The problem frequently arises of trying to decide which, if any, change known to occur at the molecular or tissue level is responsible for a given debility. It may be practically impossible to devise a study that would prove any cause-and-effect relationship. A first step might be to ascertain which of the basic changes are truly aging processes in terms of universality within the population, irreversibility, and progression. Use can then be made of postulates analogous to those of Koch relating bacteria to disease: Is the basic change always present when the debility is present and does it always precede the debility? Is the debility always present when the basic change is present? Is there a positive correlation between the extent of the two? The basic change that best satisfies such postulates should be favored as a cause of a given debility.

Difficulties in the study of aging make investigations in this area particularly challenging. Aging processes constitute exceedingly important problems both in basic biology and disease. Application of the highest talents and major resources to the solution of these problems would be fully justified.

Author Index

Subject Index